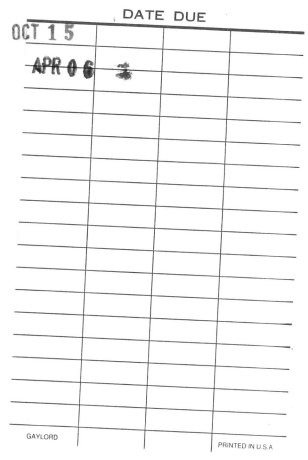

The Democratic Movement in Italy
1830–1876

The Democratic Movement in Italy 1830–1876

Clara M. Lovett

Harvard University Press
Cambridge, Massachusetts
and London, England   1982

Copyright © 1982 by the President
and Fellows of Harvard College
All rights reserved
Printed in the United States of America

Library of Congress Cataloging in Publication Data
Lovett, Clara Maria, 1939–
    The democratic movement in Italy, 1830–1876.

    Bibliography: p.
    Includes index.
    1. Italy—Politics and government—1815–1870.
    2. Liberalism—Italy—History—19th century. 3. Revolu-
tionists—Italy—Bibiography. I. Title.
    DG552.5.L68   945'.08   81–6403
    ISBN 0–674–19645–7   AACR2

For B.F.B., with love

Acknowledgments

THE CONCEPTUAL FRAMEWORK for this book was developed during the early part of 1976 in the congenial atmosphere of the Bunting Institute of Radcliffe College. Later on, archival work took me from one end of Italy to the other, to obscure collections as well as to famous ones. I received help from so many scholars and librarians that to thank each one of them individually would be impossible. However, I should express my deep gratitude to Professors Franco Della Peruta and Emilia Morelli, who opened many doors and generously shared their knowledge of sources and issues.

Much of the writing was done at the Woodrow Wilson International Center for Scholars in Washington, D.C. The Center's staff made it easy for me to work, and three of the Fellows, Gianfranco Pasquino, Paolo Prodi, and Robert D. Putnam, provided sharp and good-humored criticism. Aida Donald of the Harvard University Press, who followed this project almost from the beginning, made useful suggestions at every stage. My sincere thanks to her and her colleague Elizabeth Suttell.

The American Council of Learned Societies, the J. S. Guggenheim Foundation, and the Wilson Center provided financial support for research in Italy, at Harvard's Widener Library, and at the Library of Congress. Baruch College and the Research Foundation of the City University of New York helped with a sabbatical leave and with smaller grants.

The book is dedicated to my husband, Benjamin F. Brown, who shared his knowledge of Italian history as well as his superb editorial skills.

Contents

Introduction

NINETEENTH-CENTURY Italy produced a political movement, the Risorgimento, whose objectives, achieved in the decade 1860–1870, were to unify the country, free it from foreign rule, and give it a secular, constitutional government. By the 1840s the leaders of that movement knew that those goals could be achieved only through revolutionary means: conspiracy, insurrection, and war. By the 1850s they also realized that to unify Italy meant to challenge the temporal power of the papacy. Many of them, however, were moderate liberals, reluctant to acknowledge and to admit the radical implications of their political goals both for Italy and for the European balance of power. When their cause prevailed, thanks to the diplomatic skill of Cavour and the daring of Garibaldi, the moderate liberals went to considerable pains to deny that a revolution had taken place in Italy at all. In their political writings, memoirs, and historical accounts they avoided the term *rivoluzione italiana*, which had been widely used in the first part of the century; instead they used the term *Risorgimento* ("rebirth"), which, in their usage, implied continuity with the country's past.

The Democratic Movement in Italy

By 1870, with the defeat of the Habsburg army in Italy, the collapse of the temporal power, and the establishment of a unified constitutional kingdom, their goals of the 1840s were achieved. In the 1860s and 1870s their primary concern was to consolidate and to strengthen the institutions that they had crafted after their favorite political and social models, France under Louis Philippe and England after the Reform Act of 1832.

Other protagonists of the national struggle, however, dissented from the moderate liberal majority and flaunted their credentials as authors of subversive tracts, conspirators, barricade fighters, or guerrillas. The true Italian Revolution, they argued, had not yet come and never would until the masses were able to identify with at least some of its principles and goals. National liberation, unification, and secularization had indeed been necessary, but they were not sufficient premises for the democratization of Italian society.

These dissenters of the 1860s and 1870s were the spokesmen for a democratic movement that had thrived in the decades before the unification and contributed significantly to the national cause. As thinkers, propagandists, and militants of Italian democracy, these men had subscribed to the liberal goals of unification, secularization, and constitutional government. But they had also advocated something more: social change, whether by revolutionary or reformist means, in such crucial areas as land distribution, mass education, and women's rights. Those thinkers, propagandists, and militants — the protagonists of a democratic Italian revolution, not merely a rebirth — are the subject of this book.

The failure of the Risorgimento democrats to achieve the lead of Italy in the years of its unification and state building has usually been attributed to the abstract character of their ideology as well as to their intellectual and organizational inability to build strong ties with the Italian masses. The first hypothesis of this study is that the democrats did, in fact, make concrete and partially successful efforts to reach out to the masses both before and after the unification. Further, it brings evidence that the political failure of the democratic movement was not due to a lack of able leaders or of ideas relevant to Italian society but rather to external social, economic, and political factors that sapped the movement's vitality in the 1850s.

The second hypothesis is that, although defeated in the late 1850s, the Risorgimento democrats made a lasting impact on the development of modern Italy. Contrary to the claims of the moderate liberals and of historians sympathetic to their point of view, the Risorgimento carried within it much more than national independence, unification, and political modernization. It contained the seeds, sown largely by the thinkers and activists who are the subject of this book, for the radical transformation of Italian culture and of Italian society.

The third and final hypothesis is that the democratic movement during the Risorgimento produced — partly by design and partly by accident — the first professional politicians of Italy's history. These are, thus, the men who served as teachers and role models for the founders of both the Radical and the Socialist parties in the period between the unification and World War I, thereby assuring the continuity of an indigenous tradition of democratic protest, dissent, and participation.

The importance of this topic for the historiography of modern Italy is immediately obvious. The ideological foundations of Italian nationalism were largely cast by one of the great democratic thinkers of nineteenth-century Europe, Giuseppe Mazzini. Another democrat, Giuseppe Garibaldi, served as a model for thousands of Italians who went to prison or died for the national cause. Yet there are other democrats such as Carlo Pisacane, Giuseppe Ferrari, and Ausonio Franchi who articulated philosophies and programs of radical secularization and social revolution that had a considerable impact upon later generations.

But despite the importance of the topic, there is as yet no study of the Risorgimento democrats comparable to Raymond Grew's seminal work on the moderate liberal Italian National Society. Indeed, in the relevant literature in Italian (there is virtually no literature in English) one finds many more partisan works and semi-popular descriptive surveys than monographs based upon original sources. Intellectually, only the works of Franco Della Peruta and his disciples depart significantly from the traditional emphasis of Risorgimento historiography upon political ideology. Methodologically, even the best postwar scholarship, represented by Della Peruta, Alfonso Scirocco, Alessandro Galante Garrone, and S. Massimo Ganci, has not departed from the canons of narrative history. Nor has it given us a comprehensive interpretation of nineteenth-century Italian democracy.

In exploring the social context of democratic ideology and the politically relevant experiences that bound individuals from different regions, social classes, and religions into a nationwide movement, this study seeks not so much to revise as to complement the recent work of Italian Marxist scholars, especially Della Peruta. This is to say that at times it raises questions similar to theirs, but it is not to say that its analysis and conclusions have been bound by preconceived schemes or that they are always in tune with theirs. In employing a prosopographical approach to the subject it makes a major departure from the existing literature. This approach casts new light on some important issues, among them the socialization of young Italians to revolutionary ideology, the channels of recruitment to Mazzinian or other democratic organizations, and the effect of political involvement and persecution upon socioeconomic status and career aspirations.

Although this study arose from my desire to contribute something new and different to Italian historiography, conceptually it owes a great deal to historians of nineteenth-century political movements, particularly bourgeois radicalism, in other European countries. For instance, Simon Maccoby's classic study and more recently Hugh Emy's work on English radicals (their Italian counterparts were known as "democrats") and Alan O'Day's book on the Irish Parnellites aroused my interest in the social context of politics and in the emergence of professional politicians and modern political parties in the nineteenth century. The writings of Maurice Nordmann and Leo Loubère on aspects of bourgeois radicalism in France and of Manuel Espadas Burgos on nineteenth-century Spain suggested the intriguing possibility of comparisons between French, Spanish, and Italian democrats based not only upon the analysis of ideology but also of family and regional backgrounds. And the writings of Hans Rosenberg, James Sheehan, John Snell, and others on the ideological origins and the social bases of nineteenth-century German politics (an extension of Theodore Hamerow's ground-breaking work of the 1950s) pointed out how difficult it was for intellectuals and political activists, in Italy no less than in Germany, to strike a balance between nationalist and democratic principles, between aspirations toward national unity and a more ambitious desire to promote political equality, secularism, and in some cases, social justice within their society. In short, this study raises and attempts to answer several questions about the nature of nineteenth-century political movements that go well beyond the history of modern Italy. I hope that it will prove useful for the comparative study of political and social movements.

I also hope that it will be read with profit by policymakers, political scientists, and others interested in contemporary Italian affairs. Although my scholarly interests lie in the study of the past, I have followed closely the ongoing process of democratization of economic and cultural institutions in Italy. Again and again I have been struck by the similarity of ideas and issues, if not of strategy, between the Risorgimento democrats and later generations of Italian leftists. The three main principles of Risorgimento democracy — secularism, political equality, and the concern for social justice — have been for over a century and are still today the foundation of whatever unity of thought and action exists between Marxist and non-Marxist groups on the Left. Indeed, to ignore the legacy of the nineteenth century — and it is easy to do so in the current flurry over Marxist/Leninist/Stalinist influences on the Italian Left — is to ignore that men like Felice Cavallotti, Filippo Turati, and Antonio Gramsci owed at least as much to the founding fathers of Italian democracy as they did to the founding fathers of German and Russian socialism.

This analysis of the democratic movement's ideology, social foundations, and political behavior from around 1830 to 1876 is based upon a collective biography of 146 thinkers, propagandists, and militants. All of them played active and often conspicuous roles in the Italian Revolution. Even though not all of them achieved fame or notoriety beyond their native city or region, they were an elite of national importance. They provided the ideas and the political structures around which thousands of their countrymen rallied.

Because this type of analysis has not been previously applied to the study of nineteenth-century Italy and because I chose to study, through a select group of leaders, a movement that involved thousands of men and women, a brief discussion of methodology seems important at the outset. One question that might be raised about this kind of study is, since thousands of Italians joined or supported Mazzini and other democratic organizers during the Italian Revolution, why study a relatively small group of leaders and not a larger number of rank and filers? Why, in short, a study of a political elite and not a quantitative analysis of a statistically significant sample?

The answer to that question is twofold. First, I set out to examine not only the social origins and career patterns of the Risorgimento democrats but also their ideology and the political strategies they pursued before and after the unification. A quantitative study might have yielded good data for a social profile of the movement, but it would not have eliminated the need to study its leadership. As loosely structured as the democratic secret societies were before 1860 and as divided as the movement became afterward, political ideology and programs were formulated by a core of dedicated activists, not by the rank and file. Further, a quantitative study could not have been attempted for the entire country, but only for a specific region or, at most, for one of the preunification states. To have done so, however, would have meant to miss the significance of a nationwide democratic network born of the revolutionary failures of 1831 and 1848–49. That network, in some ways comparable to an extended family, was not built by the thousands of participants in those events, but by the members of revolutionary governments and the leaders of revolutionary armies. It was they who traveled from city to city and from region to region to spread and then to defend the principle of a national democratic revolution. The revolutionary failures separated the leaders from their grass roots, and it was a separation fraught with dangers, as many democrats discovered when they returned home in 1860. Yet those same failures, by forcing many leaders to share precarious hiding places, prison cells, and the bitterness of exile, forged bonds among them that enabled the movement to survive even in defeat and to reemerge after 1860 with redefined commitments and new structures.

Second, the survey of the available archival and other sources that I made in 1974–75 revealed that a quantitative study, even if limited to one region, would not have yielded the range of information necessary for a comprehensive analysis of the democratic movement. If they did not remain wholly anonymous, the rank-and-file participants in the Italian Revolution left few traces. The single most important source of information about them is the records of political trials, available for all the preunification Italian states. These were useful for ascertaining the sex, age, occupation, and residence of actual or alleged participants; but they revealed little, frequently nothing, about the defendants' political beliefs and motivations. In many cases it was in fact impossible to learn whether a defendant had identified with any particular ideology or group. For most defendants, the data recorded in such documents could not be verified against other sources, except for dates of birth, death, or marriage and, in some cases, tax records. Furthermore, trial proceedings and police files for the preunification era seldom contained information about the defendants' activities before their arrest or after their release. Thus, it was almost impossible to trace political careers over any significant period of time. The exceptions to the rule were publicists or organizers whose political leanings had been obvious enough to hold the attention of the authorities over several years and to warrant special attention at their trials. For those men in leadership roles, the information obtained from trial proceedings, police reports, and so on, could be verified against and complemented by other sources. Under the circumstances, an in-depth study of a sample of democratic leaders proved more manageable and more fruitful than a quantitative study of the movement's rank and file.

Because my chief purpose was to reach some generalizations about the democratic movement in nineteenth-century Italy, the analysis could not be limited to obvious figures like Mazzini or Garibaldi. Rather, I sought figures of lesser historical importance, often known only within a particular city or region even among their contemporaries. Their social origins, education, occupation, and so forth suggested that they were fairly representative of the participants in the Italian Revolution whose names had appeared more fleetingly in the archival documents.

The criteria used in selecting the 146 subjects of this study are as follows.

1. A host of secondary works and biographical dictionaries were consulted to identify the names of those Risorgimento intellectuals and activists who had been known among their contemporaries as "men of the Left." In most cases those selected had been members of Mazzini's Young Italy or similar secret societies before 1848. For each person thus identified, the information about his political preference or affiliation was checked in two or more other sources. This initial screening yielded some twelve hundred names.

2. In order to examine the development of Risorgimento democracy from its beginnings in the 1830s to the 1870s, I then eliminated from that first list those persons who, for whatever reason, had not taken an active part in the events of 1848–49. Those who remained, some one thousand persons born between 1800 and 1830, could truly be called "the Risorgimento generation."

3. In order to trace the entire political careers of these men as well as to investigate their background, education, socialization to politics, and so forth, substantial and reliable information was needed. I attempted to locate their political writings, up-to-date biographies, diaries, autobiographies, published correspondence, and personal or family papers that might be reasonably accessible to scholars. This third screening yielded a list of 227 names. For these persons enough information was available either in published sources or in the Italian archives to permit the reconstruction of full sociological and political profiles.

However, a further screening became necessary because this sample did not adequately reflect the geographical distribution and the relative strength of the democratic movement in the preunification states. Some regions were too heavily represented, especially Piedmont, Lombardy, and Tuscany, which together accounted for 62 percent of the total. This was probably because many democratic leaders from those regions had been journalists or political theorists.

A relatively permissive political climate in those regions in the 1840s and 1850s had allowed them to express their views, even on political issues. It had certainly permitted them to leave more tracks, at least in print, than did their counterparts in other regions. Conversely, the Papal Legations and the Kingdom of the Two Sicilies, both of which had produced large and militant democratic groups, appeared underrepresented. Again, this was the undesired but perhaps inevitable outcome of the criteria applied in the preceding stage of selection. The democratic leaders from the Papal States and the Kingdom of the Two Sicilies were underground organizers, conspirators, and sometime terrorists more often than philosophers or peaceful propagandists. They left plenty of tracks in police files and trial proceedings, but relatively few political writings, autobiographies, letters, and the like.

4. In order to correct this geographical bias and have a sample reflecting what was already known about the relative strength of the movement in the various regions, the list was further reduced to 146 names, distributed as follows:

Kingdom of Lombardy-Venetia	35
Kingdom of Sardinia	23
Grand Duchy of Tuscany	17
Duchies of Parma and Modena	5
Papal States	24
Kingdom of the Two Sicilies	42

Commonly held ideas, more than common social origins or specific political programs, accounted for the formation of democratic networks in the 1840s and for their survival even in defeat. Despite innumerable differences among them, the democratic leaders shared certain beliefs that set them apart from their moderate liberal and their conservative contemporaries. In the first part of this study, I shall examine the three most important of these shared beliefs: the democrats' desire to create a non-Catholic culture in Italy, their definition of political equality, and their concern for social justice.

1

The Italian Revolution as a Cultural Revolution

THE democratic intellectuals and activists who make up the dramatis personae of this book shared certain educational experiences, sociological characteristics, and personality traits. These factors set them apart from their moderate liberal and conservative contemporaries and created among them a special sense of group solidarity that survived despite powerful external pressures upon the movement and despite an awesome number of internal quarrels of a political or personal nature. But above all, the solidarity that made the democratic movement possible and that kept it alive, even in the face of persecution and of repeated political failures, was built upon a shared intellectual heritage and a common ideology.

When historians write about the losers in a major revolutionary movement or war, they almost inevitably ask, "Why did these people lose? Was there something about them, their cause, or their political or military strategy that doomed them to failure?" This approach to the problem of revolutionary "failures" seems inherently flawed, because it focuses upon the internal dynamics of minority movements

rather than upon the larger political and social realities within
which those movements operated. In the case of the Risorgimento
democrats, historical interpretations of their failure to lead the
unification of Italy and the transformation of Italian society have
placed great emphasis upon the ideological divisions within their
ranks, especially after 1848, in contrast to the rallying of liberal
opinion to the policies of Cavour. Although this approach has undoubtedly been useful in understanding the complex history of the
democratic movement, it may have distorted our view of the movement's historical significance.

In fact, if ideological divisions and personal rivalries among its
members were serious enough to diminish the movement's potential
popular appeal before 1848 and to impair its political effectiveness
in the 1850s, they neither destroyed it nor made it irrelevant to
Italy's political development after the unification. Thus, while giv-
ing due attention to important distinctions, for example, between
Mazzinian republicans and federalist republicans, one should not
lose sight of those central ideas to which Risorgimento democrats, on
the whole, subscribed rather loyally and consistently: anti-
Catholicism, political egalitarianism, and social justice. The first of
these shared ideas is particularly important to an understanding of
the movement's intellectual character and of its historical legacy.

Democratic Critiques of Catholicism

From an ideological or philosophical point of view, the democratic
movement of the Risorgimento should be defined as an anti-Catholic
movement first and foremost. The notion that the Italian Revolution
had to result in the establishment of a non-Catholic or secular culture was widely shared by the Risorgimento democrats, although
they often disagreed upon the definition of such a culture. Indeed,
anti-Catholicism was probably the single most important unifying
principle of democratic ideology.

Like their contemporaries of other political persuasions, the
democrats of the 1830s knew that to advocate the independence and
the unification of Italy or even to demand significant reforms within
the existing states entailed a confrontation with the papacy. The
unitary solution proposed by Mazzini was predicated upon the actual dismantling of the Papal States. But even the neo-Guelf federalist scheme popularized by Vincenzo Gioberti in the early 1840s
called for major changes in the role of the pope as a temporal ruler
and in the relative position of his territories vis-à-vis the other
Italian states. As for reforms within the existing order, Pope Gregory
XVI turned a deaf ear not only to the petitions of his own subjects

but also to the practical suggestions of the stability-minded Metternich. And Gregory's successor, Pius IX, departed from that pattern only in his willingness to reduce the number of political prisoners in the papal jails and to listen to the political grievances of the most influential among his subjects. His conduct in 1848–49 and the restoration of his temporal authority in Rome under French protection made it obvious to democrats and to moderate liberals alike that the Italian Revolution would have to destroy the Papal States.[1]

But the events of 1848–49 did not merely undermine the legitimacy of the temporal power in the eyes of many Italians. They also challenged the claim of the Roman Catholic hierarchy to a dominant influence upon Italian culture and Italian society. As one of the pope's rebellious subjects, Felice Orsini, put it, "Yes, we lost [in 1849]; but our downfall is concealing a great moral event, the consequences of which will soon become apparent . . .; the papacy has lost its moral authority for all times!"[2] Few moderate liberals indulged in this kind of flamboyant rhetoric; but behind their decorous restraint they, too, envisioned a future political order in which the principles of separation of Church and State and of religious toleration would be more thoroughly implemented than at any time since the era of the French revolution. A clue to their ideas on this issue and to their intentions for the future was the drive for secularization in Piedmont-Sardinia, the only Italian state with a liberal constitutional government in the 1850s. The ecclesiastical policy of Massimo d'Azeglio and Camillo Benso di Cavour was applauded by liberal exiles from every part of Italy, and it was supported by the democratic contingent in the Sardinian Parliament.[3]

In short, especially after the revolution of 1848, democrats and moderate liberals alike adopted an antipapal and anticlerical stance. But any similarity between the two major political currents of the Risorgimento ended here. For in the eyes of democratic intellectuals and political leaders the destruction of the temporal power, the separation of Church and State, and religious toleration were not the ultimate goals they were for most moderate liberals. They were only steps, necessary but not suffiicient, toward the shaping of a non-Catholic national culture.

Most Risorgimento democrats rejected the Roman Catholic tradition early in their lives. Indeed, that rejection and the ensuing commitment to the secularization of Italian culture figured prominently in their socialization as children and young adults. And it was heightened in many cases by traumatic personal experiences. But, however it was acquired, the anti-Catholic posture of the Risorgimento democrats had a long tradition behind it.

Among its intellectual ancestors in the struggle against Catholicism the democratic movement counted political theorists, philosophers, and even theologians who had condemned the temporal power as a menace to the spiritual mission of the Church. In their critiques of conservative philosophers like Joseph de Maistre or of innovative neo-Catholic authors like Antonio Rosmini-Serbati, Vincenzo Gioberti, and Alessandro Manzoni, the leading theorists of the movement often quoted from heretical sources of the sixteenth and seventeenth centuries, especially the writings of Paolo Sarpi and Giordano Bruno. And they were well acquainted with the vast array of eighteenth-century anticurialist and regalist tracts, particularly the works of Carlantonio Pilati and Cosimo Amidei. They did not delve into such literature only to find intellectual ammunition to be used against Catholic philosophers. They also looked for evidence that non-Catholic subcultures had existed and flourished in Italy for centuries alongside the dominant Catholic culture. When they found such evidence, they did their best to publicize it, even at the cost of occasional distortions and exaggerations. Conscious of the unpopularity of anti-Catholic views among many Italians of their time, they were eager to demonstrate that their own ideas were, after all, not so novel, shocking, or revolutionary.

Three democratic publicists stood out among many as masters of this genre of historical-philosophical literature: Giuseppe Mazzini, Giuseppe Ferrari, and Ausonio Franchi. Coming from different backgrounds, they often criticized each other's work; but they shared the assumption that organized Christianity, especially in its Roman Catholic form, was an unsuitable faith for the nineteenth century. All three wrote anti-Catholic tracts, usually in direct polemic with contemporary Catholic authors, but they approached their subject from different intellectual perspectives.

Unlike Ferrari, a lifelong atheist, and Franchi, a renegade priest and a rationalist, Mazzini was a deeply religious man. Although he experienced a crisis of faith in his youth, he believed in God and in human progress as the expression of God's will. He professed an admiration for primitive Christianity as he saw it, in idealized form, through the prism of his mother's Jansenist teachings. Religious belief, he thought, assured the well-being of the individual and his willingness to transcend selfish interests for the benefit of society. But Mazzini was convinced that the religious beliefs of his contemporaries had been manipulated and corrupted, particularly by the Roman Catholic hierarchy, and that

> superstition, intolerance, and clerical despotism have thus far exploited this belief [the universal belief in God]. Let us

deprive them of this prop . . . The peoples [of the world]
will free themselves from human despotism, not from divine
authority . . . As for Catholicism, it is the religion of the
dead. And we will repeat for all to hear: Catholicism is
dead; Christianity itself is an individual not a social religion
. . . Spiritualism applied to society, that must be our ban-
ner.[4]

Catholicism was dead because as a hierarchical and supranational
faith it could not adjust to the principles of democracy and nationalism that were shaping European civilization in the nineteenth century. Above all, Mazzini wanted to provide for his fellow Italians an
alternative to Catholicism; he wanted to channel their religious
sentiments away from the established Church toward a new faith
that allowed them to come face to face with their God, with their
collective persona (the Nation) as the sole intermediary. It was no
accident that many of his writings on the Italian Question were
couched in religious language. He described his revolutionary secret
society, Young Italy, as "neither a sect nor a party; it is *a faith and a
mission*. Precursors of Italy's rebirth, we will lay the first stone of
her religion."[5] But, conservative critics inquired, was it not dangerous, especially in Italy, to launch a crusade against the papacy? Did
not Mazzini run the risk of undermining the very same religious sentiments that he wished to preserve? And would not his revolutionary
propaganda destroy public morality? Not so, he answered:

The condemnation of the papacy does not come from us; it
comes from God; from God who has called the People to rise
and to establish a new Unity between the two spheres of
temporal and spiritual power. We are merely interpreting
the spirit of our Time. And our Time rejects any sort of intermediary between itself and the source of its existence . . .
The papacy and the Austrian Empire are doomed to perish,
one because for at least three centuries it has hindered the
general mission which God entrusted to mankind; the other
because likewise for three centuries it has hindered the
special mission which God entrusted to each People. *Mankind* will triumph over the ruins of the papacy and the *Nation* upon the ruins of Austria.[6]

Although Mazzini found the papacy obsolete and Roman Catholicism unsuitable for the age of democracy and of nationality, he
understood and respected the religious sentiments of those contem-

poraries who remained loyal to the Church. For this he was often criticized by his fellow democrat Giuseppe Ferrari, one of the most radical (rabid would not be too strong a word) secularists of the Risorgimento.

Influenced by Saint-Simonian and Comtian ideas during a long sojourn in France, Ferrari believed that civilizations developed through several stages, each one marked by a distinctive epistemology: theological, metaphysical, and scientific.[7] In his younger years as an expatriate and aspiring academician he believed that Europe had already entered the scientific stage. Therefore, like Auguste Comte, he regarded religion as obsolete and useless by definition. Later on his political experiences, and particularly the behavior of the French propertied classes between June 1848 and December 1851, led him to revise that hasty judgment. He realized that under certain circumstances an "established," that is, organized and officially protected religion, could not be dismissed as a quaint and harmless relic of the past. When such a religion entered a symbiotic relationship with the interests of politically or economically powerful groups, it could be used as an effective brake upon social progress. Ferrari argued that precisely such a relationship existed both in France and in Italy between the Roman Catholic religious establishment and the propertied classes. At mid-nineteenth century, he wrote, the bourgeoisie which had once read Voltaire and given up mass found in organized religion a most effective ally in the preservation of the social order. For its part, the religious establishment profited from the relationship because it no longer had to worry about its most severe critics, who ever since the early eighteenth century had come precisely from the ranks of the educated bourgeoisie.

Ferrari analyzed the relationship between Property and Religion (to use his own shorthand) in his *Filosofia della Rivoluzione* and *La federazione repubblicana*, works published in Switzerland in 1851 but sold in the Italian states through a smuggling network operated by exiles in Lugano, Turin, and Genoa. He made an important contribution to the secularist propaganda of the 1850s by calling attention to the social context of religion. Religious ideas and institutions, he argued, could only be understood (and attacked) by tracing their relationship to other social phenomena. If one assumed, as he did, that Property and Religion were complementary aspects of the European social order in the nineteenth century, it made no sense to fight one and not the other. Precisely for this reason, as a member of the Italian Parliament in the 1860s and 1870s, Ferrari insisted that an anti-Catholic cultural revolution could only succeed in Italy if it was accompanied by an anticapitalist social revolution.[8]

Although both Mazzini and Ferrari made significant contributions to the anti-Catholic ideology of the democratic movement, its most versatile and prolific secularist writer was the defrocked priest Cristoforo Bonavino, better known by his pseudonym, Ausonio Franchi. His theological background and his knowledge of ecclesiastical institutions were far more extensive than those of Mazzini and Ferrari. Thus, although he was a less original thinker than either of them, he was a more effective polemicist. Before Italy's unification he specialized in polemics against the liberal Catholicism of Charles de Montalembert and his Italian followers, which he regarded as more insidious than the conservative varieties. After the unification he agitated against a reconciliation between the Italian government and the Holy See.

There were in Franchi's anti-Catholic writings elements of both Mazzini's and Ferrari's positions. As an ex-priest, Franchi was sensitive to the importance of religious sentiments among his fellow Italians, particularly women and the poor. Like Mazzini he believed that Catholicism was no longer relevant to the needs of the masses in an age of democratic aspirations, and he argued that it lingered on mainly because of fear, superstition, and ignorance among the masses. The educated segments of the population, he observed, had already adopted "the religion of the eighteenth century," that is, rationalism. As for the Catholic piety of the propertied classes, it was only skin-deep, a means of discouraging social protest among the lower classes.

Although he resided in Turin, Franchi found it impossible to publish his works in the Kingdom of Sardinia until the late 1860s. His major anti-Catholic tracts were all published in Switzerland, and the hostility of both ecclesiastical and secular censors certainly restricted their circulation in Italy. Yet his influence within the leadership of the democratic movement was probably strengthened by the publication of his works abroad. In fact, many prominent democrats who were unwelcome in Piedmont-Sardinia settled in Switzerland in the 1850s or at least crossed it on their way to other countries. Thus, Franchi's works were not only read but also imitated by a number of exiles. Indeed, he was so successful as a propagandist that his halfhearted return to the Catholic faith at an advanced age caused clerical authors to burn incense and secularist groups to wear mourning.[9]

Mazzini, Ferrari, and Franchi were prolific writers, but the anti-Catholic literature of the democratic movement was by no means limited to their works. Several lesser propagandists tried their hand at this genre, not only in the wake of the revolutions of 1848 but also after Italy's unification. Each writer brought to the anti-Catholic crusade some special concern or twist that reflected his background and experience. Thus, Davide Levi aired the grievances and sufferings of a minority long oppressed by the dominant Catholic culture.[10] Rinaldo Andreini, Mattia Montecchi, and Giuseppe Galletti, survivors of papal jails, cried out against the most visible and odious form of clerical despotism, the papal government. For instance, in a letter to Enrico Cernuschi, Andreini declared, "I shall easily grant you the privilege of remaining an atheist; as for myself, I reserve the pleasure of signing the verdict that will have the reigning pope shot . . . to be rid once and for all of the papacy and of Catholicism."[11] Galletti wanted everyone to know how clerical compassion (*la carità dei preti*) had treated actual or alleged subversives in the Romagna. In his memoirs he described his involuntary journey from a jail in Forlì to the bleak grandeur of the Castel Sant'Angelo. He had entered Rome in an open mule-drawn cart, filthy, hungry, and bruised: "In such a disgusting and shameful way, and in broad daylight, the clerical government [*il governo dei preti*] transported to Rome an honorable citizen, a member of the most cultured segment of society, a mature man, the father of five children, a man suspected of a political crime, but not convicted, nay, not even properly indicted."[12]

Another prolific propagandist, Ferdinando Petruccelli della Gattina, had no personal experience of papal misrule. But in his heavy-handed, scurrilous satires of "popery" one could read the bitter resentment of the impoverished people of his native Calabria against the political influence and the economic privileges of the Church. With the possible exception of Franchi, Petruccelli was the only democratic intellectual of the Risorgimento to try to earn a living as an anti-Catholic pamphleteer. He was not very successful until the early 1870s, when he met Robert E. Peterson, a Philadelphia businessman bitterly opposed to Catholic immigration. In Petruccelli's writings Peterson found plenty of grist for his nativist mill. He commissioned a new anti-Catholic tract which he translated and published at his own expense.[13]

Petruccelli was a rather unusual democratic propagandist in that he was paid for some of his works. But he was by no means the only one whose writings were translated and used in antipapal or anti-Catholic campaigns outside of Italy. The Gallican intellectual Jean Gustave Wallon, for example, was well acquainted with those writings. And in the 1870s, when he became a spokesman for the Old Catholic movement in France, he kept his files up-to-date through a voluminous correspondence with his longtime friend Ferrari. In England, George Jacob Holyoake, the founder of the Secularist Society, corresponded with the exiles Mazzini, Aurelio Saffi, and G. B. Varè, and through them became familiar with the anti-Catholic literature of the Italian democratic movement. In fact, the personal correspondence of the movement's most active propagandists and the number of translated editions of their works suggest that the Risorgimento democrats from the 1840s until about 1880 were the torchbearers of anticlericalism, secularism, and irreligion in western Europe. The intellectual arguments and the emotionally charged language that they used as early as the 1840s appeared in almost identical form in the last quarter of the nineteenth century in the writings of British and French secularists as well as in those of the German democrats Arnold Ruge, Karl Vogt, and Karl Nauwerck.[14]

As the examples of Peterson and Holyoake indicate, foreign observers were attracted to the negative aspects of the Italian democratic movement's anti-Catholic position. They admired the relentless intellectual criticism by men like Ferrari and Franchi, and they obviously relished the lurid exposés of clerical despotism and corruption that were the specialty of Petruccelli, Angelo Brofferio, Giorgio Asproni, and others. But there was also a positive and constructive aspect that, though it escaped the attention of foreigners, was far more important to nineteenth-century Italian culture. The positive aspect survived as a theme in Italian politics long after the rationalist tracts of a Franchi or the impassioned anticlerical diatribes of a Galletti had been relegated to dusty library shelves. It consisted of an effort to define the cultural objectives of the Italian Revolution. Both before and after 1860 the Risorgimento democrats strove to find intellectual alternatives to Roman Catholicism and to offer constructive suggestions on how such alternatives could be popularized among the Italian people.

The Quest for Alternatives

What could replace Roman Catholicism as the basic foundation of Italian culture? This was the central question in the debate among democratic intellectuals from the early 1830s until the 1870s. Although there were almost as many answers to this question as there were intellectuals in the movement, it is possible to identify several alternatives around which a consensus was reached. An important group which was led by Mazzini himself and included among others Gustavo Modena, Mauro Macchi, Maurizio Quadrio, Francesco Dall'Ongaro, and Quirico Filopanti, rejected Roman Catholicism but not religion per se. As the basis for a new national culture, they proposed the founding of a civil religion. Mazzinian political thought provided the theoretical foundation for this alternative.

Anti-Catholic but not irreligious, Mazzini always expressed his political messages in the language of theology. He described Young Italy as a faith and a mission, and when he spoke of the Italian Revolution he used terms like regeneration, redemption, and salvation. The national revolution, he wrote in 1834, "requires a faith and that faith requires good works."[15] The "good works" of his new religion were, of course, the political or military deeds necessary to liberate Italy from foreign rule and unify the Italian states. And the martyrs of the new religion were those men and women who could say with Mazzini himself, "I have renounced even a semblance of happiness on this earth. Far from my mother, from my sisters, from everything I hold dear, I lost in prison the best friend of my youth . . . I despaired of what an individual can accomplish . . . and I told myself: 'Persecuted and misunderstood, you shall die halfway.' "[16] The mystical quality and the strong religious coloration of the Mazzinian message were, as Gaetano Salvemini and other interpreters have pointed out, important reasons for its widespread popular appeal. The language of theology, albeit in vulgarized form, was obviously more familiar to the average Italian of Mazzini's time than was the language of philosophy or political theory. But those same qualities that enabled Mazzini to touch the hearts of many Italians were a source of friction between him and other democratic intellectuals. Throughout his career, he left himself open to criticism by extreme anticlericals like Franchi and Pisacane and by uncompromising atheists like Ferrari. Particularly after his appeal to Pope Pius IX in 1847, they charged that he underestimated the pervasive influence of the Catholic hierarchy over the political outlook of his countrymen and that by catering to their religious sentiments he was, in effect, helping to preserve that which he claimed to hate. Moreover, although they could never deny his total devotion to the cause of Italian liberty, they objected to the mystique that surrounded him as the messiah of the national revolution.[17]

The criticism of Mazzini's alleged tolerance of Catholicism flared up in 1849 because of his role in the government of the Roman Republic. Andreini and other extreme anticlericals chided him and his fellow triumvirs, Saffi and Carlo Armellini, for having failed to abolish or to outlaw the Catholic religion.[18] Foreign friends of Mazzini who regarded the growth of religious pluralism in Italy as a prerequisite for political and social progress made much the same point. For the most part these were unfair criticisms. In his own way, as Metternich perceived in the 1830s, Mazzini was as coherently anti-Catholic as those democratic intellectuals who were identified with atheistic rationalism or with Freemasonry.

Three central concepts of Mazzini's political thought were basically incompatible with Christianity, especially with Catholicism. One was the concept underlying his most famous political slogan, "God and the People" (*Dio e Popolo*). The Mazzinian God did bear some resemblance to the Father of the Judeo-Christian tradition as the Creator of all things and as an active presence in human affairs. But the relationship between this God and His People, as Mazzini conceived it, was not dependent upon either a sacramental structure or a priestly hierarchy. From a theological viewpoint, Mazzini's theory of a direct relationship between God and the People was perhaps closer to the Protestant concept of the priesthood of all believers than to Catholic doctrine. But this is not to say that he ever endorsed Protestantism. Although as an exile in England he seemed quite comfortable in bourgeois Protestant circles, he refused to concede that the growth of Protestant groups in Italy could be helpful to the birth of a new Italy. Around 1850 he wrote to Dall'Ongaro, a former priest who had come under the spell of the Calvinist tradition in Switzerland, "What would be the point of proscribing Catholicism [in Italy] and of not proscribing Protestantism? They are but two variations of the same faith."[19]

Even in the absence of such clear-cut pronouncements, an analysis of the Mazzinian concept of revelation should have dispelled any impression that he wished to preserve some aspects of traditional Christianity. The Mazzinian God revealed His presence and manifested His will not through the Scriptures and the teachings and sacrifice of Christ but through the history of each People. The will of God assigned to each People a particular mission. But how, in the absence of a Savior, a priesthood, a sacramental structure, and a Holy Writ, could the People discover God's will and fulfill their particular mission? They could do so, Mazzini argued, by studying and understanding their historical development.

In the context of nineteenth-century Italian culture, this was a profoundly revolutionary message. Had Mazzini never conspired against the existing governments, had he never founded Young Italy, had he never participated in the government of the Roman Republic, his ideas would have been, nonetheless, a formidable threat to the position of the Catholic Church in his country. By challenging the need for intermediaries between God and the Italian People, the theological premises of his new religion inevitably also challenged the need for the temporal power, for ecclesiastical courts and benefices, for clerical control over education, and so forth.[20]

Moreover, the same theological premises were a potential threat to the existing political and social institutions even outside the Papal States. In Mazzini's religious outlook, a People, that is, all those who share a given area, language, and historical tradition, are capable of understanding their particular mission and all have a part to play in its fulfillment. Differences of income, status, and education might persist among them, but those differences, Mazzini argued, become unimportant before the higher form of equality that derives from the principle of "association," that is, from the common effort by the People to relate to their past and to forge their collective destiny.[21] When applied to concrete social or economic issues, Mazzini's associationist philosophy was too vague to provide the basis for specific democratic policies or institutions. But even its critics within the democratic camp (and there were many) could not deny its egalitarian character and its usefulness in the struggle against the Catholic establishment and the governments of the Restoration.

The assertion that Mazzini was a coherently anti-Catholic thinker is also borne out by his concept of the Third Rome. In the process of understanding their past, he argued, the Italian People would discover that the roots of their civilization went much further back in time than the rise of papal Rome. They would eventually conclude that the Eternal City belonged to them, not to the pope, and they would claim it as the natural capital of the new Italy. They would realize that under Roman rule Italy had been united, and they would defy the domestic and foreign skeptics who now denied the possibility of such unity. Above all, an understanding of their Roman heritage would give the Italian People the necessary stimulus to create new cultural institutions, including a political press and universities free from clerical control and censorship. By claiming Rome for themselves and by beginning a cultural revolution they would prepare the foundations for a new political order.[22]

Most Risorgimento democrats agreed with Mazzini that a major change in the attitude of their countrymen toward the Church was a prerequisite for a successful political revolution. Relatively few tried to bring about that change through the preaching of a civil religion. One who did so was the eccentric scientist and philosopher from Bologna, Giuseppe Barilli. His philosophical treatises, published under the pseudonym Quirico Filopanti, refuted a series of documents, beginning with the Syllabus of Errors in 1864, by which the pope stated the incompatibility of liberal or democratic political ideas with Catholic doctrine.[23] Filopanti argued that in the nineteenth century God no longer revealed Himself through a hierarchy preoccupied with its own worldly interests but through those who worked for political freedom and for social justice. But Filopanti's books, though interesting to historians of ideas, were much too abstruse for mass consumption. The popularization of a new religion for the Italian people was largely the work of three men, Modena, Macchi, and Quadrio, who, much more than Filopanti or Mazzini himself, possessed the common touch.

An actor, playwright, and impresario, Modena toured northern and central Italy with his company in the 1840s. His profession, and his ardent belief that the theater must be an instrument for the moral and political education of the masses, made him an ideal agent of democratic and nationalist propaganda. His articles and short plays, written in a folksy and humorous style, popularized every aspect of Mazzini's ideology, especially the concept of "God and the People." But Modena's anti-Catholicism went far beyond the Mazzinian position. He advocated, for instance, the establishment of a new Italian Church (*una chiesa repubblica*) whose leaders were to be chosen from among the lower clergy and to be elected by the people. Like other democrats, he believed that the lower clergy could be won over to the cause of the Italian Revolution and to a democratic civil religion, whereas the upper clergy was hopelessly tied to the interests of the Old Regime.[24]

Macchi and Quadrio were born organizers, activists rather than intellectuals. In the 1860s and 1870s they devoted their energies to the political education of the lower classes. Because the national revolution had succeeded not under democratic but under moderate liberal leadership, the lower classes were virtually excluded from participation in the life of the new state. Thus, in preparation for a second phase of the revolution, it was essential to carry the Mazzinian message "God and the People" to ever larger segments of the population. Although a native of Lombardy, Macchi worked primarily with labor unions and political clubs in the emerging industrial city of Turin. Despite ailments and advanced age, Quadrio traveled through much of northern and central Italy addressing working-class groups of every description in both urban and rural areas.[25]

Macchi and Quadrio were not religious men; they certainly lacked the mystical sense of divine mission that was evident in Mazzini's personality and political behavior. Yet they were well aware of the persistence of religious beliefs among the people they were trying to organize. They also sensed that Italy's urban artisans and workers, if not the peasants, were disenchanted with the Church hierarchy's indifference to social problems and were looking for an alternative to the traditional faith. Mazzini's civil religion, with its egalitarian message and its emphasis upon one's duties toward one's fellow citizens and toward the Nation, could be that alternative.

Quadrio was particularly active and successful in the preaching of civil religion to working-class groups. Like Mazzini, whom he had followed around constantly during the decade 1849–1859, he used religious terms to discuss political issues. For instance, he once addressed the Società democratica livornese on the need for a second, democratic revolution in Italy, "If [we] Italian democrats want to amount to something . . . we must live and act like a militant religious sect (una chiesa militante)."[26] Quadrio did not stop at the preaching of democratic ideas. More sensitive than other democrats to the emotional aspects of religious worship and to the importance of symbolism and liturgy, he also conjured up saints and sacred images, insignia, relics, and hymns for the new religion. In Quadrio's chiesa militante, Mazzini was depicted as Christlike (especially after his death in 1872), and Mazzini's mother became the new Virgin Mary. Banners with the motto "God and the People" stood where the papal insignia were normally found in Catholic churches. Men and women who might have been reluctant to break with Catholicism and who were distrustful of a political propaganda that addressed itself only to their material interests found here fellowship and reassurance: whatever the pope might say, God loved a good democrat.

If the civil religion preached by Mazzini and his followers gained many adherents to Italian democracy before and after the unification, it was not exempt from criticism within the movement itself. In the 1850s, for example, Ferrari, Franchi, and Carlo Cassola engaged in lengthy polemics against the religious coloration of Mazzini's democratic and nationalist program. In La federazione repubblicana, Ferrari argued that in the nineteenth century it was absurd to substitute one religious faith for another because Western civilization had developed much beyond the need for theological explanations of the natural world and of society. It was especially absurd in Italy where a large part of the population still had to be weaned from Catholicism. Instead of deceiving the masses with new forms of religion, Ferrari argued, Italy's democratic intellectuals had an obligation to teach them how to think rationally and scientifically about society. Above all they had an obligation to teach the masses that established religion in whatever form served the interests of the propertied classes, because it diverted the aspirations of the poor away from social and economic issues to some mythical rewards in the hereafter. Mazzini's civil religion, Ferrari thought, was not a useful weapon against Catholicism. For despite its egalitarian spirit, it too diverted the attention of the masses away from a rigorous critique of society by stressing faith in God and self-sacrifice for the fulfillment of a rather vague collective mission. As the first priority of the democratic movement in Italy, Ferrari urged "war against the pope, against . . . the Church enthroned in Rome and dominant elsewhere in Italy . . . No equivocations, no uncertain halfway doctrines, semi-Christian, semipapal . . . *the religion of the revolution is that which deifies man*, his reason, his rights unrecognized and scorned by the Church."[27]

In a similar frame of mind Ausonio Franchi argued for the popularization of rationalist philosophy among his countrymen. To contemporaries who argued that the philosophy of an intellectual minority was not likely to take hold among the masses, he had this to say, remembering his days in the confessional, "Brought up as they are amidst ignorance and hunger, the common people's first concern is to secure their material survival; religious worship for them is primarily a show [*uno spettacolo*]. Thus, it is easier for them than for other social classes to switch from one form of belief to another."[28] Franchi was confident that the Italian masses could be won over to rationalism and atheism if the deomocratic intelligentsia was able to expose the symbiotic relationship between Religion and Property, if it could convince them that its anti-Catholic cultural revolution was but the first step toward a total transformation of Italian society.

Thinking along the same lines, in 1864 Cassola greeted with enthusiasm the appearance of Ernest Renan's *Life of Jesus* "which [was] making its way in the Christian world everywhere blazing a trail of light among the shadows of superstition."[29] There was in Italy a great need for works of this kind, abridged and popularized so that they could be accessible to men and women of limited education. Better one Renan, Cassola argued, than all the Bibles sent into Italy by the British and Foreign Bible Society and other such groups. If the British really wanted to help, he added, instead of Bibles they could send weapons to help the Italians overthrow the temporal power.[30]

Ferrari, Franchi, and Cassola were not alone in espousing this brand of radical anti-Catholicism. But their iconoclastic ideas were not widely accepted even within the democratic movement itself. Certainly in the 1850s and 1860s their uncompromisingly irreligious position had a much smaller popular appeal than either Mazzinian civil religion or evangelical Christianity. Still, their ideas were not forgotten; they surfaced again in the 1880s and 1890s in the strongly secularist outlook of socialist intellectuals who had no qualms about linking their anti-Catholicism to their quest for a new social order.

The radical anti-Catholicism of these Risorgimento intellectuals did not lack precedents in the history of Italy. Ferrari, in particular, was inspired by the writings of Tommaso Campanella, Pietro Giannone, and Giordano Bruno. But his and Franchi's connections with the anti-Catholic subcultures of the past were indirect and purely intellectual. There were, however, Risorgimento democrats who could claim a more direct connection, organizational as well as intellectual. These were the members of various Masonic lodges.

Despite a papal condemnation in 1751, Masonic lodges had been established in all of the Italian states during the eighteenth century. As in other European countries, they had recruited their members from the educated classes, and they had been instrumental in the diffusion of egalitarian political ideas and of new scientific and social theories, which quite often had been at odds with the teachings of the Catholic Church. At the end of the eighteenth century, Italy's Masonic lodges, especially in Milan, Tuscany, and Naples, had been focal points of the reform movement within the Old Regime and later of opposition to Napoleonic despotism. Forced to curtail their activities in the conservative climate of the 1820s, they had provided recruits for more specifically political secret societies like the Carboneria. During the Risorgimento their members were found in both the democratic and the moderate liberal camps. But the most dedicated Masons and those who attained the highest ranks in the order were frequently found on the democratic side. Among them were three grand masters, Ludovico Frapolli, Giuseppe Mazzoni, and Adriano Lemmi.

The network of Masonic lodges, particularly in the Kingdom of the Two Sicilies, in Tuscany, and in the Duchies, played an important part in the democratic movement's anti-Catholic crusade. The Masonic contribution was both intellectual and practical. To the ideological struggle against the Church some lodges contributed their vast holdings of both Italian and foreign anticlerical and antipapal tracts dating back to the early eighteenth century. They also provided experienced propagandists like the Tuscans Mazzoni and Giuseppe Dolfi, and they were a breeding ground for lifelong conspirators like Francesco Crispi.[31]

The role of Masonry in the democratic movement's struggle against the Church was enhanced rather than diminished by the liberal political victories of 1859–60. After the unification, the movement's leaders (including Saffi, who had a peripheral interest in Masonry, and Ferrari, who had never joined a lodge) found the support of the Masonic network more valuable than ever before. In the 1860s the movement was weak and splintered, perennially short of funds to finance anti-Catholic newspapers, and worried about attempts by the ruling liberals to reach a compromise with the Church. It was in these times of defeat and stress that Frapolli published his controversial essay *La Franc-maçonnerie reformée.*[32] He sought an expanded and revitalized role for Italian Masonry as a center of anti-Catholic opposition and egalitarian political agitation. Masonry's goals were to be the secularization of Italian culture, the banishment of the papal court from Italy, and the establishment of a constituent assembly. The first two goals seemed within reach because the governments of the liberal Right, although seeking reconciliation with the Church, were unwilling to serve as her arm against Masonic propaganda.

Ironically, the idyll between the democratic leadership and the Masonic lodges began to deteriorate in 1876 when the parliamentary wing of the movement took over the reins of power. By the 1880s there were unmistakable signs of tension between Crispi and his Masonic brethren. As a statesman, he could not deal with ecclesiastical affairs and with the Roman Question without due regard for its domestic and foreign implications. For their part, they were disappointed to see that the advent of the democratic Left to power was having only a modest impact upon the secularization of Italian culture. Gradually, men like Mazzoni and Lemmi gave up hope of implementing the Masonic anti-Catholic program through legislation. Parting ways with their old friends in the government, they devoted more and more time to extraparliamentary political activities. By the 1890s, in the midst of serious outbreaks of social unrest, Crispi and other parliamentary democrats had moved so far away from the militant anti-Catholicism of the Risorgimento era that an indignant Lemmi declared, "Your [recent] assertion that religious authority must henceforth work hand in hand with civil authority for the defense of the state struck me as unconscionable."[33]

Finally, among the alternatives to Catholicism offered by members of the democratic movement was an interesting attempt to introduce an evangelical culture, Christian yet independent of papal authority. Commenting in his memoirs on the antipapal insurrection of 1830 in the Romagna, Giovanni La Cecilia complained, "The religion of Christ has been twisted into the religion of the pope; if the son of Mary of Nazareth, the Righteous of the Righteous, were to reappear today at the gates of the Vatican, He would be crucified again as an innovator and a revolutionary."[34] Except for a few die-hard atheists like Ferrari, most Risorgimento democrats were sensitive to charges of being irreligious. Hence, in their writings and correspondence one encounters again and again attempts such as this to distinguish between *la religione di Cristo* and *la religione dei preti*. In many cases, no doubt, these attempts to separate genuine Christianity from Catholicism were a rhetorical exercise or a defensive reflex. But there were some men in the movement who believed quite sincerely that the cultural revolution in Italy must be a "Christian revolution," a kind of Italian Reformation that was to save their countrymen not only from the clutches of the Catholic hierarchy but also from an emotionally sterile skepticism. Thus Giuseppe Montanelli warned his fellow democrats that their failure to distinguish between Christian doctrine and clerical despotism and to respect the former while fighting the latter was playing right into the hands of their adversaries: "The reactionaries are most eager to monopolize to their own advantage the conscience of those who have remained faithful to the religion of their fathers. They set themselves up as the paladins of the Catholic *faith*, when in fact they are only defending the Catholic hierarchy . . . We are playing their game if we ourselves fail to distinguish between Catholicism and clerical despotism."[35] Montanelli, a genteel and spiritual man, was different from most of his fellow democrats. He was shocked by Ferrari's proclamation that God was dead (or at least quite irrelevant to the human condition), by Mazzini's argument that Catholicism was dead, and by the scurrilous anticlerical literature which the movement and its Masonic allies produced en masse; yet he believed that a new Italian society, more just and happier, could only be built after a major religious reformation. In contrast to his liberal contemporaries Bettino Ricasoli, Alessandro Manzoni, and others concerned with a *reformatio Ecclesiae*, Montanelli was willing to defy papal authority even to the point of a schism. He faced excommunication with sadness, yet without fear for his immortal soul because, he argued, his struggle against Rome was not religious but political.

Another democratic maverick who advocated the end of the temporal power and attacked the hierarchy while professing his devotion to Catholic doctrine was Giovanni Pantaleo. A friar who left the monastery to fight with Garibaldi in 1860, Pantaleo took his excommunication philosophically. He intended to fight back. Knowing that many parish priests and members of religious orders welcomed the unification of Italy and the end of the temporal power, he dreamed of reorganizing the Italian clergy along democratic lines. With encouragement from Garibaldi, he founded the Associazione emancipatrice del sacerdozio italiano (Association for the Emancipation of the Italian Clergy). Its charter members were about seventy clergymen who had, like Pantaleo himself, traded their cassock for a red shirt in 1860. Through its newspaper, *L'emancipatore cattolico*, the association sent numerous appeals to Pius IX to relinquish the temporal power voluntarily.[36]

Given the entrenched position of the Church in Italian life, its substantial economic interests, the predominance of Italians at the top of the hierarchy, and the pope's attitude toward the unification of Italy, a tremendous act of faith was required to believe in the success of a major Catholic reform movement. But if an evangelical, nonhierarchical form of Christianity seemed beyond reach within the Catholic tradition, it might be found elsewhere. Thus, in the 1860s and 1870s, some democrats viewed sympathetically the growth of evangelical Protestant churches in Italy; and one of them, the Bolognese priest Alessandro Gavazzi, actually became a Protestant minister. These attitudes were not only consistent with the principle of freedom of worship; they also reflected a shrewd and practical realization that there was no better way to undermine the influence of the Catholic Church than to encourage the growth of religious pluralism in Italy.[37]

On the whole, the Risorgimento democrats displayed a high degree of ideological unity vis-à-vis the Roman Catholic Church. In a future democratic Italy there would be no place, of course, for the temporal power. Moreover, if Catholicism was going to survive at all, it would be just one faith among many, tolerated but never officially sanctioned. Indeed, with few exceptions, the Risorgimento democrats felt it incumbent upon themselves to discourage their fellow citizens from following even the spiritual leadership of the Catholic clergy. Before the unification their anti-Catholicism consisted essentially of propaganda, much of it aimed at obvious targets like the temporal power, the Jesuit order, and the Roman Curia. But afterward they agitated both within and without the national Parliament for specific legislation to disestablish the Church and to destroy its influence in the areas of education, charity, and family law.

2

The Italian Revolution as a Political Revolution

WHEN the Risorgimento revolutionaries explained their political beliefs, they spoke in terms of national independence, unity, liberty, and equality, usually in that order. These were code words for key political concepts. As political goals of the Italian Revolution, the concepts of national independence and unity provided the basis for a consensus between moderate liberals and democrats. But the no less important concepts of liberty and equality kept the two groups apart both before and after the unification.

In the 1830s and 1840s national independence was synonymous with the elimination of Austrian rule in northern Italy as well as of Austrian influence exercised through blood ties, dynastic marriages, and diplomatic pressure upon Tuscany, the Duchies, and the Kingdom of the Two Sicilies. Formidable obstacles stood in the way of this first objective of the Italian revolutionaries because it entailed drastic changes in the international settlement of 1815 — the foundation of the European equilibrium — and required political and military resources that they did not possess. Still, some two decades

after the Congress of Vienna, they regarded it as a sine qua non for
the political modernization and economic progress of Italy. The best
minds of the Restoration, from Filippo Buonarroti and Mazzini to
Cesare Balbo and Massimo d'Azeglio, grappled with this problem.
There seemed to be only two ways to achieve national independence. One was to train revolutionary cadres through the network of secret societies for future action against the existing governments and the Austrian troops that protected them. The other was to
rely upon the diplomatic and military leadership of an Italian ruler
who, in the pursuit of his own ambitions, might wish to challenge
Austria's predominance in Italy.[1]

Before 1848 this "diplomatic solution," as it was often called,
seemed the more realistic of the two. Hence the enduring popularity
of Charles Albert of Savoy, despite his betrayal of the Piedmontese
liberals in 1821, and hence the immense popular enthusiasm for Pius
IX in the years 1846–1848. The events of 1848–49, however, disappointed the advocates of a diplomatic solution to the Italian Question and encouraged new attempts to achieve national independence through revolutionary coups de main. As Della Peruta
has pointed out, Mazzini and other democratic activists emerged
from the revolutionary experience with enhanced political reputations and with full confidence that they would soon lead a *guerra di
popolo* against Austria. Even so, domestic and international conditions of the 1850s frustrated their attempts at insurrection and set
the stage for a return to a diplomatic solution under Sardinian
leadership.

But neither the ideological debates between liberals and
democrats on the issue of national independence nor the changes in
strategy dictated by external events should obscure the common
determination of *all* Italian revolutionaries to free their country
from Austrian influence. The behavior of Mazzini, the most consistent advocate and the most successful organizer of popular insurrections, is evidence of this common purpose. At every critical moment
from the 1830s to the spring of 1860 he stood ready to abandon his
strategy (though not his principles), if by so doing he might hasten
the day of victory against Austria.[2]

Much the same could be said with regard to the concept of
Italian unity. Used in the seventeenth and eighteenth centuries to
describe the shared cultural heritage of an educated elite, the words
"Italian unity" (*unità d'Italia*) took on a political meaning during
the Restoration. Until 1848 they were used to mean either the
merger of the existing states into some kind of league or the creation
of an entirely new political structure, whether of a centralized type

like France or of a federal type like Switzerland. Thus, somewhat paradoxically, men as far apart politically as Gioberti, Mazzini, and Carlo Cattaneo could all describe themselves as advocates of "Italian unity." The collapse of the neo-Guelf scheme, however, clarified the situation as one more ideological alternative was eliminated. Certainly after 1848 to be in favor of Italian unity meant to be in favor of an entirely new political order in which neither the continued military presence of Austria nor the continued existence of the temporal power would be tolerated.

Within the democratic camp the future political organization of Italy was the subject of a prolonged and lively debate. Mazzini, Pisacane, and many others argued for a unitary state with a central government strong enough to withstand the inevitable external pressures from powerful neighbors. An influential minority led by Cattaneo and Ferrari argued, on the contrary, that the political and civil liberties of individual citizens could best be safeguarded within a federal structure in accordance with Italy's historical traditions. Again, however, the intellectual liveliness of this debate and its importance for the history of the democratic movement should not obscure the determination of all Italian revolutionaries to sweep away not only the treaties of 1815, but the political and economic institutions of the Old Regime as well.

The broad ideological consensus between moderate liberals and democrats on the goals of national independence and unity accounted for the great accomplishment of the Risorgimento: the creation in 1860 of a modern and united Italian state. Paradoxically, though, the lack of a comparable consensus on the equally important goals of liberty and equality made it an intellectually exciting time for the men who shaped Italy. That lack of consensus generated passionate debates and has been the subject of historiographical controversy ever since the unification. The word liberty was writ large on the banners of all Risorgimento revolutionaries, who usually justified their pursuit of national independence and unity in the name of liberty. However, during the course of the Italian Revolution significant differences emerged between the liberal and the democratic definitions of that term, differences which have persisted long after the unification in debates on the most important national issues.

As Rosario Romeo pointed out some years ago, in the initial stages of the Italian Revolution "moderate liberalism presented itself as a public opinion trend more than as an actual political movement; [it was] suspended, by its very nature, halfway between its loyalty to the regional states and the Catholic religion and its

desire for progress, a desire which in nineteenth-century Europe
. . . inevitably led to the question of liberty."[3] But the events of
1848–49 demonstrated that there could be no progress without liberty, and that there could be no liberty without independence and
unity. Once the painful and necessary choices had been made, once
the inevitability of a struggle against Austria and against the papacy
had been recognized, moderate liberalism emerged as a genuine
political movement with an ideology at least as clear as that of any
comparable group in nineteenth-century Europe.

The ideology of Italian liberalism was formulated by a group of
distinguished jurists and philosophers from all parts of Italy, many
of whom in the 1850s found hospitable refuge and congenial intellectual fellowship in the Turin of Cavour, d'Azeglio, Pier Carlo
Boggio, and Michelangelo Castelli. This ideology cannot, of course,
be analyzed in depth without due regard to differences of philosophical and regional background among its proponents and
without taking into account the political realities within which it
was formulated. Still, for the purposes of this essay the analysis can
be limited to those basic concepts shared by all the leaders of Italian
liberalism from the 1850s to the end of the Risorgimento. Subse-
quently, the basic politcal concepts of liberal ideology can be compared with those of democratic ideology.[4]

For the liberal thinkers of the Risorgimento, to attain liberty
was to destroy all those institutions and traditions that stood in the
way of Italy's moral, cultural, and economic development (or "progress," to use the language of the nineteenth century). In some ways
they saw themselves as the heirs of Bernardo Tanucci, Francesco
Maria Gianni, Guillaume du Tillot, and Gian Rinaldo Carli. But
the difficulties which those famous eighteenth-century reformers
had encountered, and their own experiences of the late 1840s, led
the Risorgimento liberals to conclude that the attainment of liberty
required a complete break both with the existing regimes and with
the Church. Many objectionable institutions stood in the way of progress as the liberals defined it: various kinds of communal and
seigneurial rights that had survived the era of the French Revolution, ecclesiastical courts, schools that taught theology and Latin at
the expense of logic and science, and guilds that stressed tradition
and security for their members at the expense of economic growth.
Yet what was the ultimate purpose of destroying these traditional institutions and of teaching a new generation of Italians to think in
terms of "progress"? The eighteenth-century reformers had introduced changes, even radical ones, in order to strengthen the
authority of the state and to reaffirm its legitimacy. The Risorgi-

mento liberals proposed instead to free the individual from the bondages of tradition first in the intellectual and then in the social and economic spheres.

Once the individual had been set free, which form of government was best suited to safeguard his liberty in the Italian context? The overwhelming choice of the Risorgimento liberals was a constitutional monarchy with a parliament elected by an indirect system of representation. A constitution, preferably written by the best legal minds in the nation, would protect the individual's civil rights, while a monarchical form of government would guarantee political stability and protect, when necessary, the rights of minorities against the tyranny of the majority. Finally, an elected legislature would function as both a law-making body and a forum for public debate of great national issues.[5]

The political institutions of the Kingdom of Sardinia after 1848 did not quite measure up to the highest ideals of Italian liberalism. For example, the constitution granted by Charles Albert had been drafted hastily and had not had the benefit of a proper constituent assembly. The influence of the clergy in public life remained strong even after the passage of the controversial Siccardi Laws in 1850. Moreover, it took the Piedmontese liberals several years of political struggle to establish parliamentary control over state expenditures, including the military budget. But, on balance, Piedmont-Sardinia in the 1850s came close enough to the "reign of liberty" that the liberal exiles of 1848 such as Pasquale Mancini, Terenzio Mamiani, Antonio Scialoja, and Filippo Cordova had tried, with only fleeting success, to introduce in other parts of Italy. That was a major reason why those men adjusted relatively well to the political climate in Piedmont-Sardinia, why they were able to remain in public life, and why they supported Cavour's anti-Austrian policy in the late 1850s.[6]

There were other models of political development to which the advocates of Italian independence, unity, and liberty could turn for inspiration: the July Monarchy in France and the British parliamentary system as reformed in 1832. Cavour himself was known to admire the British Parliament (that of Sardinia was a mere shadow body by comparison) and the strong British tradition of local self-government. Mamiani and Marco Minghetti, who had spent several years in Louis Philippe's France, admired the political ideal of the *juste milieu*. Other liberals, though, doubted the wisdom of imitating a political system that in February 1848 had proved pitifully vulnerable to attack by a revolutionary minority. In any event, looking ahead to national independence and unity, the proponents of liberal ideology kept their options open. In the 1850s they certainly did not believe that the political institutions of Piedmont-Sardinia, however advanced, could simply be extended to the rest of the country. If they accepted this solution in 1859–60, it was only because domestic and international circumstances made other alternatives seem unrealistic or dangerous. But after the unification, as deputies and ministers, they labored to reform the Sardinian institutions of 1848 along more genuinely liberal lines by insisting, for instance, upon ministerial responsibility to the Chamber.

There was, however, one aspect of the Sardinian political system that was entirely compatible with the liberal definition of good government: the highly restricted electorate. The Italian liberals, like their counterparts everywhere in Europe, made a clear distinction between the citizenry (*i cittadini*) and the masses or populace (*il popolo*). In a liberal state the populace were entitled to civil rights, but only the citizenry, a minority fit for positions of responsibility by virtue of sex, age, property ownership, and formal education, could properly be entrusted with political rights. Was such a distinction between citizenry and populace compatible with the "reign of liberty"? The liberals thought that it was not merely compatible with liberty but essential to its preservation.

Everywhere, of course, the liberal position on this issue reflected the fear that political democracy might lead to unstable government and to "mob rule," that is, to uncontrollable social conflicts. In Italy it also reflected the fear that the triumph of political democracy might delay the attainment of national unity (or wreck it after it had been attained). But interpreters of the Risorgimento may have overemphasized this element of fear. In the 1850s and 1860s the Italian liberals had no valid reasons to believe that Mazzini and other leading democrats were less devoted to the cause of national independence and unity than they were. Nor did they have much reason to believe that the democrats were insensitive to the dangers of mob rule. Their opposition to democratic political ideas and their resistance after the unification to quite modest suggestions of franchise reform stemmed less from their concern for national unity than from their view of political participation.[7]

In the outlook of the Risorgimento liberals, political participation was not the birthright of every person born within the geographical boundaries of the state; it was a privilege. It could not, of course, be ascriptive like the aristocratic privileges of the Old Regime but had to be earned through individual effort, the appropriate conditions for which were established by liberal political institutions. The privileges of voting and of seeking elective office were not to be confused with such human rights as life itself or with civil rights such as freedom from arbitrary arrest. Instead, the liberals regarded those political privileges as an integral part of a meritocratic sociopolitical system within which the individual also earned economic power through the accumulation of property, and intellectual power through the acquisition of socially valuable knowledge. In short, the liberal position was an updated version of the eighteenth-century concept of equality based upon the principles of "natural rights" and of "careers open to talent." Although they imposed major restrictions upon political participation, the Risorgimento liberals could still argue in all sincerity that their position was egalitarian. They pointed out that a liberal state recognized the "natural" equality of all men. As for the barriers to political equality — necessary to assure stablity, especially in a backward country such as Italy — they were merely temporary and could be overcome by individual effort. The only exception was the obviously ascriptive barrier of sex. And significantly, the Risorgimento liberals were more ambivalent and divided on the issue of women's suffrage than were their democratic opponents.[8]

Both before and after the unification the liberals' commitment to a meritocratic view of society and politics was the focal point of their ideological conflict with the democrats. This was ironic, for it would be difficult to imagine in nineteenth-century Europe a group of men more deeply committed than the Risorgimento democrats to the principles of "natural rights" and of "careers open to talent." Their socioeconomic background, their education, and their experiences as exiles after 1848 prepared them particularly well to appreciate and indeed to demand a society that rewarded individual talent and ambition. But the leaders of Italian democracy remained critical of the liberal ideology even when they found that they could personally thrive within a liberal socioeconomic system. They remained critical, first of all, because their own concept of political participation was rather different from that of the liberals and, second, because they perceived in the restrictive political participation preferred by the liberals an implicit acceptance of the glaring inequalities of Italian society.

Liberty, defined as the destruction of the Old Regime and its replacement by constitutional government and narrow parliamentary representation, was the all-important political goal of the Risorgimento liberals, the reason for fighting a war of independence and for attempting to unify Italy. They took for granted that new political institutions of their making and under their guidance would ultimately produce important social benefits. For the democrats, on the other hand, the attainment of liberty merely by an elite was only a step, albeit an essential one, toward the attainment of more ambitious political goals: broad popular participation and, eventually, political equality.

In the initial stages of the Italian Revolution when liberty was still beyond reach, liberals and democrats cooperated in attempts to force the existing governments to reform along constitutional and secular lines. But even then they differed on political strategy. Orsini, for instance, wrote that in his native Romagna, where conflicts between moderate liberals and Mazzinian republicans developed early and were more intense than elsewhere in northern Italy, "the main thrust of [our] agitation was the reform and the secularization of the papal government, but we never lost sight of our long-range objective, national independence. Moderates and republicans, we were all united in our determination to change the status quo; but we disagreed on the means to be used."[9]

With the failure of the reform movement and the outbreak of revolutions in 1848, the precarious cooperation broke down, and it became obvious that the two groups were following different paths to liberty. If the liberals found inspiration in the accomplishments of the great Italian reformers of the eighteenth century, the democrats identified with the Jacobins of the 1790s (whose direct descendants they often were) and with the myth of a great egalitarian revolution thwarted by the militaristic ambitions of Napoleon Bonaparte. When they looked for political models outside of Italy they did not turn to the politics of the *juste milieu* or to British liberalism but to the First French Republic, to Switzerland, or to the United States. It was no accident that these were republican regimes. Although the leaders of Risorgimento democracy, with few exceptions, came to terms with the Sardinian constitutional monarchy in the 1860s, the democratic movement was born with a strong republican bias which it never really lost. The philosophical reasons for this bias were spelled out early in the history of the movement in the program of Mazzini's Young Italy:

The aim of Young Italy . . . is to conquer for Italy Unity, Independence, and Liberty. Revolutions are made with the People for the People. In order to stir up in the People an enthusiastic commitment to revolution, we must persuade them beyond any doubt that we are attempting it for their sake. In order to persuade them of this, we must inspire in them a consciousness of their rights and we must present the revolution as the path to the full enjoyment of those rights. Hence, we must propose as the goal of our revolution a

democratic system, a system that will improve the conditions of the poorest and most numerous classes, a system that
will call upon all citizens to use their talents in the conduct
of public affairs, a system built upon [the principle of]
equality, a system in which the government will be elected
by a broadly based, inexpensive, and simple method.

This system is a Republican system.

Young Italy stands for a Unitary Republic.[10]

Mazzini's republicanism was built upon two assumptions. One
was that under monarchical institutions the survival of liberty could
not be guaranteed by even the most advanced of constitutions. The
accumulation of power in the hands of the rulers over several generations inevitably produced dynastic interests that were at variance
with those of the nation. The second assumption was that monarchical institutions were inherently incompatible with the principle of equality. Both assumptions could be traced directly to the
arguments of the French regicides of 1793 and to the polemics of the
radical Jacobins in Italy. These assumptions were widely shared by
the Risorgimento democrats, including men like Ferrari and Cattaneo who never joined Young Italy and who criticized other aspects
of the Mazzinian program.

There were times before 1860 when Mazzini himself and other
democrats set aside their republican convictions because an acceptance of monarchical leadership seemed to offer a shortcut to the
cherished goals of national independence and unity. But they felt
uneasy each time they sacrificed one political goal of the revolution,
equality, to pursue the others, and each time they came to regret
their decision. In 1857 when republican stalwarts like Daniele
Manin were casting their lot with the Sardinian monarchy in an-
ticipation of another war against Austria, the Mazzinian Quadrio in
vain pleaded with them to learn from his own bitter experience:
"Twice in my life [in 1821 and in 1848] I put my trust in the monarchy, and twice I saw it renege on its promises."[11]

Besides refuting the liberal arguments in favor of a constitutional monarchy, the Mazzinian program raised the issue of political
participation in the Italian Revolution and in the postrevolutionary
state. After the failure of the reform movement and the collapse of
the neo-Guelf scheme, all Italian revolutionaries had to agree that
national independence, unity, and liberty could not be won without
some form of popular participation. Throughout his long career
Mazzini asked troublesome questions as to how this participation
could best be encouraged and rewarded, for it was obvious to him

that the Italian masses had to be called to make sacrifices for the success of the national revolution. This issue was also raised by the socialist Pisacane. In his book on the revolutions of 1848 he pointed out that the propertied classes in Italy were ready and willing to fight Austria and overthrow the Old Regime. For only the lack of political freedom and power was keeping them from the full enjoyment of what they already had: wealth, education, and social prestige. But they needed help to achieve their political objectives. What, if anything, were they prepared to offer in exchange for the support of the masses?[12]

According to most Risorgimento democrats, some form of political participation in the postrevolutionary Italian government was the least that could be promised the masses as an incentive to join the national struggle. But because the democrats were fully as conscious of their country's backwardness as were the liberals, they did not propose the immediate wholesale adoption of democratic institutions. On the issue of universal manhood suffrage, for instance, they were divided and cautious, especially after 1848. From both the Italian and the French experience they learned the hard way how an unsophisticated electorate could be manipulated by conservative notables and by the clergy.[13] After the unification they had reason to fear that this might happen again, to the detriment of national unity and of the secularization of Italian society. Nonetheless, in the democratic outlook political participation by the masses was not the distant, utopian goal that it was for the liberals. Neither was it a privilege to be earned in the same way as one earned money, university degrees, intellectual fame, or military glory. It was a right, and to withhold from the masses the enjoyment of that right could only arouse bitter resentment against the new political order.[14]

Recognizing that a minimum level of education was necessary for the responsible and effective exercise of political rights, the Risorgimento democrats generally supported literacy tests for prospective voters. In practice, this meant that in the 1860s they accepted the exclusion of a majority of the population (and in the South and islands an overwhelming majority) from political life. Still they believed that this unfortunate situation could be corrected in a few years through an intense literacy drive sponsored by private organizations as well as by the state. In fact, men like Quadrio, Macchi, and Saffi who were active in the Società operaie after the unification urged them to give priority to the civic education of their members and to adult education programs for the lower classes in general.[15]

But if the Risorgimento democrats conceded the wisdom of excluding illiterates from the polls, they did not concede the wisdom of restricting political participation to the propertied classes. There were several reasons behind their objections to the property requirements dear to the hearts of their liberal colleagues. Quite a few Risorgimento democrats were poor, though well educated. Like Don Stumbo, the revolutionary priest in Giuseppe Ricciardi's prophetic *Storia d'Italia dal 1850 al 1900*, they were "[men] of education far above [their] station."[16] That is, they were men of humble backgrounds who were unable for various reasons to use their education in the pursuit of upward social and economic mobility outside the political arena. Naturally, as participants in the Italian Revolution they objected to electoral laws that might discriminate against them. The case for educated but propertyless men was argued, for instance, by Giovanni Battista Tuveri against a liberal colleague during the debate over the Sardinian electoral law of 1848.[17] But even well-to-do democrats like Ricciardi, Ferrari, and Lemmi objected to property requirements for prospective voters. Their objections are particularly interesting as a clue to the democratic perception of Italian society.

Liberal ideology made participation in the governing of the polity contingent upon achievement of success, presumably by independent effort and merit, in other areas of life. Thus, in Italian society "the poorer and more numerous classes," as Mazzini called them, were excluded from participation not only because most of them were illiterate but also because they owned little or no real property. But no Italian revolutionary of the nineteenth century, liberal or democrat, could possibly have argued that the masses would be *forever* excluded from participation in the polity. To argue this would have meant to deny the inevitability of progress, in which Cavour believed no less fervently than did Mazini. Obviously, therefore, the liberal position on the issue of participation implied confidence that most Italians would be able to overcome both illiteracy and poverty, in the distant if not in the near future. The democrats were confident (perhaps too much so) that mass illiteracy could be overcome quickly. But most of them could not believe that the introduction of liberal institutions, however desirable on other grounds, would ever lift millions of their countrymen out of poverty. Long before the unification Ferrari expressed the skepticism of many democrats on this issue: "Liberty, sovereignty, and independence are nothing but lies wherever the rich oppress the poor, wherever the poor exist only to enhance the comfort of the rich, wherever a poor man can only feed his family by toiling hard

. . . to build a world of luxury to which he can never aspire."[18]

Ferrari, Macchi, Benedetto Musolino, and others believed that widespread poverty could only be eliminated through radical changes in the structure of property relations. Pisacane, Francesco Milo Guggino, and Tommaso Landi thought that this could be accomplished only through a full-fledged "revolution from below." In any event, the attainment of greater social equality and of a more equitable distribution of wealth (the rough meaning of "social justice" in the vocabulary of Risorgimento democratic ideology) seemed a long way off. In the meantime, to deny political participation to the propertyless majority was a double injustice. It was an injustice, first of all, to every man (and perhaps also to every woman) from the lower classes who had responded to the revolutionary appeal for Italian independence, unity, and liberty. He (or she) had already earned the right to determine the political future of Italy. Second, it was an injustice to millions of poor people because it assumed poverty to be a temporary condition amenable to individualized solutions, rather than the endemic social disease it actually was. The liberal ideology in effect penalized the poor for being poor while denying them the opportunity to change by political action the institutions, laws, and social relations that created their condition.[19]

The leaders of Risorgimento democracy had ambivalent feelings toward the masses. Their behavior toward them was paternalistic more often than egalitarian. Moreover, those democrats who themselves came from the lower classes, like Francesco Domenico Guerrazzi, Asproni, and Filippo De Boni, were much less inclined to idealize the morality and patriotism of the common people than was the solidly middle-class Mazzini. In contrast to most liberals, the democrats worried that the government's mistrust of the masses which resulted in their exclusion from political life and in the neglect of their material needs might breed social conflicts so violent as to offset the blessings of national unity and of liberal institutions. Saffi spoke for many fellow democrats when he said, in November 1860, "Mistrust is the bane of our government . . . mistrust of the revolution, mistrust of the people, mistrust of the [Garibaldian] volunteers, mistrust of every element that most vigorously embodies the growing vitality of our young nation."[20]

Interpreters of Mazzini's thought have pointed out that before the unification he often played down the more radically egalitarian implications of his political and social philosophy. It was important to him personally and to the success of his movement not to allow critics to draw any plausible parallels between his brand of democracy and that of contemporary socialist or communist intellectuals. The Risorgimento democrats were similarly vulnerable on this point. In the intellectual climate of the Restoration, republicanism was still associated in the popular mind with the excesses of the Terror in France and with the irreligious proclivities of many Italian Jacobins. An egalitarian ideology, even if restricted to the realm of politics, conjured up memories of seventeenth-century English Levellers, of Babouvist conspiracies, of Fourierist communes. And the advocates of such an ideology became, of course, all the more vulnerable to criticism if they brought up issues of social justice. Thus, the Risorgimento democrats were always on the defensive, constantly facing the danger that their republican and egalitarian sentiments might alienate potential supporters of the struggle for national independence and unity. After the unification they still had to come to terms with that problem if they wished to get elected to the national Parliament.

There were among them a few mavericks like Ferrari who had no qualms about flaunting their egalitarian convictions as well as their militant anti-Catholicism. They were the exceptions. Ferrari, as a voluntary expatriate, a French citizen before 1860, and a *rentier*, could afford not to worry about the price to be paid for his radical political pronouncements. However, most of his fellow democrats, especially during the period 1849–1860, were not so fortunate. Often they were impoverished and downtrodden exiles, subject to political harassment, to discrimination in jobs and housing, and to expulsion on short notice. Pisacane gave a pithy and accurate description of their lot in the 1850s: "We [democrats] are regarded as the plebs among the exiles. I am pleased with this label, but sorry that we do not have the finest attribute of the plebs: numbers."[21] Pisacane was able to be openly defiant because his personal lifestyle and his widely known socialist convictions placed him well beyond the pale of respectable society. But far from sharing this defiance, other democrats went to some pains to defend their political ideology and to make it palatable to respectable society. A good example of democratic cautiousness and defensiveness is found in Macchi's political writings of the 1850s.

During his youth in Milan, Macchi was a disciple of Cattaneo, and he later followed his teacher to the barricades in 1848. Afterward, as an exile in Switzerland, he contributed to Cattaneo's *Archivio triennale delle cose d'Italia*, trying to mediate the ideological conflict between unitary and federalist republicans. Expelled from Switzerland, he settled in Turin where he worked as a journalist and as a political organizer among the lower classes. His ties with Mazzini and Cattaneo and his own political activities made him an obvious target for police surveillance. Fearful of a new expulsion, he gradually detached himself from Mazzini's conspiratorial network. And in an essay of 1854 he endeavored to persuade his readers that a republican form of government did not threaten the social order but rather guaranteed stability:

> With regard to *form*, the difference between monarchy and republic consists in having a king or a president [as head of the state]; but insofar as *substance* is concerned, we should say *that a country has a republican form of government whenever public opinion there is sovereign*, whenever it is strong enough to thwart any evil designs by the prince. On the contrary, we should say that a country has a monarchical form of government whenever public opinion is not strong enough to thwart the intrigues or the arrogance of a president. From this viewpoint, England might be called the most republican of the European nations, even though she grants the firstborn child of a certain family the right to parade around in royal pomp on official holidays.[22]

As for political equality, Macchi emphasized that it was a *goal* of the democratic movement, not a *policy* to be implemented as soon as Italy became independent. His views reflected the sobering effect of the revolution of 1848 upon the democratic leadership. He lamented, "I see, alas, that the masses are still a long way from that degree of maturity which we, in our youthful enthusiasm, attributed to them in the early days of our rebirth . . . Nonetheless, I deeply believe that given proper examples and education the masses will learn to recognize their rights and to use them. I call myself a republican, because I remain unshakable in this conviction."[23] In support of his argument that republicanism and political egalitarianism did not lead inevitably to terror and anarchy, he pointed to the United States: "North America goes forth happy and tranquil in her democratic institutions, combining progress and peace, the two greatest blessings of civilized living."[24]

For democrats on the defensive, like Macchi, the myth of a democratic and independent American Republic served a useful purpose. The birth of the United States in a struggle for national identity and against monarchical despotism, its enviable political stability, and its growing prosperity were proof that a republican form of government and a democratic electoral system were compatible with peaceful progress. Having read about the United States mostly through French sources (especially Alexis de Tocqueville's classic political analysis), Macchi, Guerrazzi, Ermolao Rubieri, De Boni, Asproni, and others admired it rather less critically than they did the more familiar Swiss Republic. They were particularly enthusiastic because of the lack of any established state religion in the United States, which they regarded as the foremost contribution of American civilization to the modern age. Their idealistic belief, correct in part, that American society was more egalitarian than any found in Europe further fueled their enthusiasm.[25]

But if foreign examples seemed irrelevant or, as Mazzini argued, if they were inappropriate for the leaders of a national revolution, the Risorgimento democrats could pursue another and perhaps more convincing line of defense. They could and did argue that their republican and egalitarian principles were rooted in native traditions. Thus, reminiscing over his participation in the defense of the Venetian Republic in 1849, Orsini observed, "Wherever the people were left to fend for themselves . . . they set up republics, the only form of government suitable to Italy's traditions and to her social exigencies."[26] He noted that in Venice, at the moment when the democratic leadership had been most effective and the revolutionary spirit of the population most intense, it had seemed natural to resurrect the Republic of St. Mark. But republican governments had also been proclaimed in parts of Italy where centuries of monarchical or seigneurial rule were thought to have destroyed all traces of a republican past. There was a lesson to be learned from that extraordinary experience; and the democratic leaders were quick to capitalize on it even in defeat. They did not want their contemporaries to forget the exhilarating moment when republican and egalitarian principles had prevailed or to believe that it had been a unique, isolated moment in the history of Italy. Mazzini affirmed that the exiled leaders of the Roman Republic of 1849 were an *Italian* government-in-exile. One day, he said, they would return to Rome and resume the great task of national unification and democratization that had been interrupted by the unconscionable intervention of republican France.[27] Hundreds of lesser democratic lights wrote memoirs or historical accounts of the revolution of 1848, many of which were published by Cattaneo and his collaborators in the Lugano area and smuggled into Italy. And most important, Ferrari, Montanelli, Pisacane, and Cattaneo himself used the revolutionary experience as a starting point for new interpretations of Italian history as well as a source of political lessons for the future.

Like Orsini they were impressed by the considerable popular en-

thusiasm for the revolutionary governments of 1848–49, especially
for the republics in Venice, Tuscany, and the Papal States. That experience inspired them to write works that did much to legitimize
the republican and egalitarian aspirations of Risorgimento democracy and that became part of its intellectual legacy to later generations. Cattaneo and Montanelli traced the origins of those aspirations not to foreign models, not even to the impact of the French
Revolution in Italy, but to the Italian city-states of the late Middle
Ages. In a widely read and acclaimed essay of 1858, Cattaneo
argued that Italy's intellectual and economic life had been at its
vigorous best when the Italian people had been able to establish independent republics around major urban centers. He saw in the
leaders of those republics the ancestors of the industrious and self-
confident bourgeoisie that had initiated the economic modernization of Italy and that was already playing a major role in its political
emancipation. The republican city-states, he thought, had enjoyed
some of the political blessings for which the democrats of the
modern age were fighting: broad popular participation and freedom
from monarchical and clerical despotism. He was aware that the
governments of the city-states had been oligarchical, not
democratic. Against the partisans of constitutional monarchy and of
Sardinian leadership he argued that the tradition of republicanism
and independence of the city-states was very relevant to Italy's needs
in the nineteenth century: "The people of Italy's cities, even without
any knowledge of military science, are stronger than the armies of
the monarchs. Monarchy in Italy is an exotic and feeble plant, an
unnatural thing."[28]

In his analysis of the revolution of 1848 in Lombardy, Cattaneo
commented that it was not enough for the Italian people to rise
against their oppressors. Once liberty had been earned on the barricades or on the battlefield, it was necessary "to keep one's hands on
it," as he put it. Liberty could easily be lost again unless the people
were vigilant and careful to preserve it. Given the primitive political
consciousness of the masses and the strength of their attachment to
local traditions, Cattaneo doubted that a nationwide revolution
with its focal point in Rome could be successful. He feared that there
might be more moments of popular excitement and glory followed
by more moments of confusion and disappointment. Against Mazzini's unshaken belief in a national movement for independence and
unity, he could cite the course of events in Lombardy after the successful Milanese uprising of March 1848. The people of Cattaneo's
native region had fought enthusiastically against Austrian troops until they had realized that they were actually fighting for the greater

glory of the Sardinian king and of the patricians who had urged him to intervene. At that point, the Lombard people had lost interest in the struggle.[29]

This Lombard experience led Cattaneo to conclude that it was more in keeping with the Italian tradition of the free city-state (a distinctly republican tradition) to work for revolutions of relatively limited scope. Only thus could the local or regional loyalties of the masses be aroused and channeled in a positive direction, instead of becoming an obstacle to change as had happened in 1848–49. A federation of revolutionary republics and eventually an all-Italian constituent assembly were sure to follow as an inevitable response to common needs for defense against foreign powers and for economic development. Above all, Cattaneo believed that a federation of small, democratic republics of the Swiss type would make it easier for the people to understand political issues, to participate in discussions and elections, and to become accustomed to civic responsibilities. As the liberals realized very well, in a large and complex polity, especially one created by the merger of states that were historically quite distinctive, it would be difficult for the masses to acquire that kind of political education. The liberal solution to this problem was the restriction of political participation to enlightened men of means. Cattaneo's solution was to create a federation of independent republics small enough for the masses to keep a watchful eye on their elected leaders, if not to govern directly.[30]

Cattaneo's defense of Italy's republican traditions vis-à-vis the supporters of constitutional monarchy and his federalist arguments against Mazzini were centered around the issue of political liberty. As S. J. Woolf has pointed out, Cattaneo defined liberty in roughly the same terms as the liberals, stressing how the destruction of the Old Regime and the release of individual energies would eventually benefit society as a whole. He disagreed with the liberals and with his fellow republican Mazzini primarily about the means most appropriate to the attainment and the preservation of political liberty. But his contemporaries and friends Ferrari, Montanelli, and Pisacane drew rather different lessons from the same revolutionary experience. They came out of it convinced that the leadership of the revolution had slipped out of their hands not so much because they had initially succumbed to the general enthusiasm for Charles Albert and for Pius IX but because they had failed to define and emphasize clearly and adequately the concept of equality, the democratic principle of greatest importance to the masses. In their writings on the revolution of 1848 they faced this issue and confronted their fellow democrats with it.

In his *Rivoluzione d'Italia*, Montanelli urged his fellow democrats, especially Mazzini, to stop being defensive about their preference for a republic and their commitment to political equality. It was most unfortunate, he wrote, that in 1848 the leaders of Italian democracy, caught up in their patriotic enthusiasm and in their eagerness to cooperate with the liberals, had neglected to emphasize "two fundamental principles. The first one [is] that our Revolution [is] not merely a *national* revolution . . . The second one [is] that the European revolution of which the Italian Revolution is a part will result in a *restructuring of Europe's economic and social conditions.*"[31] It was incumbent upon all Italian democrats, he added, not to repeat the same error. The argument that political egalitarianism was a dangerous philosophy of foreign, especially French, derivation could be answered by an analysis of Italian history. As Cattaneo had done to defend its republican bias, Montanelli justified the democratic movement's egalitarian position by tracing its origins back to the city-states of the late Middle Ages. Those Italian communities, he argued, had provided political ideas and models of political participation and social equality that had later been adapted in other countries, most recently by French republicans and socialists. Thus, instead of denying any affinity between Italian democracy and French socialism — as Mazzini and others were doing defensively — every democrat had the duty to publicize the Italian roots of republicanism and egalitarianism, especially in those regions where monarchical and clerical despotism had become most deeply entrenched. It was also the democrats' duty to explain to the masses that the Italian Revolution, though it had particular objectives (like the destruction of the temporal power), was part of a much broader European movement for political liberty and equality.[32]

If Montanelli's work pointed to new directions for democratic propaganda, however, it did not deal with the question of how the masses were to be attracted to those new avenues. To publicize the historical roots of Italian democracy and the international context of the political struggle in Italy might be an effective way to reach young people from the educated classes, but it was obviously not the way to reach millions of illiterates. Two democrats with very different backgrounds, Ferrari and Pisacane, tried to deal with this question, which both Cattaneo and Montanelli had left unanswered. Reflecting upon the events of 1848–49 in Italy, Ferrari and Pisacane came to the conclusion that the promise of political equality in a postrevolutionary state was unlikely to arouse more enthusiasm among the masses than the promise of national independence and unity or the promise of liberty as the liberals defined it.

Discussing the Mazzinian program in an essay of 1845, Ferrari had written, "If [material] means without ideas cannot arouse the masses, ideas without means are worthless weapons. Mazzini relied on ideas and he proclaimed liberty to rally the people. Unfortunately, he forgot that the only enduring liberty is that which corresponds to the true needs of the masses."[33] Ferrari had left it at this without defining "the true needs of the masses." Presumably he had meant the social and economic needs of the lower classes, which were in those days the foremost concern of his French friends Philippe Buchez, Georges Sand, Pierre Leroux, and others. He returned to this issue in the early 1850s with a more thorough and biting critique of what he called "Mazzinian abstractions." In his letters to Mazzini and in *La federazione repubblicana* he argued that in 1848–49 the leaders of Italian democracy had made two serious errors. If repeated, he predicted, those errors would cost them the leadership of the Italian Revolution for which they (and Mazzini more than anyone else) had made enormous sacrifices. The first error had been to leave the Roman Catholic establishment intact; the second had been the failure to give the masses any concrete incentive for identifying with the revolution and defending its leaders against domestic and foreign enemies. Could the promise of political rights be an adequate incentive? Ferrari doubted it, especially after witnessing how Louis Napoleon Bonaparte had profited from and even exploited universal manhood suffrage in France. But a commitment to social justice on the part of the democratic leadership might come much closer to the mark.[34]

While asking fellow democrats to redefine equality and make a stronger and clearer commitment to it than they had made in 1848, Ferrari did not argue that it should be the only or even the most important objective of the Italian Revolution. He agreed with other democrats on the need to pursue national independence and a new political order, although, like Cattaneo, he preferred a federation of democratic republics to a centralized state. Pisacane, however, saw the democrats' reluctance to deal with the issue of equality as the key to the revolutionary failures of 1848–49. His analysis of the events of those years led him to conclude that he and his fellow democrats had been working with the wrong set of priorities. They had generally followed the liberal leadership in the pursuit of independence, unity, and liberty. Equality, vaguely and narrowly defined in political terms, had appeared last, if at all, in the democratic program. In 1848 the masses had responded well to the advent of democratic governments, but their enthusiasm had evaporated quickly. From their point of view, he argued, the bourgeois revolutionary governments had not proved to be very different from the traditional ones. It was time for the democratic leadership to reverse its priorities, to place the pursuit of equality (social and economic as well as political) ahead of all other goals.[35]

Although their works were widely read and debated in democratic circles, Montanelli, Ferrari, and Pisacane never achieved a large personal following much less political parties that could rival the Mazzinian organizations. Even so, they played an important role in the development of Risorgimento democracy. Through their writings they made fellow revolutionaries rethink the meaning of political liberty and equality and thus articulate that concern for social justice which was the third distinctive feature of democratic ideology.

3

The Italian Revolution as a
Social Revolution

COMMITMENT to social justice was not only an important component of democratic ideology in the Risorgimento but also an important part of its legacy to the program of both the Radical and Socialist parties in the last quarter of the nineteenth century. It arose from the realization, common to nearly all the leaders of the movement, that the Italian masses, poor, backward, and ignorant, could not be emancipated merely by disestablishing the Catholic Church and introducing liberal or even democratic government. The condition of the masses could be improved only by a more or less radical transformation of Italian society. The sensitivity to social and economic issues that was characteristic of the Risorgimento democrats stemmed from several sources. In many cases it reflected their own experience of poverty or of limited opportunities for upward mobility during their youth, or it arose from their direct observation of poverty cultures in specific localities or regions. In a few cases it stemmed from intellectual experiences, such as the reading of French or British works on the social question. Whatever its

origins, this sensitivity developed early in the lives of the leading Risorgimento democrats, and though at times a major source of controversy, it became an important intellectual and emotional bond
among them.

Before 1848 Mazzini tried to develop an organic and coherent
relationship between his insights into issues of social justice and his
revolutionary goals in the realms of culture and politics. In this as in
other respects he was well ahead of his fellow democrats. It was inevitable that he should raise questions about the structure of Italian
society, for he was committed to a revolution "with the People and
for the People." Obviously, the national and democratic state for
which he struggled could never come about unless the masses were
given some incentive to contribute to its creation and its support
later on. The incentives that Mazzini offered were moral and political in nature. He was critical of those among his contemporaries
who emphasized the class struggle between rich and poor or the socialization of land and capital. Indeed, he was as eager to strike a
blow against "the materialism of the eighteenth century" as he was
to undermine the conservatism of the privileged classes. Thus, he defined the social objectives of the Italian Revolution as follows: "the
abolition of all privileges other than those derived from the eternal
principle of ability applied to good ends; the gradual reduction [in
the number] of men who sell their labor . . . ; a gradual rapprochement among social classes, so as to form one People and to promote
the maximum development of individual abilities; and the attainment of laws that meet the People's needs."[1] In the 1830s and 1840s
the followers of Buonarroti and some independent intellectuals such
as Ferrari and Ricciardi criticized Mazzini's social ideology for being
utopian and vague, even if their own attempts to formulate the
social goals of the Italian Revolution were not significantly more
profound or successful. The revolution of 1848–49 was the catalyst
that brought many individual insights into focus and stimulated the
formation of alternatives to Mazzini's social ideology.

The revolution of 1848 marked a turning point with regard to
the social goals of the democratic movement. First, the revolutionary upheaval gave many leading democrats an opportunity to
travel and to observe firsthand — and even to become involved
with — the problems of regions quite different from their own. The
Tuscan Montanelli, the Ligurian Nino Bixio, and the Neapolitan
Pisacane, for instance, all fought against Austria in Lombardy. During the campaign they noticed the widespread indifference of the
Lombard peasantry to a war that was being fought for Italian independence, unity, and liberty. In 1849 democrats from every part

of Italy participated in the government of the Roman Republic. Such was the pressure of events in that remarkable year that shortly after their arrival in Rome, and with little previous knowledge of the Papal States, they were drafting legislation designed to transform every aspect of Roman society. As the Venetian Dall'Ongaro said upon accepting the nomination to a seat in the Roman Assembly, "from the Alps to the sea there [was] but one Italian citizenship." Although their efforts were muddled and their accomplishments short-lived, the experience of a national, republican, and democratic government was exhilarating and unforgettable.

Second, the experience of government in a revolutionary situation forced many democrats, often for the first time in their lives, to face the poverty and backwardness of the masses and the social antagonisms that hindered the pursuit of national unity. The social tensions that the democrats of 1848 had to confront were particularly severe in the rural South, but they also surfaced elsewhere. In trying to deal with these tensions many democrats learned how difficult it was to bring about the "gradual rapprochement among social classes" advocated by Mazzini.

Most important, the revolutionary experience convinced many democratic activists that it was impossible to enlist the support of the masses for a cultural and political revolution without articulating the social goals of that revolution in more coherent and specific terms than Mazzini had done. Thus, in the midst of the Roman Republic De Boni wrote, "We are doing badly, very badly. And it is largely our own fault . . . It was incumbent upon us to get the poor involved in our revolutionary effort. But we did nothing at all for them."[2] And two weeks later, commenting on the course of that same revolutionary episode, Giuseppe Camillo Mattioli observed, "I am not happy with the new Municipal Law, which is, in part, undemocratic; most of all, I am not happy with the exclusion of the peasantry [from the vote]; it is both a violation of [our] principles and a tactical error, because it will further alienate from us this class so large, so important, and so oppressed."[3]

If Mazzini's associationist philosophy was inadequate to overcome the antagonism between social classes, if even the promise of political rights for all people (or at least for all those who were literate) was not sufficient incentive, what could the democratic leadership do to promote the interests of the masses and win their support? In the 1850s the democratic veterans of 1848 debated this question at length. To reach a consensus, even a vague one, on the social goals of the Italian Revolution proved much more difficult than to agree upon its cultural and political objectives. Indeed, both before and after the unification the issue of social justice was the major cause of dissension in the democratic camp.

In the debates of the 1850s, the leading democrats tried to define their own relationship to the masses. Although their definitions varied according to their own social background, regional origin, or intellectual formation, they were in agreement on one critical point: for the sake of the revolution, it was incumbent upon them to *lead* the Italian people. For many years, of course, Mazzini had proposed to lead the people in the discovery of their collective mission and hence in the establishment of a new moral and political order. More militant democrats had proposed to lead them in a patriotic *guerra di popolo* against Austria or to the barricades against the governments of the Restoration. In 1848 they had dreamed of guiding the politically emancipated masses in the proper exercise of their political rights. A typical statement of this ambition was expressed by the charter of the Florentine Circolo del popolo, "a gathering of honest men from all social classes who [professed] democratic prinicples," whose purpose had been to promote Italian liberty and independence by "instruct[ing] the people about their rights and duties."

The attitudes of the leading democrats revealed a characteristic mixture of genuine solidarity with the masses and paternalism. Guerrazzi expressed this ambivalent attitude particularly well in a letter to his friend Niccolò Puccini:

> You have no faith in the masses and you are wrong; because you were not born among them, you are not in touch with them. Not that I would ever want to defend the past errors and sins of a people who have been left to languish in poverty and ignorance; but when I think about the masses I am always reminded of that darling picture by Albano, of Love riding a lion and playing a lyre to spur him on. Certainly, much thought and much chiselwork will be necessary to sculpt this marble to perfection; but one day a god will spring from it.[4]

Several democratic intellectuals, among them Macchi, Montecchi, Rubieri, De Boni, or Asproni, could have inserted this passage in one of their letters without changing a word. They too had been "born among the masses," and they too, on that basis, claimed to be in touch with them. But even those who could not boast plebeian origins would have concurred with Guerrazzi's image of the masses as a lion to be tamed by sweet song or as raw marble. Someday that piece of marble would have a life of its own, but not until a sculptor with a vision, the democratic intellectual, had shaped it to perfection. Democrats who did not share Guerrazzi's predilection for artistic or literary allusions used a homier and even more revealing metaphor, that of the head of a household. "The leaders of a well-governed society," Asproni wrote, "must radiate the loving concern of a good paterfamilias."[5]

This paternalistic definition of the relationship between the educated elite and the masses was a constant source of difficulties for the Risorgimento democrats. It was obviously difficult to reconcile such a relationship with their commitment to political equality. Aware of the contradiction, however, they explained that their role as leaders would cease when the masses had acquired political rights and political maturity. Alas, this argument was dangerously similar to those used by the liberals for excluding the masses from political participation. One might be tempted to dismiss it as a convenient rationalization were it not that the democratic activists, especially after the unification, became personally involved in scores of projects for the emancipation and education of the lower classes.

Another source of difficulty was the question of legitimacy. On what basis could the democrats justify their claim to the leadership of the Italian masses? Guerrazzi based his claim upon his own humble social origins. Obviously, however, democrats of more privileged backgrounds, such as Mazzini, Ricciardi, or Pisacane, could not do so. They could only justify it on the basis of a superior understanding of Italy's conditions and destiny. And again, this attitude was most difficult to reconcile with egalitarian ideals. Whatever its basis, the democratic claim to leadership certainly implied an ability, as Ferrari put it, to discern "the real needs of the masses," to analyze the origins of those needs, and to suggest appropriate remedies. In the minds of the veterans of 1848, of course, the attempt to understand these issues was never separated from their desire to secure mass support for a new phase of the revolution. After the unification, it was never separated from their desire to challenge the political hegemony of the liberals.

The causes of and possible remedies for the masses' poverty and ignorance were addressed by the leading democratic intellectuals. Their solutions can be arrayed along an ideological spectrum that goes from the basically liberal position of Carlo Cattaneo on the right to the revolutionary socialism of Pisacane, Luigi Pianciani, and Tommaso Landi on the left.

The son of a goldsmith, Cattaneo was not born to wealth or

fame. He owed his respected place in the Milanese society of the 1830s and 1840s to his considerable intellectual talents. He could therefore claim on the basis of his social background to be at least as much "in touch with the masses" as was his contemporary Guerrazzi. Moreover, he was one of the most careful students of the social question of his time, and he wrote seminal essays on the condition of agriculture in Sardinia as well as in his own Lombardy and in Ireland, his wife's native country. He was as well informed as any Italian of his generation (and much better informed than most democrats) about the socioeconomic conditions of rural populations, especially in backward areas of Europe. Indeed, his reputation as an expert was such that in the 1840s Richard Cobden consulted him about a solution to the Irish agricultural crisis, and in 1860 Garibaldi asked his advice about a possible land reform in Sicily. Still, as a resident of Milan and a friend of pioneer social reformers like Giuseppe Sacchi, he was also sensitive to the problems of the urban poor and of the early industrial workers.[6]

Despite his sensitive social conscience, Cattaneo did not believe that a social revolution was necessary to eliminate poverty and ignorance. The structure of Italian society did need to be changed, and the social and economic conditions of the masses obviously did need improvement. But he believed that the improvement would come naturally and gradually, through the elimination of all obstacles to freedom of trade and investment and through the ensuing expansion of opportunities for employment and upward mobility. "The working man," he wrote, "must work hard and live well." His ideas on the social question reflected his economic thought, which was a great deal closer to the economic outlook of Cavour than to that of other leading democrats. Despite a barrage of criticism from fellow democrats, especially Ferrari, Cattaneo maintained this position even after the revolution of 1848. The revolutionary experience taught him the importance of mobilizing the masses; and afterward he insisted that such a mobilization was essential to the creation of secular and egalitarian republics. He also believed that the advancement of popular education (secular, of course) and the promise of political rights would be sufficient to secure mass support for a new revolutionary effort. Once the political and cultural revolution had succeeded, the introduction of economic freedom would achieve the rest.

To the left of Cattaneo on the issue of social justice was a rather large group of democratic intellectuals that included Ricciardi, Petruccelli, Rubieri, Guerrazzi, and Asproni. These men were much less sanguine than Cattaneo about the social benefits of economic freedom and much less certain that the development of a modern capitalist economy, more or less on the British model, would lift the Italian masses out of poverty and ignorance. Yet they were ideologically close to Cattaneo in that, like him, they attributed the backwardness of the masses to the lingering of ascriptive privilege, to outdated economic practices, and to reactionary political leadership. Although they lamented the wretched conditions of the rural masses and denounced a social system that placed blue blood and money above intellectual merit, they explained social injustice in political or moral terms without much thought to the actual sources of economic inequality and to the structure of property relations. Somewhat illogically, they called for the abolishment of ecclesiastical property even when they did not otherwise question the legitimacy of private ownership of land or capital. They sincerely believed that the solution of Italy's social problems lay in the establishment of a secular and democratic polity under new leaders who were "in touch with the masses." These leaders would ensure that laws were passed to help the oppressed and to protect the weak. A characteristic expression of this idea is found in the diary of Giorgio Asproni, a Sardinian who loved his native island fiercely and knew well the grinding poverty of its people:

> Good policies will mean good fiscal laws; good fiscal laws will mean simple and bearable taxes; indeed, [most people] will not even feel the burden, because the taxes will be paid by the rich and not by the poor. Good policies will mean more extensive and more careful cultivation, and the land will yield better crops to those who give it the sweat of their brow. Good policies will mean a more equitable distribution of wealth and therefore an end to the blight of mendicity. Good policies will put an end to privilege, and people of merit will be placed in those positions in which they can be most useful to society. There will be no more violent revolutions, because there will be a continuous revolution, and the state will run as smoothly as a locomotive in its tracks.[7]

This view of the future, whose millenarian flavor perhaps reflects Asproni's peasant roots and his theological education, rested upon two assumptions: good policies made good laws, and good laws could transform Italian society. Such laws, however, could only be the handiwork of "people of merit," that is, of enlightened men capable of acting for the good of society. That these men could only come from the ranks of the democratic intellectuals was stated em-

phatically by Ricciardi in an essay of 1850. He lamented that in
1848–49 the masses "[had] often stood by, passive witnesses to the
events." But he also noted that the Italian rulers and the upper
classes had shown greater fear of social upheavals than of Austrian
guns. Thus, they could not be counted on to introduce laws that
diminished their wealth or their political influence. The task obviously fell upon renegades from the upper class, like Ricciardi
himself, or upon other educated men, the Don Stumbos of the
Italian Revolution who had no vested interest in preserving
"privilege."[8]

Asproni mentioned the need for "a more equitable distribution
of wealth" in the postrevolutionary society; Ricciardi and Petruccelli
depicted in bold colors the exploitation of the southern peasantry by
Bourbon officialdom, by the clergy, and by greedy bourgeois landowners; Guerrazzi brooded all his life over social injustices which
"[had] nurtured disillusionment . . ., cast a pall over [his] youth
. . ., and hardened [his] soul." Their genuine outrage (and occasional slips into demagoguery) should not, however, obscure that
these men were moderate social reformers, not social revolutionaries. The limits of their concern for social justice, sincere
though it was, were clearly defined. In fact, in 1848–49 the two
Tuscans in this group, Guerrazzi and Rubieri, clashed with extremists who demanded radical social legislation. And the two
southerners, Ricciardi and Petruccelli, refused to approve the occupation of state lands (*terre demaniali*) by landless peasants.

Although these reformers wanted the elimination of privilege,
especially ascriptive privilege, and of extreme economic inequalities, they accepted the existing social structure with its class
divisions as a permanent feature of Italian life. Mazzini and his
followers, by contrast, advocated a "classless society," that is, a
society in which the term "class" would have no social significance,
in which there would be only citizens and producers.

Mazzini never wrote a major work specifically dealing with
social theory. His definition of the social goals of the Italian Revolution must therefore be reconstructed from his numerous essays and
letters of the period 1830–1850. Like other aspects of his thought, his
social theory was vulgarized for popular consumption by the inven-
tive Modena before the unification and by Saffi, Quadrio, Federico
Campanella, and others in the 1860s and 1870s. Around 1840, Mazzini edited *L'apostolato popolare*, a London newspaper designed to
reach a hodgepodge of working-class Italians, from household servants and craftsmen to organ-grinders and other street performers.
He also organized a free school for these fellow exiles and their

children. The articles he wrote for this audience provide excellent clues to his perception of Italian and European society and to his view of the social question of his time.

Obviously influenced by the contemporary political and intellectual debates in England and France, Mazzini categorically rejected the liberal argument that freedom of trade and investment produced benefits for the whole of society. On the contrary, he observed, the experience of countries more economically advanced than Italy suggested that their much-vaunted freedom was, in fact, "the freedom of one class; their power [was] in the hands of a small group of people; their growing wealth in the hands of a few families." He feared that this type of economic development, which was not "true social progress," would inevitably breed violence. He was hopeful that Italy could avoid such a situation, given the "naturally generous disposition of her people and the traditions of an ancient republican equality, still alive despite the nefarious governments that [had] followed."

But if the Italian workers could count on such valuable psychological and historical assets, in other respects they lagged far behind the most exploited workers of other countries. In England, in France, and in Belgium, the workers were conscious of their condition and importance, while in Italy they "suffered and complained, but without thinking of remedies, without even suspecting that there could be remedies." They were passive, Mazzini argued, because they did not yet realize "that God had given them twenty-two million brothers . . ., that a unity of purpose [and] a common resolution were sufficient to sweep aside all obstacles to the improvement of their condition."

The ideological arguments presented in Mazzini's articles of the early 1840s remained at the heart of his social thought in later years. When he altered them or played them down, especially in the 1850s, it was for tactical reasons, not because his ideas had really changed. His first argument was that in Italy as in the rest of Europe there was a crying need for social justice, which he defined as follows: "There must not be on this earth either *masters* or *slaves* but only *brothers* in the same faith, associated, each according to his calling, in a task to which all must contribute; [they must be] rewarded according to the difficulty, the importance, and the fruits of their labor [and] willing to choose and to follow as leaders of society the most virtuous, intelligent, and altruistic among them." Second, Mazzini argued that the preconditions for a just society already existed in Italy, but that only the workers themselves could bring about the full development of those preconditions. Social justice like political freedom could not be the gift of rulers; it had to be earned through a collective struggle. Third, Mazzini believed that this collective struggle, which had already begun in other countries, required common bonds of ethnic consciousness, language, and customs, that is, the bonds of nationality. In Italy these bonds were to be found as yet only among the educated classes. It followed that the most urgent task for the democratic intellectuals was to promote a sense of nationality among the Italian workers because there could be no collective struggle for social justice without national unity.

Mazzini's dream of replacing competition with interclass cooperation as the guiding principle of society was well attuned to the prevailing trend of thought among the reformers and social revolutionaries of his time, from Charles Fourier and Louis Blanc to Robert Owen and the Chartists. Indeed, at least in the 1840s, his social theory was much more a part of the European intellectual mainstream than were those of Etienne Cabet, Marx, or even Pierre Joseph Proudhon. Yet, at almost every step in his career, Mazzini denied any affinity with even the most moderate currents of socialist thought. His reasons for doing so were quite valid, though his contemporaries often failed to understand them and attributed them to his intellectual arrogance or to his political ambition. The misunderstanding developed in part because Mazzini formulated his social theory in terms that were familiar to all intellectuals of his generation, yet he used them idiosyncratically.

What did he mean, for instance, when he wrote that "a radical change in the organization of society [was] in the air" and that "questions concerning work and the working masses [were] more and more overshadowing all others"?[9] His contemporaries had every reason to believe that like other intellectuals, he was focusing on labor and capital, wages and working conditions, the development of modern industry, in short, on *homo oeconomicus*. But in fact, Mazzini was very uncomfortable with the prevailing emphasis of social theorists upon things economic. He rejected the view that material interests were the mainspring of human behavior, and he rejected Jeremy Bentham's contention that the best society was the one most able to harmonize the interests of the greatest number. His sharpest criticism was reserved for the French socialists, children of "the materialistic eighteenth century," whose influence on Italian culture he fought all his life. Of them he wrote:

Fourierists, Saint-Simonians, Communists, I know you all. By whatever name you clothe yourselves, whatever may be the formulas of universal brotherhood and love that you

may borrow from our democracy . . ., you are all worship-
pers of *utility*, you have no other moral than that of *interest*,
your religion is that of matter . . . You have accepted the
chosen weapon of the enemy; you have said: "They preach
the interest of the class [to which they belong]; we will
preach the interest of the whole." Absurd and unrealizable
dream![10]

Mazzini did not take issue with the socialists' desire to improve the
material conditions of the working classes and to protect them from
the greed of their employers. In fact, he described the miseries he
had seen in working-class London with the same sense of outrage
that pervades Friedrich Engels's work. According to Mazzini, the
problem with the socialists was that they were fighting with "the
chosen weapon of the enemy," class interests. Thus, they were
leading the workers to emulate the tactics and the moral errors of
the propertied classes. For his part, Mazzini wanted to teach the
Italian workers that the real enemy was not "the bourgeoisie but
egotism," whether in its individual or collective forms.

Mazzini maintained that the interest of the whole could not be
served by the replacement of one economically dominant group by
another. Indeed, if the largest class ever became economically dominant by emulating the acquisitive spirit of a privileged minority, it
might establish a form of tyranny far more vicious than any
previously known in history.[11] When he contemplated this dreadful
prospect, he sounded, in fact, very much like his friend Thomas
Carlyle. But he did not propose to combat the prevailing emphasis
upon *homo oeconomicus* by a return to the supposedly heroic values
of a preindustrial and predemocratic age. He prescribed instead a
"moral revolution" aimed at eradicating the very concepts of
domination, exploitation, and competition from the consciousness of
future generations. In contrast to Carlyle, he believed that it was
precisely "the upward movement of the popular classes" to political
power and the economic development of western Europe which, by
creating new forms of association, were making such a revolution
possible. His moral message was, of course, directed at *all* social
classes. But he thought that the new social consciousness would more
easily take hold among the workers because they were the class most
alienated from existing social and economic arrangements.

Mazzini's social theory was shaped by his encounters and
debates with intellectuals who had fled to London or Paris from
nearly every European country to escape persecution and
philistinism. If he had been British or French or if, as happened with

other exiles, he had lost interest in his native land, he might well have become a social theorist of European importance. But even while he reflected upon the social question in its western European context, his thoughts and emotions remained focused on Italy and its ongoing cultural and political revolution. He therefore found himself in a curious intellectual predicament. On the one hand, the European context of his social theory, his ongoing polemic with the French socialists, and the firsthand experience of the first Industrial Revolution in England blinded him to the social realities of his own country. His appeals to the Italian masses and his definitions of social justice were couched in language appropriate for literate workers in advanced countries and probably also for the artisans and sailors of his native Liguria, but not for the Italian peasantry. Other urban intellectuals, most notably Ferrari and Montanelli, came to see during the course of the revolution that in Italy "the masses" were peasant masses and that the social question there was primarily a land question. Mazzini, however, never understood this.[12]

On the other hand, his absorbing preoccupation with Italian problems and his very success in promoting the *political* goals of the Italian Revolution limited both the scope and the depth of his social analysis. In great part this limitation was self-imposed. Before the unfication, time and again he toned down his appeal for social justice and his critique of *homo oeconomicus* for the same reason that he toned down his anti-Catholicism in 1846–47 and later his republicanism, first in 1848 and again in the late 1850s. He was afraid of losing the support of the propertied classes for the political aspect of the revolution. In vain Pisacane and others argued with him that those classes needed no special incentive to support the revolution because under any circumstances they stood to gain the most from the creation of an independent, united, and constitutional Italy.

After the unification, however, Mazzini's pronouncements on social issues became more frequent, more forceful, and were no longer affected by political considerations. In the 1860s he gave a great deal of thought to the Società operaie, which he regarded as the instrument of the new social consciousness among the lower classes. Even then he paid little attention to the rural masses. Moreover, his most trusted agents within the Società operaie, Saffi and Quadrio, were less interested in making converts to the revolutionary dimension of his social thought than they were in promoting civil religion, voting rights, and other practical reforms. Although in theory they continued to preach Mazzini's philosophy of moral regeneration and interclass cooperation, in practice they identified with the workers' interests, or at least with the interests of the most articulate and politically conscious among them. Like the socialists, who inherited their social and political mission, the Mazzinians were practical reformers with a revolutionary ideology.[13]

Particularly before the unification, the sharpest criticism of Mazzini's social theory came from a group of democrats who had no qualms about advocating a radical transformation of Italian society on behalf of the lower classes. In fact, they regarded such a transformation as necessary to the success of the cultural and political aspects of the Italian Revolution. Most of them came from northern Italy: Ferrari, Macchi, Agostino Bertani, Carlo De Cristoforis, and Pietro Maestri from Lombardy; De Boni from Venetia; Enrico Guastalla from the Duchy of Parma; and Montanelli from Tuscany. Carlo Rusconi came from the Papal States and Domenico Mauro and Musolino came from Calabria. Although they never formed a distinct party, these men constituted an ideologically well-defined and important force within the democratic movement. Despite regional, social, and intellectual differences, they shared the conviction that the Italian Revolution must be a social revolution, and they spelled out the social goals of that revolution in more concrete terms than Mazzini did.

In the 1850s the ideas of this group were best expressed by Maestri, De Cristoforis, Guastalla, and Rusconi in the form of theoretical works with limited circulation, and by Ferrari and Macchi in polemical tracts designed for mass consumption. The theorists in the group argued for equal economic opportunity and for the right of producers to control the accumulation as well as the social uses of capital. They were "Proudhonians," as Della Peruta has pointed out, in a philosophical though not in a literal sense. Like Proudhon, they advocated political and financial institutions that would protect the rights of small producers in both agriculture and manufacturing from the encroachments of monopoly capitalism. Without such protection, they argued, the small producers stood to lose their economic independence and with it their social status and personal dignity. If, however, the small producers could organize and play a role in the shaping of a new Italian state, they had a good chance of becoming the cornerstone of Italian society and of the Italian economy. When these theorists wrote about "the Italian masses," they had in mind primarily the landowning peasantry, the *mezzadri* of central Italy, and the urban artisans, who were more numerous and more economically important at mid-nineteenth century than the relatively few large producers.[14]

The same distrust of the growth of monopoly capitalism and its cultural and political implications pervaded Ferrari's *La federazione repubblicana*, which argued against large concentrations of land and capital in the hands of a few and suggested the modification of inheritance laws as a means of preventing such concentrations. In direct polemic with Mazzini, Ferrari insisted that unless the leaders of the democratic movement made a firm commitment to a more equitable distribution of wealth in Italian society, they would never be able to undermine the political influence of the notables, whether these were conservative supporters of the Old Regime or advocates of a national/liberal state.[15]

Macchi stressed the same theme in an essay of 1856, in which he attacked Mazzini's associationist ideals. He also took issue with Mazzini's fear that any talk of a social revolution in Italy was foolhardy and premature because it might alienate the propertied classes from the national cause. Macchi's words carried considerably more weight within the democratic movement than did the theoretical works of the "Proudhonians" or even the arguments of Ferrari. Macchi was known to be personally fond of Mazzini, and unlike Ferrari he could not be accused of parroting French social theories without regard for Italian realities. Macchi questioned whether the democrats, especially after the failures of 1848, had to work for national independence to the exclusion of all other goals. In particular he questioned that the Italian masses' low level of political maturity made it inevitable and imperative that the democrats postpone to the distant future any attempt to deal with economic and social issues. To these Mazzinian theses of the late 1850s Macchi replied:

> You are telling us: "Nothing can be done for the people as long as there is no Italy." But what is keeping you from thinking right now in the privacy of your study or, better still, in the nurturing sunlight of a public debate through the press, about the most expedient ways of dispelling the clouds of ignorance that still shroud the masses, to lift from their shoulders the crushing burden of poverty, to alleviate at least some of the unspeakable sorrows which brutalize their souls and destroy their bodies prematurely . . . You are telling us: "The stirrings that are heard among the common people [*i popolani*] are patriotic stirrings and nothing else." Your statement might be accurate, in part, if by "common people" we mean a few workers in a few cities, organized in a few [patriotic] associations. But if by "common people" we mean the great majority of the population,

including the least educated segments of the urban and especially of the rural population, I am afraid that it would be closer to the truth to say that they have just about everything on their minds *except* patriotism . . . To these wretched people who do not know how to read, who do not want to read (and I am not saying that it is their fault), the government that levies the lowest tax on salt seems preferable to the government that grants the greatest freedom of the press. Nor is it surprising that these same people prefer a despot who exempts them from the hated head tax to a patriot who is sacrificing everything in the name of a "unity" which they do not understand.[16]

Macchi observed that the Italian democrats had a long and proud record of concern for the welfare of the masses. In the 1840s Mazzini himself had given touching evidence of that concern when he had published *L'apostolato popolare* in London surrounded by the affection of Italian workers and their families. Macchi appealed to Mazzini to understand that a willingness to work for economic and social change was precisely what set the democrats apart from other advocates of a national revolution, and that to ignore the material needs of the lower classes, even for a time, was to betray the democratic program and to make it irrelevant for the future.

Macchi's plea did not alter Mazzini's long-standing opposition to *any* program that pitted the masses against the economically privileged classes. Nor did it alter Mazzini's tactical argument of the late 1850s, that the attainment of Italian independence and unity required cooperation with the moderate liberals, albeit within limits. Yet Macchi's essay is significant because it stated clearly that if the democrats neglected to pursue economic and social change they would lose both their ideological identity and their political effectiveness. After the unification, Ferrari, Musolino, and Bertani issued the very same warning to their colleagues of the parliamentary Left. Risorgimento democracy, they argued, would lose its raison d'être unless its leaders remembered their responsibility as spokesmen for the oppressed and unrepresented masses.

Unlike Cattaneo and his fellow moderate social reformers, the democrats advocating a radical transformation of Italian society did not believe that the introduction of constitutional government and political equality would ipso facto produce social change. They argued that it was not possible to improve the material condition of the masses except at the expense of the privileged classes. For this reason they rejected Mazzini's associationism, even though they were in substantial agreement with him and with most other democrats on one important point: Any restructuring of Italy's economic and social relationships would have to be done *for* the masses, not *by* the masses. Behind their sympathy for the sufferings of the lower classes and their willingness to endorse, for instance, far-reaching fiscal and land reforms, was a deep concern for the stability of Italian society. Although their statements before the unification and some of their legislative proposals after 1860 had a revolutionary ring, their intent was basically conservative. Ideologically, they were closer to the Tory reformism of a Disraeli or to the social paternalism of a Bismarck than they were to the leaders of Italian liberalism. Perhaps the most revealing examples of the mentality of these conservative revolutionaries are found in the parliamentary speeches of Ferrari and Bertani and in the editorials of Rusconi's *Rivista d'agricoltura.*

Returning from a tour of the rural South which he had taken in order to understand the causes of banditry and peasant unrest, Ferrari urged the ruling liberals to get on with the distribution of the *terre demaniali* to landless peasants and to send the still popular Garibaldi to them "with a message of loving concern," instead of sending more soldiers and tax collectors. The appalling poverty of the southern peasants, he argued, posed a far greater threat to the security of the new Italian state than did the bandits or the few partisans of a Bourbon restoration. A decade later, Bertani urged a nationwide investigation of the conditions of the rural masses. The liberals, he observed, were quite free to ignore economic and social injustices; but he doubted that they ever paused to think what might happen in Italy if millions of downtrodden peasants "[lost] their patience."[17]

This problem had already been addressed by Rusconi in the first editorial article of his Florentine *Rivista d'agricoltura, industria e commercio.* The title foreshadowed Rusconi's thesis that Italian agriculture must be given higher priority than other sectors in any planned economic development. And planned development, which he regarded as essential in a backward country like Italy, must include technical assistance and tax credits for landowners to stimulate productivity and agricultural schools for all rural workers.[18]

Haunted by the prospect that the oppressed classes might indeed lose their patience and destroy the new state, Ferrari, Bertani, and others in this group became involved in many radical social causes from land reforms and labor legislation to women's rights. In the 1860s and 1870s, however, the moderate liberals failed to perceive the conservative purpose behind those radical causes which they generally opposed. Ironically, after 1876, when the moderate parliamentary wing of Risorgimento democracy came to power, its leaders made a similar error with regard to the emerging Socialist party and the phenomenon of Christian democracy. They failed to distinguish between the revolutionary ideology and the reformist practice of the former and to appreciate the latter's potential contribution to the integration of the Catholic masses in the cultural and political life of united Italy.

Mazzini's position on the social goals of the Italian Revolution was unique because he believed in the moral roots of social change and also in the possibility of cooperation across class lines. Most other democrats were either social reformers or social revolutionaries with a conservative intent. Most of them either believed the masses incapable of initiating a social revolution or else feared them *too* capable. But the democratic movement also produced a few extremists, such as Pisacane, Pianciani, Milo Guggino, and Landi, who did not share the reformist or the conservative-revolutionary inclinations of their colleagues. Although they did not have as great an influence on the Risorgimento as did their more moderate colleagues, they should not be ignored, for they represented a tradition of revolutionary protest and rebellion which their followers Saverio Friscia, Giuseppe Fanelli, and others kept alive within the anarchist movement and within the maximalist wing of the Socialist party after the unification.

These ultraradical thinkers differed substantially from their fellow democrats on the issue of social justice. They wanted the Italian Revolution to be a social revolution first and foremost. They did favor the establishment of a new political order and the secularization of Italian culture, but they thought that the pursuit of those goals could be left to the liberals or perhaps to Mazzini, who spoke for the social classes that stood to gain the most from a cultural and political revolution. The dissidents argued that their special mission was to speak on behalf of the masses who were interested in things quite different from constitutional government and a secular culture. Their attitude toward the masses was distinctly less paternalistic than that of other democrats.

Pianciani, for instance, whose family operated a textile mill in the Spoleto area, believed that the masses were quite capable of initiating a revolution. The middle-class democratic intellectual could be their advisor and teacher, but not for very long their leader. The prospect of spontaneous and autonomous actions by the workers did not frighten him, however, for he believed that the Italian masses were by nature inclined to nonviolent protest. Thus, he was confident that their just aspirations to economic well-being and social dignity would ultimately be satisfied without class warfare and bloodshed. His belief in the innate goodness of the most oppressed classes was shared by Pisacane who, in fact, sacrificed his life to that belief. Convinced to the end of his life that the Italian Revolution must be a social revolution, Pisacane saw the downtrodden rural masses of his native Kingdom of Naples as the most logical recruits for a revolutionary army led by democratic intellectuals. He believed that although no revolution could succeed without the use of violence, the violent phase of the revolution in Italy would end soon after the overthrow of the Bourbons. For without the protection of Bourbon laws, police, and army, the bureaucrats and landowners would not be able to resist the establishment of a democratic republic and the seizure of land by the peasants.[19]

There were a few dissonant voices in this chorus of optimistic and even idyllic predictions. Perhaps the most apocalyptic vision of the Italian Revolution as a social revolution was that of Tommaso Landi of Messina. The scion of an urban middle-class family, he was at once attracted and repelled by the mysterious ways of the Sicilian peasants. Under their traditional reserve and passivity he sensed a seething rage against government officials and the propertied classes. If that rage were ever unleashed, for instance by a liberal political revolution, it would be accompanied by large-scale violence. Ironically, Landi's chilling vision resembled the worst misgivings of the Sicilian liberals. Unlike them, he regarded peasant violence as inevitable and cathartic.[20]

Although Landi's vision was relevant to other regions besides his native Sicily, it was neither widely known nor discussed among the democrats. In many ways it remained unique. Among northern democrats, only the Mantuan Francesco Siliprandi addressed himself so directly to the peasant question, which he analyzed in historical perspective. However, his tract *La rivoluzione dei contadini* appeared only in 1883. Unlike Landi, he did not regard peasant violence in Italy as inevitable, for he believed that simply the threat of it would force the propertied classes to make concessions. Siliprandi and most of his colleagues remained confident that Italy could be transformed peacefully, provided that democratic intellectuals could direct—if not actually control—the process of change.[21]

Whether their intent was to revolutionize the social order or simply to make it more responsive to the needs of the lower classes and whether they had been born poor or rich, the Risorgimento democrats were determined to play a significant role in the transformation of Italy. Experiences in the family environment and at school gave them the first clues to the structure and problems of Italian society. Later, participation in secret societies and political networks allowed them to explore aspects of the social question in more systematic fashion, through the filter of social theories developed by Italian and foreign thinkers. And finally, the process of political unification and development opened up to them valuable opportunities to work amid and for the lower classes.

4

Family and School: Patterns of Political Socialization, 1830–1848

SEVERAL related questions about the Risorgimento democrats of the years 1830–1847 throw light on social patterns and on the beginning of political involvement. Why did these men become militant opponents of the existing governments? Why did they become specifically interested in political democracy and social change? Who were their role models? And finally, by what means were they recruited for political activity? Like any other aspect of the socialization process, an individual's socialization to politics does not occur in a vacuum. Thus, to explore why the Risorgimento democrats joined the Italian Revolution is to explore the social institutions and milieu within which they were reared and which most affected their view of life and their understanding of political issues. It can be argued that the political consciousness of these men was shaped by the interaction of experiences to which they were exposed within the family and at school.

The Family

The intergenerational transmission of political values and of role models of appropriate political behavior is a vital concern of every society. It is important not only to those individuals and groups who wish to preserve and to legitimize already existing political arrangements but also to those who are preparing the ground for change either by reform or by revolution. In the literature on modern Western societies, the family emerges as one of the foremost agents of political socialization, although its importance in relation to other agents has been the subject of extensive debate.

One theory of political socialization concludes that young people who become involved in political activities, including revolutionary movements, do so in keeping with what they perceive to be the family tradition. They therefore expect their elders' approval even when engaging in different, more extreme forms of political behavior. Another major theory holds, on the contrary, that rebellion against a particular political establishment or against political authority in general is an acting out of hostile feelings toward parental discipline and authority. The rebel's real targets, according to this theory, are his parents or other immediate relatives who controlled his life in its early stages and against whom he could not strike without violating powerful social taboos.[1]

An inquiry into the family background of the Risorgimento democrats, or at least into those aspects of it that were relevant to their political socialization, provides substantial evidence in support of the first theory. But before discussing specifically how the intergenerational transmission of political values and role models took place, the type of family in which the Risorgimento democrats were reared must be examined.

One sociological generalization that can be made is that the Risorgimento democrats came from "the educated middle classes." Although this generalization is essentially correct, it is, however, too broad to be useful as a tool of analysis. The democrats were indeed "educated men," in the sense that they were the beneficiaries of formal instruction far beyond the average from their contemporaries. They were "middle class" in that most of them were born and tended to remain within that large cross section of Italian society that was neither very wealthy and prestigious nor poor and downtrodden. But if the term "middle class" is a kind of convenient shorthand to describe where the Risorgimento democrats and their families stood vis-à-vis a privileged minority on the one side and the Italian masses on the other, it should not be used as a substitute for the word "bourgeois," as Italian historians, particularly Marxist ones, have frequently done.[2]

Among the Risorgimento democrats we do find men whose families owed their economic and social position to modern forms of commerce, manufacturing, and farming or to some well-defined profession. These families were representative of a modern bourgeoisie in the classic sense of the word, that is, they were the backbone and the beneficiaries of a developing capitalist economy. But others owed their economic security and social stability to crafts with an ancient tradition, such as printing, to bureaucratic jobs, to service occupations for the wealthy, and so forth. For these families the development, such as it was, of the Italian economy in a capitalist direction was at best irrelevant, at worst disastrous.

In short, it can be said that the families of the Risorgimento democrats shared a certain "space" in a social hierarchy, whether defined in terms of wealth or social prestige. But they certainly did not display the relative harmony of interests and values that sociologists and historians have generally assumed when discussing a social class. In addition to marked regional differences, there were among these families, for instance, significant differences of income, of status in the community, and of religion.

To determine the social status of these families data was sought about the main source of family income (landownership, salaried jobs, business enterprise, and so forth), about the occupation of the head of the household and other adult males, and about the relative status of the family within its town or province. Over one half of the 146 families under consideration derived their income from more than one type of economic activity, frequently from combining profits from landownership or other investments with professional salaries or fees.

In a society where precapitalist notions of status and stability had by no means been pushed aside by modern notions of economic expansion, mobility, and change, landownership was still a desirable source of income and social prestige. Yet only 32 of the 146 families derived all or a substantial part of their income from landownership. Of these 32, 24 lived in the Kingdom of the Two Sicilies. No matter how small or infertile his estate, an owner could style himself a *possidente*. The term carried considerable prestige in every part of the country, and in some preunification states, such as Lombardy-Venetia and Tuscany, it carried a measure of political power at least at the local level. Despite this, the 108 families in the sample whose income came from commerce, manufacturing, or the professions do not seem to have favored land purchases over other forms of investment. Exceptions to the rule were the salaried farm managers, like the Depretis family in the province of Novara or the Siliprandis in the province of Mantova, who not surprisingly aspired to ownership. As for the important fringe benefit that had traditionally accrued to the buyer of an estate — an aristocratic title — it seemed of little interest to those families who did not already have one. Indeed, of the 146 families studied, only 12 belonged to the aristocracy and of these 12 only 3 or 4, like the Piancianis of Spoleto and the Anellis of Lodi, could boast long family trees and substantial assets. The others in this group either held titles of very recent vintage, like the Ricciardis of Naples, or had long since lost their estates, like the Milo Gugginos of Sicily. In fact, in the variety of their situations, these twelve families reflected the heterogeneous character of the Italian aristocracy and its relative weakness vis-à-vis both the preunification dynasties and other, more cohesive groups within Italian society.

The 108 families whose heads were neither *possidenti* nor peasants can be separated into two subgroups, unequal in income, prestige, and social mobility. The first subgroup comprises 63 families whose income came entirely or primarily from commerce or from professions such as medicine, law, and university teaching that in the first half of the nineteenth century were becoming well defined, specialized, and socially respectable, if not always lucrative. The second subgroup comprises 45 families that could be called "middle class" in terms of their relative position within the social hierarchy and of their aspirations, yet whose heads were engaged in precarious and poorly paid occupations. For instance, they were performers, artists, tutors, notaries, public school teachers, and journalists.[3]

By far the smallest group in the sample, only six families were peasants. The biographical profiles of the six democratic leaders who were of peasant background, like Filippo De Boni of Venetia and Giorgio Asproni of Sardinia, strongly suggest that these families, even if they owned some land, were significantly poorer and had fewer opportunities for advancement than all the rest. Although generalizations cannot be made about such a small group, it might be pointed out that of the six democrats of peasant background four were enrolled by their families in seminaries and encouraged to pursue upward mobility through an ecclesiastical career, and the two others entered the professional class at its lowest rung as peddlers of occasional verses and of articles for popular magazines.

In sum, most of the Risorgimento democrats were reared within urban families. Predictably for nineteenth-century Italy, even those families that drew their income from land rents lived in urban centers, migrating to a country residence, if they had one, only during the summer months. To say that the Risorgimento democrats were predominantly of urban background, however, is not to say that they came solely or primarily from Italy's largest cities. Only forty-five of them, in fact, were born in or spent most of the years prior to the revolution of 1848–49 in cities like Milan, Genoa, Turin, Venice, Florence, Rome, Naples, and Palermo. Many more spent their formative years in provincial towns: Mantua in the Kingdom of Lombardy-Venetia; Alessandria in the Kingdom of Sardinia; Pisa, Pistoia, Lucca, and Livorno in the Grand Duchy of Tuscany, and so forth. The relatively wide range of ideas and experiences to which the Risorgimento democrats were exposed in their childhood and youth, and particularly their political education, suggest that these towns, though small (ten thousand to fifty thousand inhabitants in the 1840s), were not cultural and intellectual backwaters. Like the capitals of the smaller Italian states, they indulged in *campanilismo*, particularly at the expense of the larger cities, yet they also bore witness to the continuity and vitality of ancient urban traditions of learning and self-government.

Finally, in order to understand fully the role of the family in the political socialization of the Risorgimento democrats, family structure and composition must be examined. In general, the Risorgimento democrats came from nuclear families and had relatively few siblings (an average of 4.3 for the entire sample, but with lower figures for professional and commercial families in the major cities of northern Italy). It should be borne in mind, however, that many of them spent their youth in small centers, where contact with other relatives was a common occurrence. Thus, though the families in question were nuclear, unlike many contemporary ones they were not isolated from the larger web of kinship ties by blood and marriage. Again, as is the case for the economic base of their families, the life histories of the Risorgimento democrats offer interesting examples of ambivalent modernity.

For a significant minority in the sample (63 out of 146) there is direct evidence in correspondence, memoirs, and other sources that the family was an important source of political values and of role models of political behavior. Of the 63 democratic leaders for whom this can be documented, 53 were unquestionably the children and grandchildren of politically conscious parents, the conspirators and rebels of an earlier era: Jacobins, Carbonari, Veri Italiani,

Apofasimeni, and so forth. The remaining 10, however, were rebels against a conservative family tradition, and they became involved in the Italian Revolution very much against their elders' wishes.

To understand the socialization of those democratic leaders for whom revolutionary politics was a family tradition, two questions must be asked: How were political values transmitted within their families, and what socializing functions did their families perform above and beyond the transmission of values?

In politically conscious and active families the transmission of significant values and emotions, such as hatred of censorship and despotism or a sense of national identity and social justice, was undertaken deliberately, and it began at an early age for the future protagonists of the Italian Revolution. This process of early socialization within the family seems to have occurred in two stages, visual and verbal, that corresponded roughly to the stages of a child's cognitive development.

In their preschool years the young scions of families who had participated actively in the political upheavals of the 1790s or in the liberal conspiracies of the 1820s learned, first of all, to distinguish and to revere some material objects that embodied the struggles and the hopes of their elders. Mothers and grandparents played the key role in this first phase of socialization to the family tradition of dissent and of opposition to the existing regimes. The memoirs of the Piedmontese democrat Angelo Brofferio and of the Neapolitan Giuseppe Ricciardi illustrate particularly well how very young children were introduced to politically significant objects.

Before his father, a country doctor with scientific aspirations, moved the family from Castelnuovo Calcea to Turin, Brofferio spent much time with his paternal grandfather.[4] They took long walks in the countryside, during which the youngster was given informal lessons in the natural sciences. But the teacher in this case was not interested only in the natural world. He also happened to have been one of Castelnuovo's most prominent Jacobins. From time to time, his eyes misting with pride and frustration, he paused during those walks to point out to Angelo the liberty trees of the revolutionary era. Years went by, of course, before Angelo Brofferio learned the history of the French Revolution and understood what it meant to be a Jacobin in Piedmont or when and why those trees had been planted. But even as a young child he came to realize that the liberty trees were dear to his grandfather as symbols of past achievements and of hope for the future, while to others in the community they symbolized all that was evil. During those country walks, in short, the future revolutionary did not merely learn to recognize an object that was important to his closest relatives; he also began to perceive differences of outlook and tradition between them and other adults with whom he came in contact, for instance, the village school-teacher.

The Neapolitan publicist Ricciardi learned similar lessons between the ages of approximately five and ten. The setting for Ricciardi's first lessons in the family tradition of revolutionary politics was, however, quite different from the bucolic one of Brofferio's experience. Ricciardi's mother came from an old aristocratic family, and his father, a magistrate, had earned a title and most of his wealth in the service of King Joseph Bonaparte. Ricciardi was an only son and a sickly, overprotected child. Because he suffered from a congenital weakness of the hips and legs, he was tutored at home and spent much time indoors. Besides his mother, his only steady companions were his sisters and the housemaids. To entertain him they occasionally allowed him to play with family memorabilia that were kept in a special chest. Among those cherished objects were the insignia his father had worn in the service of King Joseph and various gifts he had received from the Bonapartes.

These family treasures played the same role in Ricciardi's political education as the liberty trees did in Brofferio's. As a child Ricciardi not only learned to revere those objects because they meant much to his parents but he also came to realize why they could not be worn or displayed in public, at least while the Bourbon government remained in power. Although tucked away in a chest, those objects symbolized a revolutionary tradition of which his family was proud and which he was expected to carry on.[5]

In a second stage of the socialization process, sometime between the ages of ten and fifteen, the future democratic activists began to associate the concrete symbols of the family tradition with words and concepts that came up frequently in conversation among members of the household and visitors. The words liberty, constitution, and independence were perhaps the most frequently heard in the homes of former Jacobins and liberals. Their children and grandchildren grew up to think of these as positive words long before they actually understood their meaning and implications. By the time the future activists were old enough to stay up with their elders around the hearth to hear them recount past experiences or discuss current events, they began to understand why these words evoked positive responses within the household whereas they could not be used outside of it without risking a reprimand.

The memoirs and family correspondence of the Piedmontese democrat Riccardo Sineo and of the Tuscan Giuseppe Mazzoni provide illustrations of this growing level of political consciousness. For instance, Sineo learned from his father, a former Jacobin mayor, that the slogan "Long live liberty" (*Viva la libertà*) which was frequently used in toasts and discussions at home, could not be used on the outside because it was associated with memories of the French occupation of Piedmont and of French revolutionary legislation. Those were positive memories for the Sineo family, which had endorsed and profited from the revolution, but they were negative for many others and certainly anathema to the restored Savoy monarchy.[6]

But what was behind that elusive word "liberty"? And why did it evoke such strong emotions among one's relatives and other adults? By the time he was a student at the *liceo* of his native Pistoia, Mazzoni understood that "liberty" was used as shorthand to describe rights that the adult members of his community and class did not have but wanted to enjoy. Foremost among these was "the right to choose one's rulers and one's laws."[7]

In similar fashion Aurelio Saffi, a native of Romagna who was to become one of Mazzini's best-known followers, learned the meaning of "constitution." The word occurred often in conversations between Aurelio's father, Girolamo, who was later proscribed by the papal government for his role in the revolution of 1831, his uncle Pietro, a prominent Carbonaro, and their closest friends and associates. At first young Aurelio simply sensed that the word had positive connotations within the family circle, though very negative ones outside. But by the time of his father's proscription, when Aurelio was fifteen, he had already become aware of what it meant to be a constitutionalist. It meant to favor restrictions and limitations upon the power of a government that claimed absolute authority in temporal as in spiritual matters. It meant putting a stop to policies and practices that had inflicted both moral and physical suffering on the people he held most dear. Constitutional government would mean an end to arbitrary police searches and arrests, to a censorship as stifling as it was capricious, to compulsory religious observance in the schools, in short, to all those aspects of papal rule that discouraged inquiry, initiative, and experimentation.[8]

The family played a key role in the socialization of many Risorgimento democrats not merely as a source of political symbols, language, and concepts but also as the first source of role models of political behavior. Many scions of families with a tradition of revolutionary politics were socialized to value nonconformity, the ability to work with other people toward a common goal, and courage in the face of physical threats. Within their own families the future democratic leaders found many examples of nonconformist behavior in political as well as other matters.

Banished for his role in the revolution of 1848, the Calabrian Casimiro De Lieto, for instance, urged his son "to steel [himself] for adversity . . . [remembering] that the De Lietos had always spoken out against tyranny, superstition, and ignorance."[9] Doubtless, this statement exaggerated the political merits of the De Lieto family, reflecting as it did the nostalgia of the exile for familiar places and the frustrations of a father forced by circumstances to guide his son's education from afar. Yet it was true that for three or four generations this family had produced political reformers and rebels as well as scientists. Before Casimiro De Lieto made his mark in the revolution of 1848, other De Lietos had made theirs in the reform movement of the 1770s, in the revolutionary governments of the 1790s, and in the scientific circles of Reggio Calabria and Naples.

For families like the De Lietos, political dissent usually went hand in hand with nonconformist behavior in other matters. The experiences of two democrats of quite different backgrounds and temperaments, Felice Govean and Maurizio Quadrio, illustrate this point. A journalist and playwright, Govean when still in his teens joined the group of Piedmontese democratic-republican intellectuals of which his better-known contemporaries Brofferio, Lorenzo Valerio, and Sineo were also members. In Govean's view, to take a position against the literary establishment of his day was to follow in his father's footsteps. The elder Govean had not only been the Jacobin mayor of Racconigi, near Turin, but he had also been the black sheep of his family, having renounced his religious vows to participate fully in the revolutionary upheaval of the 1790s and to marry the woman he loved.

If Govean could argue that his involvement in the literary avant-garde of the 1840s had been inspired by his father's political and social nonconformism, Quadrio might have argued that his own interest in overthrowing conservative governments was the political equivalent of his father's pioneering efforts in science and public health. Although he had practiced medicine in the mountainous and isolated province of Sondrio, the elder Quadrio had kept up with the development of eighteenth-century science, and he had been the first to introduce smallpox vaccination in his community. In the 1790s the local civil and religious authorities had reacted to his scientific theories and medical innovations in much the same way as they were to react thirty years later to his son's anti-Habsburg and antimonarchical ideas.[10]

Especially in small communities like De Lieto's Reggio Calabria or in rural areas like Quadrio's Valtellina, nonconformist political behavior entailed not only the risk of antagonizing powerful people but also the risk of intellectual and psychological isolation from peer groups and community. The families of the Risorgimento democrats seem to have been aware of this danger, for they emphasized to their children the importance of seeking out and of working with people of similar outlook.

One of the common traits of the democrats selected for this study is that they joined revolutionary clubs and secret societies when they were still quite young. The available evidence suggests that at least for the sixty-three who came from revolutionary families, the secret society was in some ways an extension of the family circle, a logical setting in which to develop and to apply the political values learned in the early stages of socialization. For some future activists the transition was particularly smooth and natural because they were introduced to the secret societies by members of their immediate family in what might be called an initiation rite. Acceptance in a Masonic lodge, a *vendita carbonara*, and the like marked one's passage into the world of adult responsibilities. And what better way to make that passage than with the help of one's relatives!

The Calabrian democrat Francesco Angherà, for instance, wrote to his sister that he had "left behind the charm and irresponsibility of childhood" when he had first accompanied his uncle Domenico on a tour of several villages in the region's interior.[11] Domenico Angherà, a priest and founder of a secret society that promoted at once evangelical religion and political revolution, did not undertake such tours in search of picturesque scenery or other delights. Rather, he visited his disciples and sought to attract new ones. If he took Francesco along on such hazardous missions, it was probably on the assumption that the youngster already knew enough about the revolutionary network to be of help and to take care of himself in case of trouble. It also seems probable that Domenico wished to groom one of his nephews to succeed him as the leader of this particular society.

Another Risorgimento democrat for whom the transition from family circle to secret society was easy and natural was Augusto Elia of Ancona, the only son of a sailor. At the age of ten Augusto began working as a deckhand on the same ship as his father. Like many others of his city and class, by entering the adult world of work he was expected to assume other adult responsibilities as well. One of these was to spy and deliver messages for a Mazzinian group of which his father was a member. Another was to help political suspects attempting to escape Ancona by boat. At the outbreak of revolution in 1848 Augusto was only eighteen; nevertheless, he was already well versed in the art of conspiring and of working with others toward a common goal.[12]

Finally, the children of Italian revolutionaries of earlier times were socialized to endure physical hardship, perhaps because family members and close friends had experienced harsh imprisonment and worse. Giuseppe Petroni, for instance, wrote that as a youngster he had often overheard his father's friends, many of whom had been in jail, discuss ways of enduring torture and solitary confinement. The lessons thus learned served him well, because he spent seventeen years in Roman prisons known to be among the worst in Europe.[13]

The adult males in the family usually provided role models of political behavior and supervised the political rites of passage. They were the authors of revolutionary tracts, the members of secret societies, the barricade fighters, and often the victims of censors and police spies or the casualties of unsuccessful unrisings. There were times, however, when adult females were called upon to be role models for adolescents and young adults as well as vehicles for the political socialization of the very young. When the need arose mothers, grandmothers, and older sisters proved equal to the challenge. The Sicilian Marietta Campo wrote that her politically minded parents had expected her to be no less aware of the family tradition and no less committed than her brothers to the struggle against Bourbon despotism. Her picture of a family in which political ideas and activism were not an exclusively male preserve is borne out by the experience of several men who, like her brother Francesco, played significant roles in the democratic movement of the Risorgimento.[14]

As adults a few of them recollected that their mothers had been more politically active than their fathers, bolder in expressing subversive opinions, more supportive of their children's involvement with secret societies or demonstrations. The Genoese firebrand Nino Bixio, for instance, almost certainly learned more about political issues from his young and dynamic mother, Colomba Caffarelli, who moved in Mazzinian circles, than from his father, who worked for the state mint and was fearful of losing his job. Likewise, the Risorgimento's foremost advocate of women's rights, Salvatore Morelli, paid tribute in his writings to his well-educated mother's influence on his own ideas.[15]

Women who took political positions independently of their husbands were quite rare in nineteenth-century Italy. When adult females served as political role models for their sons, it was usually because the males were absent. Saffi, for instance, observed that in one generation political tragedy had twice struck his family, forcing first his maternal grandmother, the widow of a prominent Jacobin, and then his own mother to become heads of the household. After 1831, Saffi wrote, when his father had fled into exile, the two women had seen to it that the children were brought up in the republican and democratic tradition of their ancestors. A similar situation occurred in the family of the Piedmontese Lorenzo Valerio. Having lost his father at the age of twelve, Valerio apparently grew up without any male role models, at least in his immediate family. But he remembered that his mother, who had liberal ideas, had supported him in several disputes with conservative school authorities.[16]

The political significance of family ties did not diminish as the Risorgimento democrats entered the adult world. The family, in fact, not only performed an important socializing function during their childhood and adolescence but it also played a crucial supportive role in later years as they became more and more deeply involved in risky ventures. The support was both moral and material, and for some Risorgimento democrats it would be difficult to tell which was the more important.

A visit in prison or a letter expressing affection, approval, or solidarity acquired enormous importance in the eyes of an activist separated from his community and branded as a peril to society. For some, these signs of support made a difference between total despair and psychological survival. This feeling was expressed with poignant clarity by an exile of the revolution of 1831, Giuseppe Lamberti of Reggio Emilia. Intensely attached to his small hometown, he could never adjust to the anonymity, the crowded streets, the great distances of the French capital. Although he was busy with his duties as Mazzini's lieutenant in France, he could not avoid despondency and depression. The only bright spot in his life were the letters of his father, Jacopo, a revolutionary of an earlier era who urged endurance and hope. The letters of his illegitimate daughter, Sofia, who lived with his sister, were much shorter and not political at all, but no less important to his psychological survival.[17]

Those who were stronger or perhaps more fortunate never became quite so dependent on their families' emotional support as Lamberti apparently did; yet they gratefully acknowledged its importance. Among these were two of the movement's most revered figures, Giuseppe Mazzini and Benedetto Cairoli. Beloved oldest sons, both of them had extremely close relationships with their mothers and from them received unfailing encouragement at critical points in their long revolutionary careers.[18] But like their fellow democrats Nicola Fabrizi, Musolino, Salvatore Calvino, and many others, Mazzini and Cairoli received more than emotional support from their families. They also received subsidies that often made the difference between indecorous poverty and relative comfort, particularly when they wandered about in exile in the 1850s.

As for those democratic activists who avoided exile, they were usually not lucky enough to avoid long jail terms. In prison they became even more of an economic burden to their families than were the exiles; there were bribes to be paid to spies and guards, food and other necessities to be purchased, and lawyers to be hired. Indeed, some of the families never recovered from the economic sacrifices they made on behalf of relatives persecuted for their political activities. It is not surprising, then, that in the 1860s some of the former political prisoners and exiles sought compensation for their personal contribution to the Italian Revolution not for themselves alone but also for surviving relatives who had helped them in the years of struggle.

Even those Risorgimento activists who joined revolutionary secret societies in defiance of their parents' wishes and sometimes in open rebellion against their values found that they could count on their families for support in times of particular stress and hardship. For example, as their voluminous correspondence reveals, Luigi Pianciani of Spoleto and his father, Vincenzo, were at odds politically. In the 1830s and early 1840s the elder Pianciani tried hard to keep his son out of involvement with revolutionary groups, predicting that Luigi would someday come to grief. In the early 1850s he continued to plead with his exiled son to abandon political activities and to petition the papal government for permission to return home. But if Vincenzo Pianciani abhorred his son's republican and anti-Catholic convictions and grieved over his errors, he never refused to give financial help. And requests for such help came frequently, not only because Luigi could not find steady employment but also because he shared what he had with needy fellow exiles and contributed generously to Mazzini's propaganda campaigns. Thus, financial help from his family did more than keep Luigi Pianciani alive and well. It also enabled him to remain active in the revolutionary movement. And in this respect his experience was no different from that of the children of revolutionary parents.[19]

That some activists, such as Pianciani, the Sicilian Rosolino Pilo, or the Tuscan Piero Cironi, became involved in the democratic movement against their elders' wishes might be taken as prima facie evidence of a latent rebellion against parental authority extended later to public authority. But in fact, the experiences of Pianciani and others do not support such a theory. The bonds of affection between them and their families survived years of disagreement and separation. With a few exceptions, like the maverick Barnabite priest Gavazzi, the young rebels did not hate their elders, turned reluctantly against them, and never broke their ties with them. In the experience of the Risorgimento democrats, in short, the family played a politically significant supportive role even when it was not the source of political values and of role models of political activity.

Schooling

The educational system, particularly at the elementary and secondary levels, was the source of important political experiences for a large majority (105 out of 146) of the democrats in the sample. Not surprisingly, the Risorgimento democrats received formal instruction far above the average for their times. In a country where the illiteracy rate varied from a low of perhaps 50 percent in the urban centers of Habsburg Lombardy to a high of over 90 percent in much of the South, 141 out of the 146 individuals studied here had some schooling beyond the elementary grades. And 85 of them (58.2 percent of the sample) had at least some university training. To understand the origins of their political ideas and activities, however, it is less important to know how many years of schooling they had than to explore the type of education they received and their motives for wanting it.

For nearly all the individuals under discussion the elementary and secondary schools were the first settings of important social experiences outside of the family circle. Although a handful of them were born to families wealthy enough to hire private tutors for their elementary and secondary education, the great majority attended day or boarding schools between the ages of seven or eight to eighteen. Four or five hours of instruction at a day school not far from home seem to have been the norm in the early grades. Whether a youngster who wanted education beyond the elementary level continued to attend a day school or was sent away to boarding school depended largely on where his family lived. Of the 141 who attended school beyond the elementary level, at least one third left home for a boarding school at the age of ten or eleven, because they lived in communities too small to have secondary schools.

Ginnasi, licei, and universities, whether secular or Catholic, were privately financed and generally expensive. For all but the wealthiest families, therefore, to educate one or more sons entailed considerable sacrifices, particularly if boarding school fees were added to the cost of tuition and books. Because the Risorgimento democrats were the beneficiaries of formal education far above the average for their country and time and because they came mostly from families of modest means, it is reasonable to assume that formal education was important to their families. Why it was important offers interesting clues to the social values by which the Risorgimento democrats were reared.

The educational profiles of these democrats suggest that their families had a basically utilitarian view of education; they regarded it as the most accessible avenue of social mobility for their sons. In early nineteenth-century Italy, the ideal of the educated gentleman of leisure, free to cultivate his mind without worries about the practical application of poetry or the market value of a doctorate in philosophy, was by no means dead. Among the Risorgimento democrats there were, in fact, a few who lived according to that ideal. Such was the case, for instance, for the Lucanian Giacinto Albini, the son of a highly regarded doctor and a well-to-do noblewoman. Expecting an adequate income from the family properties, he studied law to please his father while writing poetry to please himself.[20]

But only one out of ten of the democrats studied here came from families whose economic and social position was solid and secure. Many more came from families that had slowly climbed the socioeconomic ladder thanks to business acumen or specialized skills and that had little reason to feel secure. Such families put considerable pressure upon their children to achieve and thus to continue the trend of upward mobility. The career of the prominent Tuscan democrat Francesco Domenico Guerrazzi offers an excellent example of this concern with educational achievement as the key to upward mobility. A lawyer by training, he was acutely conscious of his family's slow climb from the ranks of the Tuscan rural poor to those of the urban middle class. Guerrazzi's grandfather, Donato, had been a soldier of fortune of peasant origins. In his forties he had married a woman much younger than himself, whose meager earnings as a spinner he had largely squandered on drink. Despite this unpromising background, Guerrazzi's father, Francesco Donato, had done much better by himself than the old soldier. Inspired perhaps by the example of his hardworking mother, he had become a skilled woodworker. Furthermore, he had learned to read and write, though it is not known whether he ever attended school. Although he remained poor, as a literate artisan he had achieved a secure and respected position in Tuscan society, something that his father could never have claimed. But he had wanted his own sons to do even better. For a family such as the Guerrazzis, unable to accumulate enough capital to go into business, "doing better" meant to gain access to some profession. Francesco Domenico Guerrazzi fulfilled his father's expectations. When he began to practice law in Florence the family seemed well on the way to a second generation of upward mobility. Political activism, however, disrupted the young lawyer's professional life. For his part in the illegal distribution of republican-democratic propaganda and in demonstrations against the grand ducal government he was arrested at least twice before 1848. Aware of the professional opportunities he was missing, yet unwilling to renege on his political convictions, he agonized over the prospect of disappointing his family. If adverse political circumstances doomed him to failure, it was imperative to impress upon the next generation of Guerrazzis the need to achieve success in life. From the Volterra fortress where he was imprisoned after the failure of the revolution of 1848, he urged his nephew and heir, Michele Francesco: "Blood of my blood, I no longer keep a vigil during the night, but I cry; even as I write my eyes fill with tears . . . You will soon tread the path of painful experience . . . [Don't forget . . .] *Sis fortis ac constans et dabo tibi coronam vitae.* Study, study . . . The Austrians are winning because they apply themselves more than we do."[21]

While he was thus prodded to apply himself and to make his elders proud, the young Michele Francesco was also warned to be prepared for unpleasant experiences at school. His uncle and mentor carried throughout his life vivid and bitter memories of his first years in school. His teacher's behavior, he wrote, had given him the first direct clues to social distinctions and to social injustice. The scions of wealthy and powerful families had been treated with deference and given better marks than their performance warranted, whereas he and others of humble social origins were constantly reprimanded and made to feel out of place.[22] One might dismiss Guerrazzi's recollections on this subject were it not that other democrats described their school experiences in almost exactly the same terms. Brofferio, for instance, although his family was much more securely rooted in the middle class than was Guerrazzi's, wrote of his first teacher: "Don Nosenghi's school was a microcosm of human society as it has always been and probably always will be. There were two or three students in that school who could quite properly be called 'whipping boys.' Such were the children of nonrich and noninfluential parents; such was I above all."[23] Although Brofferio was occasionally sent home or beaten by his teachers for rebelling against what he perceived as unjust, arbitrary behavior, he stayed in school and went on to earn a law degree at the University of Turin. But other youngsters of similar or lower social background were unable to adjust, and they left even if it meant disappointing their parents. According to a friend and biographer, for instance, Lorenzo Valerio "was driven out of school when he was about fifteen . . . by the beastly temper of a teacher" whose political views he had challenged. Valerio's widowed mother was probably unhappy about her son's decision to leave school, but she respected his feelings and helped him find a job in a textile mill, where eventually he rose to a managerial position.[24]

From these school experiences the future democratic leaders learned two lessons that were to color their outlook thereafter: first, that under the existing social arrangements intellectual merit and diligence, although valuable in themselves, were less important to success in life than a privileged background; and second, that the schools, whether secular or ecclesiastical, were instruments of social control, designed to legitimize and to preserve other institutions equally unjust and outmoded. Nino Bixio, for instance, learned these lessons at an early age and under particularly trying circumstances. The youngest of eight children in a family of modest means, he was sent to school by his father and stepmother

> because it was customary [in the artisan class of Genoa] and also because they did not want him underfoot at home. Once he was out of the door and enrolled in some school, no one paid the slightest attention to him. They forgot to pay his teacher [and] to buy the required books and notebooks. Thus the poor lad became the target of reprimands and of cruel taunts by teachers and classmates that destroyed his love of learning and made him ever more irritable.[25]

One day the pressure became intolerable, and the young Bixio threw an inkwell at his teacher. Naturally, he was expelled; his parents then forced him to take a job as a deckhand.

Among the future Risorgimento activists who, like Bixio, rebelled against their teachers were several seminary students. Their rebellion against a particular authority figure in the classroom took on a special meaning, because it could be and often was construed as rebellion against the entire framework of ecclesiastical discipline, and therefore against the Church itself. When, for instance, the Roman Mattia Montecchi stood trial for conspiracy in 1844, his having run away from a seminary at the age of thirteen or fourteen was cited by the prosecution as evidence of an incorrigibly sinful nature.[26]

Some thirty of these democrats received their secondary education in a seminary. In a few cases, the choice of an ecclesiastical rather than a lay-oriented institution was determined by the desire of devout parents to nurture in their sons the signs of a precocious religious vocation. Thus, the Venetian Francesco Dall'Ongaro recollected that his very pious mother had watched eagerly for signs of such a vocation. The poor woman misread the signs, however, because her Francesco turned out to be a most recalcitrant seminary student and ultimately an embittered renegade priest. For a few others, such as Alessandro Gavazzi and Luigi Anelli, the choice was determined not only by a precocious vocation on their part but also by the family tradition. Both of them, in fact, came from illustrious families which for generations had produced learned clergymen and bishops, and it was expected that they would continue that tradition.[27]

For the most part, however, the choice of a seminary education was evidence neither of religious zeal nor of a cultural tradition. Rather, it was dictated by necessity. Vocation or not, for youngsters from relatively poor families a seminary education was still, as it had been for centuries, a ticket out of fields and workshops. Moreover, it was generally cheaper than a secular education, particularly if the prospective seminarian came from a devout family and found a clerical sponsor. The problem was that especially in the intellectual and political climate of the Restoration youngsters enrolled by their parents in a seminary in the hope that they would qualify for white-collar occupations in the secular world came under pressure to become priests. Great as the pressure could be in Roman Catholic seminaries, it seems to have been even worse among religious minorities, especially the Greek Orthodox communities in the Kingdom of the Two Sicilies.[28]

The profiles of fourteen Risorgimento democrats who were subject to this pressure and who did not run away or rebel speak eloquently to the folly of such ecclesiastical recruitment methods. One of them, the Venetian Filippo De Boni, completed his theological studies only to refuse ordination in the end. Of his thirteen colleagues who were actually ordained, two (Gavazzi and Pantaleo) were excommunicated for heresy, and five (Dall'Ongaro, Luigi Miceli, Asproni, Giuseppe Sirtori, and Franchi) gave up the priesthood. Another three (Gregorio Ugdulena, Atto Vannucci, and Vito Ragona) remained within the Catholic Church, but they devoted almost no time to pastoral care or theology. And finally, one priest who did both, Enrico Tazzoli, was excommunicated just prior to his execution for his role in the Mantua conspiracy of 1853.

Many children of revolutionaries exhibited rebelliousness against teachers and resentment of school discipline. Having been exposed to revolutionary political ideas and role models at an early age, they often found their teachers' values at odds with those of their families. Yet the encounter with bigoted, authoritarian, and antiegalitarian teachers seems to have had the greatest impact not on them — for they may have been forewarned by their elders — but on future activists from politically conservative or apathetic families. Reacting to negative school experiences, especially the stifling discipline of seminaries and military academies, youngsters who had been socialized to respect established authority or at least to be passive and compliant in its presence developed attitudes quite similar to those of their more politically precocious peers. Once common ground had been established between the two groups, the children of revolutionaries might perhaps share with their schoolmates the best kept of the family secrets: membership in some revolutionary society dedicated to the overthrow of the existing regimes.

Ninety-seven out of the 146 democrats became members of secret societies such as Mazzini's Young Italy or Benedetto Musolino's Figliuoli della Giovine Italia ("Sons of Young Italy") before 1848. Among them were Saffi, Angherà, Elia, and others, who were almost certainly brought into the secret societies by close relatives. But others, like Mazzini himself or the brothers Fabrizi and Usiglio of Modena, joined during their student days at a *liceo* or a university.

Revolutionary secret societies that espoused anti-Catholic and antimonarchist ideas had flourished in Italy, as elsewhere in Europe, ever since the eighteenth century. Other societies, adding national independence and unity to secular and republican aspirations, had flourished during the French Revolution and in the early years of the Restoration. These — and particularly Young Italy — were growing larger in the 1830s after the failures of the liberal *moti* of 1820–21 and 1831. As the experienced police observers of that era knew very well, the secret societies recruited their leadership cadres and most of their members from educated young men; hence the need to keep a watchful eye on the schools.

Of the various aspects of the Risorgimento none have been explored with greater care and in greater detail than the history of its secret societies, particularly the Carboneria, Young Italy, and the Italian National Society. One reason for this is the intrinsic appeal of these societies, whose mysterious rituals, heroic deeds, and colorful leaders continue to capture the imagination of even the most skeptical contemporary readers. Another is the abundance of historical records on the secret societies, enduring evidence both of the effective propaganda networks they built and of the fear they inspired in the preunification governments.

The historical scholarship on this subject, however, has focused on the programs of the secret societies or on their relationship with the Church and the governments of the Old Regime. The question of what it meant for a young Italian of the early nineteenth century to join a secret society has been largely ignored. Yet, for the Risorgimento democrats the act of joining was of tremendous significance. It marked a crucial step in their transition from the "charm and irresponsibility of childhood" to political maturity.

As the memoirs and letters of several democrats illustrate, the schools were an important source of social and political experiences. Their authoritarian structure and the attitudes of teachers like Brofferio's Don Nosenghi certainly contributed to the development in the future revolutionaries of an awareness of intellectual and political censorship, of class differences, and of class discrimination. They were also responsible for the growth of a distrust of authority and of feelings of frustration and powerlessness. The secret societies offered a refuge where these feelings could be expressed and shared with contemporaries. Moreover, they channeled the energies and the anger of young rebels away from individual acts of defiance, destruction, and self-sacrifice toward collective action to change the existing institutions.

For the children of revolutionaries the secret societies were but a logical extension of the family circle. They joined because they had been socialized to work for change and because they knew that this work could not be carried out in isolation. Moreover, membership in a secret society was usually already a part of their family tradition. For these young men, therefore, the experience of membership was less exciting and probably less significant than it was for contemporaries from conservative or apolitical backgrounds who could expect neither sympathy nor support from their families if they rebelled against school or other authorities. Montecchi, for instance, did not return directly to his Roman home after running away from a seminary. For he knew very well that in his father's eyes he had squandered his only realistic chance of getting an education. Like others of his background, Montecchi stood alone and powerless in his defiance of existing institutions until he was approached by some followers of Mazzini. Membership in Young Italy gave him the emotional support that was not available within his family. More important, it enabled him to control his youthful anger and to resume his studies (though no longer in a seminary). Nothing less would do: a future leader of the Italian Revolution had to learn to keep his passions in check and to choose the long-term interests of his cause over the short-term satisfaction of personal urges and desires.[29]

Regardless of family background, for all the future democratic leaders membership in a secret society was a broadening experience. Because *licei* and universities were the primary recruiting grounds for such organizations, new members joined when they were in their late teens or early twenties. Many democrats were recruited by Mazzinian or other underground organizations shortly after they had left home for a boarding school or a university, which were usually located in communities larger than their native one. In most cases, this was their first experience away from familiar people and places, and it was often intimidating. Again, the secret society offered emotional support; but it also opened up to the young recruit new ideas and new horizons. The secret societies of the 1830s and 1840s, especially Young Italy, recruited members of both sexes from many age groups and walks of life. Social class, religious affiliation, and formal education mattered much less within their ranks than in Italian society at large. And only the persistence of accents and solecisms gave away differences of regional origin among the members.

The life of Alberto Mario reveals the impact all this could have on a young man newly arrived in a university town from the sheltered and confining life of a *possidente* in the rural Veneto. Born in 1825, Mario was the oldest child of a couple who boasted intellectually and politically distinguished ancestors and who were related to several aristocratic families in the Rovigo and Ravenna areas. But his parents were far from wealthy; indeed, they worried about securing the economic future of their children through professional training and advantageous marriages. The strict discipline that prevailed in the Mario household reflected these economic and social pressures as well as the parents' adherence to Catholic morality and religious practice. Young Alberto's upbringing was particularly strict, both because he was the oldest child and because he was a bit frail. Having lost to illness four of their seven children, his parents were understandably concerned and probably overprotective of him.

This peaceful but stultifying way of life came to an end when Mario, at the age of eighteen, left the cornfields of Lendinara to continue his education in Venice and Padua. In the 1840s Padua with its large and restless student population was a hotbed of political activism and anti-Habsburg sentiment. Mario was impressed by the political sophistication of some of his fellow students, and even more so by their origins: they came from every part of the Kingdom of Lombardy-Venetia, from other Italian states, and from foreign countries. He found the politicized and cosmopolitan environment so new and exciting that he neglected his academic work. He read Rousseau and Saint-Simon instead of Justinian, and he wrote articles for the underground press instead of studying for exams. As a result, to his father's dismay he failed to graduate before the events of 1848 took him away from Padua and from university life altogether. But if he neglected academic subjects Mario did not fail to learn political lessons about the need for national independence and for new democratic governments. At the university, moreover, he made friends with young political activists from other regions, some of whom he met again during the revolution or during the years of exile. In short, during his student days Mario developed the ideas, the style, and the network of contacts of the conspirator and radical journalist that he was to remain for the rest of his life.[30]

Among the eighty-five university-trained democrats there were a few, like Mario, who neglected their books for political activism. In Mazzini's view, for instance, earning a degree from the University of Genoa was less important than recruiting from among his fellow students the cadres of a future revolution.[31] Others in this group, however, cherished the opportunity of a university education, particularly if they came from humble social backgrounds, and they were torn between their desire to change the political status quo and their desire to conform to and profit from it. Certainly, many democrats who became professional revolutionaries in the 1850s, and later on deputies or full-time organizers, prepared seriously for quite different careers before the revolutionary events of 1848–49.

An analysis of the democrats' career aspirations and training is useful for understanding their position in nineteenth-century Italian society. It is particularly useful for appreciating to its fullest extent the disruptive effect of their political activities during the 1840s and 1850s on their lives and status.

Only 9 of the democrats studied here were children of wealthy *possidenti;* they could realistically expect to live off the profits of landownership without engaging in anything more demanding than casual supervision of their tenants or sharecroppers. Fifteen others worked at a variety of jobs during their adult lives, without ever securing either a dependable source of income or a well-defined place in the social order. But a large majority (122 out of 146) expected both to earn a living and to secure their social position by practicing some specific profession or trade. Their career goals required either several years of schooling or long apprenticeships.

As might be expected of nineteenth-century political leaders, many Risorgimento democrats prepared for careers in law, secondary teaching, and belles lettres. Of the 122 who trained for specific careers, 69 had strongly humanistic educational backgrounds, and 14 were trained for the clergy. Given the required intellectual ability and some means, would-be lawyers, teachers, writers, and clergymen aspired to graduation from a *liceo classico* or a seminary, to be followed by at least some university training.

A substantial minority (39 out of 122), however, did not receive a humanistic education beyond the secondary level. Rather, they attended scientific faculties (including medical schools) or they learned skilled trades such as printing. On the whole, these men fared better during the years of political turmoil and persecution than did their humanistically oriented colleagues. This is not to say that the democrats who became doctors, chemists, businessmen, and printers suffered no disruption of training or careers; but they did suffer less than their counterparts in other professions. The difference can be explained in a number of ways.

The ability to treat disease, to teach the hard sciences, or to manage an estate or a factory may have been in greater demand in Italian society than the ability to write a philosophical tract or to prepare a legal brief. But more important, the history of the Italian and other nineteenth-century revolutions suggests that some professions and crafts—notably medicine and printing—were useful during revolutionary upheavals and wars. And they could be practiced without much difficulty in foreign countries, a great advantage for some political exiles of the 1850s. Thus, men with those skills maintained and even improved their professional standing during the years of most intense political struggle. When the revolution was over, they could, if they so wished, turn their full attention to the careers for which they had trained in their youth. This was rarely the case for the democrats with a purely humanistic background. At the close of the Italian Revolution they found themselves at a great disadvantage compared to contemporaries with similar training who had built their careers instead of conspiring and fighting for the national cause.

Regardless of intellectual background and training, over one half of the democrats studied here experienced politically related interruptions of their schooling and early careers. The disruption was most severe among the oldest democrats, born in the decade 1800 to 1810, and among the youngest, born between 1825 and 1830. Most of those in the former group never quite recovered from the consequences of actual or alleged participation in the abortive uprisings of the 1830s. Those in the latter group for the most part were spared arrest, imprisonment, and exile before 1848, but the outbreak of revolution interrupted their schooling or damaged their prospects for steady employment and successful careers.

In sum, school experiences contributed directly to the political socialization of the Risorgimento democrats in at least two interrelated ways. First, the schools were the setting for the first challenges to and confrontations with the political institutions and the social arrangements of the Old Regime. Second, they were the locus of recruitment for the secret societies of the 1830s and 1840s that prepared the ground for the Italian Revolution.

In the democrats who came from families with a liberal or Jacobin tradition, the encounter with the Don Nosenghis of the educational system served to reinforce the notion that the existing social order was obsolete and unjust. By joining a secret society during their student days, they demonstrated their readiness to turn into revolutionary action the political consciousness acquired through home and school experiences. As for those democrats who came from obviously conservative or conformist backgrounds, the same educational experiences perhaps strengthened already existing and repressed impulses to rebel. They certainly were a source of value conflicts. For these young men to join a secret society was more than an act of political protest against the existing governments; it was also a defiant statement of their willingness to break with their families, whose political attitudes they could no longer tolerate, and to find alternative sources of values and of support.

5

The Emergence of a National Democratic Network, 1846–1848

To EXPLORE the lives of the Risorgimento democrats is to discover a complex network of close ties more reminiscent of an extended family than of a political party. Like members of a family, the leaders of the democratic movement knew and supported one another in a display of solidarity that cut across differences of age, education, income, and geographical origin. Like family members, they quarreled bitterly and frequently among themselves, yet they were inclined to close ranks whenever attacked by political adversaries.

The correspondence and the works of the democrats studied here offer plentiful evidence of such close ties. A few examples tell the story. The Roman Scipione Pistrucci, for instance, addressed Mazzini's mother as "my dear mama," and he spoke of Gustavo Modena's wife, Giulia, as "beloved sister." After Pisacane's tragic death in 1857, Giovanni Nicotera took care of his longtime companion, Enrichetta Di Lorenzo, and paid for the education of their daughter. In a similar spirit, Agostino Bertani and others helped the family of their fellow democrat Giovanni Acerbi.

Frequently, democratic intellectuals dedicated their works to colleagues in the movement whom they particularly loved and respected. Thus, for instance, Alberto Mario's wife, Jessie Meriton White, dedicated her biography of Nicotera to the children of the activists Elena and Achille Sacchi. Enrico Gentilini dedicated his most important political tract to Felice Govean, and Ferdinando Petruccelli similarly honored the memory of a fallen comrade in arms of 1848, Costabile Carducci. Benedetto Musolino and Filippo De Boni both dedicated works to a mutual friend, Luigi Miceli.

These ties of friendship and solidarity among the leaders deserve closer attention by historians of the Risorgimento than they have received thus far. For these ties not only enabled the democratic leaders to survive the disappointments and hardships of the 1850s but more important they provided the foundation for the development of democratic political structures in the 1860s both within and without the framework of the liberal monarchy.

The emergence of such ties can be traced in the events that brought together isolated individuals or regional groups into a national democratic network and in the forms that the network took. The period between the election of Pius IX to the papal throne in June 1846 and the fall of the Venetian Republic in August 1849 was crucial to the development of these ties and the network. The events of those years brought together men of democratic inclination from every part of Italy. To acquire visibility and credibility as political leaders, they had to sharpen the focus of their social and political critique in relation to existing institutions. To some extent, they also had to find ways to cloak this critique in slogans that might evoke an emotional response from the masses without, however, spurring them to independent action. The democrats found those slogans during the revolution, thus acquiring unprecedented influence in Italian society and even actual political power in some cities. They then proceeded to use both to experiment with democratic/ republican forms of government. Although short-lived, those experiments were significant, for they provided models and set precedents for future generations of Italian democrats.

Italian Democracy before 1848

The emergence of a national democratic network was a result of the revolution of 1848. In the period 1830 to 1846 Italian democracy was not a national movement; rather, it consisted of small groups that operated on a local or regional basis under a number of leaders. Even such widespread underground organizations as the Carboneria

and Young Italy, which had thousands of members and branches in
several regions, were loosely structured. Communication between
individual members and between branches was informal and subject to frequent breakdowns because of police harassment, the hardships of travel, inadequate leadership, and so forth. Moreover, no
democratic activist, not even Mazzini, could claim to be a nationally
known figure, although by the late 1830s a few names did begin to
appear regularly in the police files of the preunification states.
Governments were warned to look out for men like Mazzini, the
Fabrizi and Mauro brothers, Musolino, Quadrio, and others
dedicated to the overthrow of the Catholic faith, of monarchical
government, and of social stability.

But the decentralized and loose structure of the democratic
groups was not without advantages. First, it allowed for coexistence
and cooperation among men with rather different political goals and
ideological orientations. For instance, the group of left-wing intellectuals that met in Turin in the 1830s and early 1840s included
men like Brofferio, committed to a republican revolution yet socially
conservative, as well as the protosocialist pamphleteer Gentilini,
whose interest in the democratization of Piedmontese society far
outweighed his hostility to the Savoy monarchy.

Second, the more loosely structured and independent these
groups, the less vulnerable they were to repression and persecution.
Thus, for instance, Mazzini's attempt in 1834 to promote an insurrection in Savoy failed miserably, with dire consequences for the
leader himself and for his closest associates. Yet even a political
disaster of that magnitude did not halt the spread of democratic republicanism. If Young Italy suffered a major setback in Piedmont
and Liguria, it continued to proselytize in the neighboring Kingdom
of Lombardy-Venetia, in the Papal Legations, in the Marches, and
in Apulia and Calabria.[1]

Third, the decentralized character of Italian democracy before
1848 allowed the leaders to interpret revolutionary theories in a
manner compatible with local traditions and to adapt their
strategies to local needs. These advantages explain why the
democratic groups of the 1830s and 1840s — a very small fraction of
the Italian population — were able to sustain an intense propaganda
effort throughout the country and to organize dozens of guerrilla actions as well as some full-fledged armed insurrections against the
preunification governments.

Nearly all the democrats studied here had a hand in the revolutionary turmoil of that period. As members of revolutionary families
or of various secret societies, they as a group participated in every

revolutionary event of those years. But very few of them did so outside their native city or region. Their first experiences as propagandists or activists occurred within a social context that was familiar to
them and in association with relatives and close friends. They were,
of course, informed about events and issues in other regions, and
they had a cultural identity as Italians. If they were Mazzinians,
they certainly looked forward, in theory, to a united Italy with a
republican and democratic constitution. But in practice, until the
events of 1848–49 they focused their efforts less upon the formation
of a national movement than upon the transformation of their
native states or communities. Their family and professional backgrounds and their social and political experiences at the local level
often determined the issues in which they became involved and the
actions they took. This relatively narrow focus of thought and action
was perhaps the main reason behind the success of the democrats as
spokesmen for the grievances of their communities. For to some extent they were able to relate the abstract principles of secularism,
political equality, and social justice to concrete issues of immediate
interest to their apolitical and less educated contemporaries.

The biographical profiles used for this study provide many examples of how personal experiences and the analysis of local problems and conditions colored the outlook of the Risorgimento
democrats before they were thrust by circumstances onto the stage
of national politics. And the profiles also suggest ways in which the
democrats tried, more or less successfully, to secure the support of
their contemporaries. Three regional groups are of particular interest in this regard.

The first one consisted of democrats from the province of Mantua. It included Siliprandi, Sacchi, Acerbi, and Tazzoli, all of them
important figures in the political development of that area, in the
anti-Habsburg opposition of the 1840s, and in the revolution of
1848. Before the revolution they all were connected with Mazzinian
organizations and were known to the Habsburg police as probable
conspirators and potential rebels. Aside from their hostility to the
Habsburg government on the one hand and a generic commitment
to democratic republicanism on the other, these four men seemed to
have little in common. Although they knew one another, they were
not close friends. Of different social backgrounds, they came from
different parts of the province, and they chose quite different
careers. And yet an interesting pattern emerges from the reconstruction of their political profiles. In their writings and letters all of
them, at one or more points in their lives, justified their anti-
Habsburg activities and their advocacy of an Italian revolution by

pointing to problems typical of their province and in urgent need of solutions. Lack of capital, of transportation facilities, and of government assistance for middle-class and peasant landowners were among the problems they recounted. Habsburg economic policies, these men argued, favored the large landowners, who were socially prominent, politically conservative, and indifferent to more efficient production.

Another and obviously related problem was the appalling poverty of the sharecroppers and farmhands of lower Lombardy. Throughout their lives these men never forgot the shocking contrast that had been part of growing up in Mantua: emaciated bodies disfigured by pellagra, mentally retarded children, and lice-infested hovels amidst stretches of opulent fields and luxuriant meadows.[2]

The strength of the Mantua democrats, who established one of the liveliest political groups of the Risorgimento, lay precisely in their ability to convince others that a successful political revolution was necessary to solve these problems. Their attitude and their approach are illustrated particularly well by a memoir that Tazzoli wrote for General Karl von Culoz, the military governor of Mantua in 1852. Culoz was troubled and puzzled by the subversive activites of this priest from a cultured and well-to-do family. He wanted to know, in particular, why the Lombard clergy seemed to meddle constantly in political issues, while the Venetian clergy usually did not. Tazzoli reminded him, first of all, of the Lombard tradition of greater learning and intellectual sophistication, a tradition shared by clergy and laity alike. But he also pointed out that in his view the pastoral mission could not be fulfilled by caring only for souls. It had to address the whole man, and that meant addressing moral problems within the context of concrete economic and social conditions.[3] In this memoir Tazzoli presented the religious counterpart of secular arguments made by others in the Mantua group. Writing about the peasantry, for instance, the physician Sacchi observed that it made little sense to establish government-funded centers for the treatment of pellagra unless one was also prepared to tackle the economic and social roots of the disease.[4]

While the Mantua democrats placed their political opposition to the Habsburg government within the framework of social and economic grievances, the group around Andrea and Felice Orsini and the brothers Barbetti in the Romagna focused upon the popular issues of declericalization and prison reform. Until 1846 they had a valuable but unwitting ally in Pope Gregory XVI. His obdurate resistance to reforms gave credence to their arguments that the higher echelons of the papal bureaucracy would not be opened up to laymen by anything short of a major upheaval. This was a strongly felt issue among the population as a whole but especially so among young men from the educated middle classes. As laymen they felt excluded from jobs for which they were otherwise qualified. Even more than in the other Italian states, they made logical and willing targets for revolutionary recruitment.

From 1831 to 1845, more republican insurrections occurred in the Romagna than in any other part of Italy. The leaders were usually young, well educated, and thoroughly alienated from the clerical regime. But the Felice Orsinis of that region could not have kept the fires of rebellion constantly smoldering without widespread support from all social classes in their communities. More than the political issue of declericalization, which was primarily the concern of an educated minority, the humanitarian issue of prison reform was ideally suited for mobilizing public opinion against the papal government. Archaic penal codes, barbaric prisons, and the slow and erratic implementation of justice were a threat to all citizens regardless of sex, age, social class, or political conviction.[5]

Declericalization and prison reform were not necessarily democratic issues; they were supported by moderate liberals and even by the Austrian government. As long as no concessions from the papal government were forthcoming, though, the democratic groups, as the foremost enemies of that government, were in the best position to exploit these issues. And exploit them they did, until the advent of Pope Pius IX gave new hope to the advocates of moderate reforms within the framework of a constitutional monarchy.

Yet another example of the importance of personal experiences and local issues for the development of democratic strategies is found in the history of the Kingdom of the Two Sicilies. Several of the southern democrats in the sample were from Greek Orthodox communities. Descendants of refugees from Albania and Epirus, they lived in the interior of Calabria, Basilicata, and Sicily. Their native villages differed from Roman Catholic towns in language as well as in traditions. These communities struggled to preserve their unique cultural identity and were constantly fending off Bourbon threats to their autonomy. Moreover, some villages claimed to have been shortchanged in the distribution of *terre demaniali* ("state lands") to the advantage of old Catholic landed families or of new speculators from the towns.[6]

As was the case with reform in the Papal States, the particular grievances of the so-called Albanians of southern Italy could have been exploited by many political groups for a variety of purposes. But democratic activists like Musolino were the first to assess the revolutionary potential of those communities and to establish ties with respected Albanian leaders like the Mauro brothers and Giovanni Mosciaro. The highly successful democratic propaganda of the 1840s among the Albanians was aimed at convincing them that a secular and democratic republic offered the best guarantee of religious freedom and cultural autonomy. These things were important to the Albanians and as such they were stressed. Before 1848 Musolino and others said little about the broader goals in which they believed, Italian independence and unity.[7]

To the extent that the democratic leaders of the 1830s and early 1840s built a popular following, they did so by relating their ideological principles to concrete issues strongly felt by the people of their regions or states. But the relatively narrow focus of democratic propaganda—a distinct advantage in recruiting new activists and in mobilizing potential supporters—became a drawback when the democrats set out to translate their social and political critique into acts of rebellion. The price to be paid for failed attempts to overthrow the governments of the Restoration and the temporal power was always heavy; none but a few dedicated zealots were willing to pay it year after year.

Many promising young democratic leaders were lost in the unsuccessful uprisings of the 1840s. More often than not, those who died in these ventures or escaped abroad were men not trapped within narrow provincial concerns but potentially able to create and to lead a national democratic movement. And that is precisely why Mazzini, the one Italian intellectual most clearly committed to a national democratic revolution before 1848, grieved inconsolably over their fate. Under any circumstances these losses would have weakened the democratic cause. Worse, though, was that democratic republicanism, particularly in its Mazzinian formulation, became associated in the minds of many Italians with violence, bloodshed, and heroically futile sacrifice.

Three revolutionary episodes in particular contributed to a crisis of confidence among the leaders and to adverse shifts of public opinion in areas where democratic groups had previously been successful. The first of these was the Bologna conspiracy of 1843. It involved the local lawyer Giuseppe Camillo Mattioli, Livio Zambeccari, who had contacts with Tuscan democrats, and Nicola Fabrizi of Modena, already a seasoned and well-traveled conspirator. Although moderate liberals participated in the conspiracy, the Mazzinians were held responsible for the failure of their supporters—mostly artisans and petty bourgeois—to take to the streets on the appointed day. And they were also blamed for the lack of coordination between the Bologna revolutionary organizations and the democratic-led groups of the rural Romagna. Those blamed for the revolutionary debacle took refuge in the Apennine mountains or escaped across the border into Tuscany.[8]

A year later, in the summer of 1844, the country was shaken by news of a much bloodier democratic failure, the attempt of the brothers Bandiera of Venice to set off the Italian Revolution by overthrowing the Bourbons of Naples. The brothers chose the province of Cosenza for their daring and tragic attempt, for they knew of the democratic groups there, and they counted on the support of the nearby Albanian communities. When they landed in Calabria, however, they found neither friends nor foes among the local population. Isolated and betrayed by one of their own, they became easy targets for the Bourbon troops. Significantly, of the seven revolutionaries who faced the firing squad with the Bandieras, none were citizens of the Bourbon Kingdom. They were all outsiders, indeed foreigners by the rules of international law, eager to join kindred political spirits in the South. The problem was that they misunderstood both the thrust and the significance of what fellow democrats like Musolino had accomplished there. Expecting to find enthusiasm for the ideal of an independent, united, and democratic Italy, they found instead leaders preoccupied with local problems and a populace as suspicious of outsiders as it was fearful of repression.[9]

Finally, democratic activists like Orsini, Andreini, and the printer Massimiliano Grazia of Rimini figured prominently in the Romagna uprisings of 1845. More than the Bologna conspiracy and the Bandiera expedition, *i casi di Romagna* served the revolutionary cause by attracting attention once again to the shortcomings of the clerical regime. Thousands of Italians agreed with the compassionate and astute analysis of a Piedmontese observer, Massimo d'Azeglio: The papal government had to undertake major reforms or else perish. But d'Azeglio's readers also agreed, it seems, with another facet of his analysis: that the violent tactics of the Romagna democrats were counterproductive. Those tactics, he wrote, invited repression instead of prodding the clerical government in the direction of basic reforms. Thus, it behooved the moderate liberal subjects of the pope to break with hotheads like Andreini and to extricate themselves once and for all from the murky and dangerous world of the secret societies.[10]

However perceptive, d'Azeglio's comments on the impact of democratic-led uprisings did nothing more than to say publicly and in print what the exiled Mazzini had been saying for some time in private letters to his followers. While d'Azeglio exhorted his fellow liberals to engage in a constitutional "conspiracy in broad daylight," Mazzini tried to convince other democrats not to take unnecessary risks. Mazzini's advice was not persuasive, however, for ever since the 1830s he had advocated armed uprisings as a prelude to a nationwide guerrilla movement. Having recognized to what extent each revolutionary failure drained the slight resources of the democratic groups, he now counseled caution. But, contrary to the hyperbolic police reports concerning his activities, he had no real means to control the various groups which in the Romagna and elsewhere claimed to act upon his principles.

If Mazzini's pleas were not enough, the Romagna affair and d'Azeglio's critique of it brought home to many democratic activists the need for a reassessment of goals and strategies. For many years they had kept the caldron of Italian politics bubbling. Yet they had not succeeded in toppling a single one of the Restoration governments since 1831. They had sympathizers in every social class in the towns and even among the rural population in such areas as Basilicata, Calabria, and the Romagna. Still they seemed to lack the critical mass of supporters needed to turn coups de main into opportunities for revolution. Such was the precarious state of the Risorgimento democrats upon the death of Pope Gregory XVI. The policies of his successor, elected in June 1846, and the mystique that surrounded those policies threatened to isolate the democrats even further and to condemn them to oblivion.

The advent of Pope Pius IX held forth the promise of a golden age of reform not only in the Papal States but throughout Italy. Earlier in the decade, the Piedmontese philosopher Vincenzo Gioberti had suggested that the papacy should be the focus of a national movement of cultural renewal and political reform. This neo-Guelf idea had appealed to many politically conscious Italians who wished to reconcile their desire for constitutional government and national unity with their Catholic faith. Both moderate liberals and democrats had, however, dismissed it as utopian and impractical, for they knew Pope Gregory XVI to be as hostile to Gioberti's call for a *renovatio Ecclesiae* as he was to the political demands of his own subjects.

After years of waiting and frustration, Gioberti's sympathizers were too quickly seized by enthusiasm for the new pope. His every word and gesture were noted, discussed, and praised in the press and in public meeting places. His amnesty for political prisoners, his willingness to discuss some political issues with prominent laymen, and above all, his touching invocation for a special divine blessing upon Italy were taken as signs that the Giobertian dream was about to become reality. *Viva Pio Nono* became the slogan of all those who opposed the political status quo. It was a convenient slogan because it signified approval of the pope's reforms and of his public pronouncements as an Italian. It was also a safe slogan, for the Catholic rulers of Italy—whatever their private thoughts on the matter—could not very well restrict public expressions of love for the head of the Church.

The political elite of the Papal States was quick to capitalize upon the liberal image that Pius IX projected in the first months of his pontificate. Moderate liberals such as Marco Minghetti hoped to use the mounting wave of popular enthusiasm, to which the new pope was by no means insensitive, to pressure him into a full-fledged transformation of his government into a constitutional monarchy. Some liberals also hoped to pressure him to become the head of an Italian federation. Their counterparts in other Italian states shared these hopes for major initiatives from Rome because, as they correctly perceived, their own rulers would not be able to resist a reform movement under the aegis of the pope. In the latter part of 1846 and in early 1847 they worked feverishly to draw up petitions, proclamations, and legislative proposals acceptable to their governments. They became highly visible during this period, and they gained the expertise and self-confidence that they were to show at the outbreak of revolution.[11]

The experience of the Risorgimento democrats, on the other hand, was quite different. The increasing popularity of Pius IX and of moderate reformism was an additional cause of dissension within groups not noted for their coherence and unity. Several democratic intellectuals, for instance, were clearly swept away by the myth of the liberal pope. Not surprisingly, those most inclined to relinquish the weapons of anticlerical propaganda and insurrection were the proponents of evangelical Christianity. From Pius IX they expected not only political reforms but also a redefinition of the Church's role in Italian life. No one had greater expectations in this regard than Montanelli, the foe of Austria and of the Jesuits, who had long dreamed of a Christian republic in his native Tuscany. He rushed to Rome at the first opportunity for a papal audience, which he described as follows: "My heart sank when I began to probe into his views on freedom of the press, on a war of independence, on the Jesuits . . .; these were the burning issues which we [Italian] revolutionaries wished to see resolved . . . [but, for all that] my love of Italy proved stronger than my republican convictions, and I went down on my knees before him."[12] Even Mazzini, for all his conviction that Catholicism was incompatible with democratic republicanism, could not ignore the significance of the pope's new role. If Pius IX could bring the Italians closer together and hasten their liberation from foreign rule, then his popularity was welcome. Indeed, Mazzini wrote, he deserved the good wishes and the support of every Italian patriot.[13]

Some democrats found this sentimental cult of the liberal and patriotic pope both dangerous and disgusting. Writing in a French magazine, for instance, Ferrari issued a warning: The reforms set in motion by the pope threatened to isolate the democratic groups completely and to destroy the preconditions for a genuine revolution in Italy. Mazzini and others, he declared, apparently did not realize that the aim of this, as of all previous reform movements, was to prolong the life of the Old Regime by making it somewhat more efficient and more tolerable. In fact, within the Papal States Pius IX was now carrying out the very same administrative and legal changes that Metternich had recommended in vain to his predecessors.[14]

But intransigent anticlericals like Ferrari were almost an extinct species in the euphoric neo-Guelf climate of 1847. The purveyors of folk wisdom agreed with the most learned statesmen of the day: Italy was to be a federation of constitutional monarchies led by the one sovereign whose authority nearly all Italians held sacred. Of course, Austria would have to be reassured and placated, but this did not seem an insurmountable obstacle. As for the advocates of a secular, democratic, and united republic, they had served the country well as vehicles of popular protest and rebellion in the darkest days of political reaction and religious obscurantism. The liberal Italy about to be born would not have need of them.

The events of 1848 proved otherwise. Although flattered by the adulation of chanting crowds and by the torchlight processions in his honor, the pope moved slowly and cautiously toward substantive reforms. Men who had spoken with him about political issues, like Montanelli, knew how concerned he was about the possible impact of an Italian revolution upon the European balance of power. They also knew how reluctant he was to tamper with such institutions as censorship and the ecclesiastical courts, which had assured the stability and the special character of the papal government for centuries.

Quite aside from the pope's uneasiness about his new role, in the latter part of 1847 the millennial federal ideal of Gioberti did not seem to be coming any closer because the other Italian rulers were at once jealous of the pontiff's popularity and afraid to outbid him by granting constitutions. By the year's end, the advocates of constitutional government in the various states had grown very restless. Peaceful assemblies, street corner posters, and newspaper editorials no longer provided adequate outlets for their impatience.

Outside the pope's own territories, the expectations of change had been greatest in the Bourbon Kingdom. Unwilling to wait any longer for the success of a nationwide movement or for concessions from Ferdinand II, liberals and democrats in Reggio Calabria and Messina joined hands in a short-lived revolutionary experiment late in 1847. Then, in January 1848, the more numerous and better-organized opposition groups in the Sicilian capital decided to take matters into their own hands as their ancestors had done under the Bourbon and other dynasties. Their rebellion and the subsequent overthrow of Louis Philippe in France were the sparks that turned the expectations and tensions of 1846–47 into a major revolution in Italy.

Unlike the February Revolution in Paris, which was initiated by intellectuals, students, and workers acting out the democratic myths of 1792–93, the Italian Revolution began with quite moderate demands. Prominent citizens with liberal views reluctantly turned demonstrator, even rebel, to obtain basic political rights that had long been available to their counterparts elsewhere in western Europe. Initially they shunned the support of the democratic groups and, of course, that of the masses because they feared the implications of putting weapons into their hands. But events showed that the moderate liberals could not go it alone. By the early months of 1848, the domestic and international situations were such that the successful achievement of even limited political goals required insurrections and war with Austria. At the barricades and on the battlefields the revolutionary experiences of the democratic leaders made them indispensale if often mistrusted and dangerous allies.

Thus, the first phase of the Italian Revolution was marked by uneasy cooperation between moderate liberals and democrats. With few exceptions, the former remained in control of the situation until the summer of 1848. But during that same period the latter had unprecedented opportunities to meet and exchange ideas among themselves and to build national reputations as revolutionary leaders.

Local and Regional Networks

In the late 1840s the capital cities of the Italian states were inevitably the focal points of political unrest. Most of the democrats

studied here participated enthusiastically in the rallies and demonstrations that preceded the granting of constitutions and the insurrections of March 1848 against Austrian rule in Lombardy-
Venetia. Some of them did so in the capital cities where they had
been born or where they had spent their student days and started
their careers. Men like Brofferio in Turin, Bertani in Milan, Bixio in
Genoa, or Crispi in Palermo were no strangers to political activity.
But even for them this was a time of intense emotions and new experiences. It was also a time for reexamining one's own political
beliefs, for making new contacts, and for developing strategies to
break down conservative institutions. The democratic networks that
emerged on the eve of the revolution and became consolidated during its first phase took different forms, depending upon the local circumstances and the character of their leadership. But a close look at
some of these networks reveals significant common patterns.

First, they were highly informal and relatively open. If conditions permitted, their members met in public places. One such place
was a popular watering hole in Milan, the Caffè della Peppina,
where progressive businessmen and intellectuals had crossed paths
for years. Late in 1847 a dozen longtime customers, among them the
brothers Pezzotti, who were in the leather goods trade, the physician Attilio De Luigi, and Carlo De Cristoforis, began to meet there
more frequently, defying police surveillance and sometimes openly
reading forbidden newspapers. Although aware of the risks, the
members of this and of similar groups in other cities were not
secretive about their political opinions and their goals for the future.
In the tense yet hopeful climate of those prerevolutionary days, they
ceased to be underground conspirators and began instead to act like
citizens conscious of certain basic rights which they were now willing to assert.[15]

A second characteristic of these embryonic networks was that
they did not coincide with any previously known organization but
rather drew their membership from several sources. Members of
secret societies who participated in network building did not forget
their revolutionary past; indeed, they continued to value the secret
societies as training grounds for future leaders and as shelters in case
of trouble. But they operated independently of their previous affiliation and alongside men who had never joined a secret society.

For obvious reasons, personal introductions by one or more
members and elaborate initiation rituals were needed to gain acceptance into a secret society. By contrast, although most of the
members did have conspiratorial backgrounds, the democratic networks of 1847–48 were easily accessible to outsiders. The Sardinian

priest Asproni, for instance, was welcomed in the Piedmontese network of Brofferio, Govean, and Costantino Reta on little more than his own statement of democratic faith and his previous reputation as a critic of clerical privilege.

Because they were rather easily accessible, groups such as Brofferio's provided a natural rallying point for democrats newly arrived from the provinces. Young men who had become politicized at home or at school during the preceding years flocked to the capital cities of Italy in search of greater political wisdom and of opportunities for advancement. They were joined by other immigrants, the political suspects of an earlier era whom the Italian governments had kept away from the capitals and forced to reside where they could do no harm. More than the younger men, who often came out of simple curiosity, these older democratic activists were eager for action and perhaps for revenge. Among them, for instance, was the famous physician from Arezzo, Carlo Pigli, who reappeared in Florence at the outbreak of revolution and then went on to become the governor of "red" Livorno.[16]

The small democratic groups that were meeting in the various Italian capitals became networks upon the influx of both young recruits and of experienced men from the provinces. Through these new members they developed direct ties with potential supporters in the smaller towns and even in villages. By the spring of 1848, they had established contacts at all levels of society in both urban and rural areas. These contacts, although elusive and short-lived, warrant close attention because they are the best and often the only clues to the democratic movement's social basis and to its impact upon Italian society.

In the 1850s the democratic leaders often blamed one another for having failed to exploit what popular support they had enjoyed during the revolution. Most interpreters of the Risorgimento — including those sympathetic to the democrats — have taken this self-indictment at face value. And from it they have generally drawn the conclusion that the links between democratic activists and the masses had been weak and ephemeral, if indeed they had existed at all. But the experiences of the democrats studied here point to a different conclusion. They suggest that major cleavages developed *during* the revolution itself, when the democratic leaders found themselves between the hammer of uncontrollable social and economic demands from the lower classes and the anvil of their own class interests and meritocratic views on society and politics.

Particularly in Turin and Florence, the democrats sometimes welcomed within their ranks exiles of similar political views who had fled the more repressive states. But on the whole, until the summer of 1848, the democratic networks grew slowly and cautiously, branching out from the capital cities to the provinces and maintaining a strong regional flavor. They proved particularly useful and effective during the early phase of political cooperation between moderate liberal and democratic opponents of the existing governments. Through the experiences of several Milanese democrats it is possible to trace the structure and activities of a large, basically urban network which played an important role in the anti-Austrian insurrection of March 18-22, 1848 (the Five Days of Milan). As for links between urban groups and small-town or village activists, they are best illustrated by the experiences of several Florentines and Neapolitans.

At least three centers of democratic opposition to Habsburg rule were active in Milan on the eve of the revolution: that of Pietro Maestri, one clustering about Carlo Cattaneo, and another around Mauro Macchi. The Maestri group, composed of literate middle-class tradesmen, civil servants, and professionals, met at the Caffè della Peppina. With good reason, police spies suspected them of republican sympathies and of illicit connections with the exiled Mazzini. Toward the end of 1847 Maestri, perhaps influenced by De Cristoforis's social theories, began to proselytize more openly in favor of democratic republicanism. He challenged intellectuals like Cattaneo, arguing that economic progress and social justice were not realistic goals so long as Lombardy was ruled by the Habsburgs. A free-trade policy, including Zollverein membership, was of little interest to the imperial government which regarded Lombardy as a rich source of revenues, not a region needing development. Social reforms on behalf of the peasantry and urban lower classes, issues dear to Maestri, were viewed with particular suspicion by the very members of Milanese society most likely to be heeded in Vienna. As manufacturers and large estate owners, these were the people who argued that without cheap labor they could not compete with foreign industries.[17]

Cattaneo and his friends were less politically militant than Maestri's Peppina group. Several former disciples of the late jurist-philosopher G. D. Romagnosi, some well-known social reformers like Giuseppe Sacchi, and a distinguished sprinkling from the Milanese intelligentsia made up this second group. Generally they subordinated strictly political issues, such as the achievement of constitutional government, to economic and social ones. Cattaneo, for instance, had made his scholarly reputation as an advocate of free trade and land reform. Sacchi was known for his innovations in the education of young children and in the regulation of factory work.

Although the radical political and social arguments of Maestri and others were not persuasive enough to turn Cattaneo into a militant republican, they did influence younger men in his circle, especially Mauro Macchi. Macchi was much more sensitive than Cattaneo, his former teacher and role model, to the need for social action. He had grown up in a poor section of Milan, to which he returned when he was about twenty to teach school and to organize mutual-aid societies. At the outbreak of revolution he led many members of his working-class community, women as well as men, to the barricades to fight alongside the middle-class groups.[18]

Early in 1848, during a successful popular boycott of the Austrian tobacco monopoly and of performances at the Teatro alla Scala, the personal contacts among these activists became more frequent and intense. By March 1848 these three groups which had formed spontaneously around different issues and leaders became a network of democratic opponents of the Habsburg regime. However, no effort was made to formalize these highly personal connections and to work out a common program. Thus, after bearing the brunt of the insurrection side by side with the lower-class elements they had mobilized, the Milanese democrats ended up playing understudy to the moderate liberals in the provisional government. For the moderate liberals, led by the mayor of Milan, Count Gabrio Casati, were at least united in their determination to achieve political liberty and social stability under an Italian constitutional monarch. But the democratic camp was marked by the uneasy coexistence of Italian nationalists, Lombard separatists, and protosocialist thinkers like De Cristoforis, for whom social justice was a more important goal than political change. The persistence of these divisions had a major impact on the course of the revolution, not primarily because it doomed the democratic leaders to a secondary role in Milanese politics, but because it greatly diminished their potential input into the policies of the moderate liberals, whose leadership went virtually unchallenged from late March to the end of July 1848.

The Milanese democratic network was not at all provincial in outlook. Cattaneo, as editor of the highly respected *Politecnico*, and other network members corresponded with democratic groups in other Lombard cities, in Turin, and in Florence. Moreover, they kept in touch with social and political trends in France through the expatriate Giuseppe Ferrari, who returned briefly to Milan after the Five Days. As for the Mazzinian members of the network, particularly the brothers Pezzotti, they were known by reputation well beyond the boundaries of their native region. As self-conscious members of an international revolutionary movement, however, the Milanese democrats did not show much interest in the small towns and villages of Lombardy. Their network maintained a strong urban bias even though democratic thinkers and activists from the provinces, such as Luigi Anelli of Lodi and Gabriele Rosa of Iseo, were welcomed within its ranks during the revolution. The presence of such men in the Lombard capital, however, usually reflected pre-revolutionary ties between urban and provincial intellectuals or business associates. It was not indicative of any effort to reach the lower classes in provincial towns or the peasantry, and in August 1848, the Milanese democrats paid the price for not having made such an effort.

Another major network, organized by Florentine democrats in 1847–48, also had an urban bias and rather tenuous connections with the Tuscan peasantry. Yet it differed markedly from the Milanese group in that it was able to reach and mobilize the urban artisans and laborers not only in the capital but also in several provincial towns, especially Livorno, Pistoia, Prato, and Siena. Although urban based, the Florentine network had a regional rather than a local character, which was reflected in the geographical origins of its leaders. The most prominent among them, such as Guerrazzi, Mazzoni, and Montanelli, were living and working in Florence at the outbreak of revolution, but they still maintained close ties with relatives and colleagues in their respective hometowns. Thus, while the Milanese network could be described as a loose coalition of local groups, its Florentine counterpart reflected in a microcosm the rich diversity of democratic life in Tuscany and the centuries-old determination of the region's provincial towns not to be overshadowed by the capital.[19]

The seventeen Tuscan democrats studied here represented not only all of the important urban centers of the area in their day but also quite a variety of social and occupational groups. Two residents of Florence, Enrico Montazio, who grew up on the Tosco-Emilian Apennine, and Ermolao Rubieri of Prato, were journalists and playwrights. Their professional activities brought them into contact on the one hand with middle-class literati in other cities, for instance, Gaetano Tallinucci in Barga, near Lucca, and Piero Cironi and Atto Vannucci in Pistoia, and on the other, with the printer Luigi Ricci and other members of the important and articulate Florentine artisan class. One of these, the master baker Giuseppe Dolfi, was instrumental in mobilizing his fellow artisans and their shophands, not only in Florence but also in his native Siena.

An equally important link in the democratic network was the renowned and ever restless University of Pisa, which attracted faculty and students from all parts of the grand duchy and from other states. Two democrats on the faculty there, Montanelli and Pigli, shared with colleagues and students more than their respective knowledge of philosophy and medicine; they shared political lessons that bore fruit during the revolution when their students followed them to the battlefields of Lombardy and the barricades of Livorno.

And finally, the Florentine network also included a conspicuous number of professionals and businessmen, from the progressive landowner Leopoldo Cattani-Cavalcanti of Castelletti a Signa, near Florence, to the lawyers Guerrazzi and Mazzoni and the brothers Sgarallino, owners of a small shipping firm in Livorno. Despite its social and geographical diversity, this network lacked any substantial support among the peasantry.

Of the Tuscan democrats studied here only Vannucci came from a peasant family. He escaped from his poor mountain village near Pistoia via the well-trod path of a seminary education and of priestly vows, and thereafter lived and taught in Pistoia and Florence. Other intellectuals and professionals despised the peasantry as hopelessly reactionary or spoke of them with condescension. Montazio, for instance, claimed to understand the plight of the peasantry because he had grown up in an impoverished Apennine village. Yet his articles in the revolutionary newspaper *Il popolano* were always based on the assumption that the peasantry had to follow the political values and leadership of the democratic intellectuals and of the urban lower class. Ultimately, the only Tuscan democrat who took direct responsibility for the political education of the peasantry was that rare exception in the democratic camp, the aristocratic landowner Cattani-Cavalcanti. And he went no further than to promote literacy on his own estate and to preach the gospel of Italian unity and independence. The principles of political equality and social justice in which he believed abstractly were kept mostly to himself.[20]

Despite a common urban bias, the Florentine and Milanese networks differed considerably in ideology. Both networks included a wide spectrum of political opinions; but ideological differences were more strongly felt within the Milan groups. During the revolution the Milanese network split along political and ideological lines, particularly on the question of whether to support Charles Albert's war effort against the Austrians. By contrast, in Florence and other Tuscan cities the really serious cleavages developed around social and economic issues. At least two factors account for this difference: first, the social composition of the networks, which were more homogeneous in Milan than in Florence; and second, the attitudes prevailing in each region toward the Restoration governments. Like others in their city, the Milanese democrats perceived Austria as the enemy, and they were inclined to seek in the Italian nationalist movement a remedy for their political and economic frustrations. The Tuscans, on the other hand, had few comparable grievances. They could not criticize the economic policies of the grand ducal government on the grounds that they reflected a harmful foreign influence. Nor could they complain, as the Lombards did, about foreign domination of the bureaucracy and of the army. Hence, while the Milanese democrats questioned both the structure and the legitimacy of their government, the Tuscans were more pragmatically concerned with their government's actual performance in the areas of civil and political liberties and of social justice. Only when it clearly failed to "deliver" in these crucial areas did they demand the ouster of the grand duke.

At the outbreak of revolution, the Milanese democrats had two assets on which to try to build their political success: the increasing popular dissatisfaction with the Austrian regime and the support of some lower-class neighborhoods. But they also faced two major obstacles. The first, evident in the early months of the revolution, was the considerable political and social influence of the moderate liberal patricians. The second, evident in the crisis of July-August 1848, was their own failure to agree on anything beyond the need to keep the Austrians out of northern Italy. The "balance sheet" of Florentine democracy also pointed to the possibility of an impasse. On the positive side were the truly regional character of the democratic network and its fairly broad social basis; on the negative was the difficulty of mobilizing public opinion for revolutionary action against a relatively benign despot, particularly when he surrounded himself with Tuscan liberals from prestigious old families.

One democratic network in the Italy of 1848, however, seemed to enjoy ideal conditions for success. Centered in Naples, it had all of the advantages of the Milanese and Tuscan networks, yet it was free from their worst handicaps. Or so it seemed at first. At the core of this southern network were three democratic groups that had developed in Naples itself during the 1840s. One such group revolved around the quixotic publicist Giuseppe Ricciardi; a second consisted of university students; and a third, led by Giuseppe Dassi, brought together literate tradesmen and artisans. The intellectuals in Ricciardi's group were primarily inspired by the writings of French social theorists, whereas the members of the other two groups were strongly attracted to Mazzinian revolutionary propaganda.[21]

As in Milan and Florence, there was considerable overlap among the members of these groups, but none of them were able or willing to reach out for the support of the large Neapolitan underclass. Known as the *lazzaroni*, this class found the Bourbon tradition of religious piety, cheap pasta, and free public festivals more relevant to their lives than the opposition's promises of political liberty and economic development. Even so, the democratic network in Naples covered nearly as large a cross section of the urban population as did its Milanese equivalent. In the composition of its leadership, however, the Neapolitan network resembled the Florentine more than the Milanese model. For it included not only intellectuals and activists brought up in the capital itself but also prominent men from provincial towns. Thus, like the Florentine network, it had at once an urban and a regional character.

However, the emergence to leadership positions of intellectuals and professionals from places like Salerno, Potenza, and Lecce did not reflect, as it did in Tuscany, the determination of those smaller towns to compete with the capital. Rather, it was the accidental—and from the government's viewpoint certainly the unwelcome—by-product of political and cultural centralization. Of the twenty-four democrats examined here who were born in the provinces of the Kingdom of Naples (the continental part of the Kingdom of the Two Sicilies), at least nineteen moved to the capital when in their late teens or early twenties to pursue higher education and begin their careers. Naples was not just the first choice of young men from the provinces aspiring to university degrees and to professional or business opportunities, it was the only choice. Alerted by the unsuccessful uprisings of 1843 and 1844, the Bourbon government increased its surveillance of students. It tried to curb the migration of educated young men to the capital, but its halfhearted efforts created resentment without really stemming the tide.[22]

The high concentration of educational institutions and business activities in Naples made it easy for young men from the various provinces to establish contacts among themselves and with existing opposition groups. And the repressive policies of the regime provided both willing recruits to the network and fertile soil for its political propaganda among the public at large. While becoming active in the capital, however, the young immigrants did not sever ties with their native communities. Indeed, at the outbreak of revolution they flocked eagerly back to lead their fellow citizens in uprisings, revolutionary assemblies, and provisional governments.

In the Kingdom of Naples, centralization was characteristic not only of the political system but of some sectors of the economy as well. The kingdom's most important industries, for instance, were clustered in and around Naples and Salerno. Even before Italian unification, the concentration of skilled workers (for example, glove cutters, ceramists, and coral finishers) in those areas favored the work of democratic propagandists like Dassi and Giuseppe Fanelli. Similarly, the experiences of the Mauro brothers and of Musolino in the province of Cosenza suggest that the political work of the democrats in rural areas was facilitated by the typically southern pattern of large and dense villages surrounded by nearly deserted fields and pastures.

This demographic and geographical pattern made it possible for political organizers to focus their propaganda efforts on relatively large communities instead of trying to reach scores of small villages, where hostile local notables might intimidate the peasantry, or isolated compounds where the resident peasant families might be closely watched by the owner himself or by his overseer. This same pattern also made it relatively easy for revolutionaries and outlaws of all sorts, and therefore also for several democrats on the run, to evade police searches and escape arrest. In the 1850s, in fact, the only democrats studied here who avoided arrest and exile and continued their underground political work in their native provinces were those bold or desperate enough to take advantage of the primitive roads, rugged mountains, and forests of the southern interior.[23]

The three democratic networks described thus far and similar ones in Rome and Venice were the more active and important of all the networks on the eve of the revolution. Their development and activities were reported in the correspondence and diaries of the major protagonists and were reconstructed later in scores of historical accounts. Inevitably, an assessment of the democratic contribution to the revolution of 1848 must revolve around this body of evidence on the major democratic networks. But it should be kept in mind that smaller networks of similar origin and composition existed in other cities and provinces in the late 1840s. Their actions were less spectacular and their leaders less famous than those of networks based in the Italian capitals. Nonetheless, they too did their part in overthrowing the existing regimes and in building grass-roots support for democratic ideology.

The Bond of Revolution

Although they defined and publicized their commitment to democratic ideology, in 1847–48 the men studied here did not attempt to draw any rigid line between their own and the moderate liberal position. Political theorists like Cesare Balbo and d'Azeglio, on the one hand, and Mazzini and Ferrari, on the other, did engage in a lively debate over the merits of a reformist versus a revolutionary solution to the Italian Question, and they did discuss the objectives and the limits of the ongoing movement for political change. On a practical level, though, democrats and moderate liberals continued to work side by side, organizing rallies, gathering petitions, and writing columns for the newly unshackled political press. In Milan, for instance, on the eve of the Five Days the democratic firebrands Cernuschi and Macchi were in and out of Cattaneo's home, as were also the brothers Porro, members of Milan's liberal patriciate and later supporters of Charles Albert's military intervention in Lombardy.

Throughout this tense and exciting period, in Milan as elsewhere the democratic leaders deferred to moderate liberal political initiatives. Their attitude, which persisted with few exceptions until the summer of 1848, reflected a realistic assessment of their society's stage of development. They were ideologically committed to far-reaching political and social changes, but they knew that they lacked the strength to achieve their goals. Their networks, though promising, were of recent origin and socially heterogeneous. Besides, they themselves lacked certain qualifications which public opinion in those days regarded as important for leadership: administrative experience, national visibility, high social standing, and maybe wealth.

Although by no means universally present or evenly distributed, such qualities were more evident in the moderate liberal camp. Its leaders had either served on judicial or advisory bodies under the Restoration governments, like Casati of Milan, or else, like Cavour, they were experienced in the management of substantial estates and businesses. Even though they did not become formally organized into a political movement until the late 1850s, the liberals already enjoyed national visibility before the revolution as the promoters of seven successful Congresses of Italian Scientists and as the advocates of an Italian Customs Union and of other initiatives for Italian economic development. But quite apart from these tangible achievements, in the early phase of the revolution they enjoyed a distinct social advantage over the democrats. In every region of Italy there were in the moderate liberal camp many names to which people still wedded to traditional social norms automatically bowed their heads. The most ardent democratic believers in political equality and social justice could not ignore a reality of Italian life.

To cite but one example, it was much easier for the liberal Duke of Serradifalco to command attention and respect in Sicilian society than it was for middle-class democrats like Crispi or Calvino.

For all these reasons, the democrats thought it tactically wise not to take independent revolutionary actions. The democratic consensus that emerged on this point in 1847 was strengthened by the liberals' shift from demands for administrative and legal reforms to demands for specific political changes. As Giorgio Candeloro and others have pointed out, the exasperatingly slow pace of papal reforms convinced leading liberals in Rome as well as in other states that the time had come for a direct confrontation with the existing governments. Once the Italian rulers had been pressured into accepting a constitutional framework, all other changes would follow. This shift in liberal tactics set in motion the revolutionary chain of events between January and March 1848 and transformed the Italian states into constitutional monarchies. The exceptions were revolutionary Lombardy, which did not have a representative assembly, and Venetia, which returned briefly to its tradition of republican government.

By accepting a subordinate role in the constitutional movement, however, the democrats did not intend to defer to liberal initiatives indefinitely. Rather, they expected that the creation of representative assemblies and the introduction of freedom of the press would allow them to challenge the social advantage of the liberal elite and to acquire comparable experience and visibility. Thus, at the outbreak of revolution the stage was already set for major disagreements between uneasy allies. In the late spring and summer of 1848, several issues and incidents began to point to the emergence of an ideological dividing line that was crossed repeatedly by both sides in the ensuing years yet was never erased.

Of the moderates' posture at the beginning of 1848 Mazzini wrote, critically yet not unfairly, that it was aimed not "at conquering a government for Italy but at conquering the governments of the Italian states."[24] Confident of their ability to modernize Italy, he pointed out, the moderates intended to replace the old oligarchies and transform outmoded institutions without altering basic social relationships and without endangering the continuity of monarchical governments. This moderate ambition and the democratic challenges to it surfaced everywhere during the revolution. But they first became evident in the Kingdom of Sardinia, where an intense political debate between moderate liberals and democrats followed the announcement on February 8, 1848, of Charles Albert's decision to grant a constitution. The debate focused on two issues: the treat-

ment of the religious minorities of Piedmont and the electoral law
that was to be the foundation of the new constitutional regime.

In contrast to the conservative oligarchy that had dominated the
Savoy court since 1815 and had steered Charles Albert away from
his youthful flirtations with romantic liberalism, the leading Piedmontese moderates were firmly committed to religious toleration for
the Waldensian and Jewish minorities. In the debates of 1846–47
over political reform, however, democratic intellectuals like Sineo
and Valerio and social theorists like Gentilini had argued that the
minorities were entitled to full civil equality as well, including access to military and bureaucratic positions and to the unrestricted
practice of all professions. These arguments had won them many
sympathizers among the Waldensian mountaineers of northwest
Piedmont as well as among the predominantly urban Jewish communities.[25]

In the debates of early 1848, the democrats again insisted on a
very broad interpretation of civil equality for these groups, whereas
some liberals favored the retention of religious restrictions for public
officeholders. The democrats' position on this issue was certainly
consistent with a commitment to equality and justice in a broader
sense, even if it also reflected quite practical concerns. Uneasy with
the first article of the constitution, which proclaimed Roman Catholicism to be the state religion, they were reluctant to challenge it
directly, knowing that they would lose. Thus, they tried instead to
water it down by pushing the concept of religious toleration as far as
it could be pushed by legislation. Moreover, they expected to benefit
from the lifting of all educational and employment barriers against
Protestants and Jews. Although mostly poor, these religious
minorities had literacy rates much above the average for Piedmont.
Among them were many young men ready and eager to qualify for
admission to the universities of Turin and Genoa and for professional or civil service careers. These young men were already attracted by the anti-Catholic theme of democratic propaganda, and
it seemed likely that if allowed to leave their native ghettos and
become integrated in the larger polity, they would become a main-
stay of the Piedmontese Left, as the artisans and sailors of Genoa
had been ever since the 1830s.

Because they sought primarily the support of educated but not
wealthy men, that is, of men like themselves, the Piedmontese
democrats insisted on low fiscal requirements for the right to vote.
They won at least a partial victory in this area, for the *Statuto* of
1848 (later to become the first Italian Constitution) had much lower
fiscal requirements than the Orleanist document after which it was

patterned. This was the democrats' reward, albeit grudgingly given, for the role they had played in the six or seven weeks preceding the announcement of the *Statuto*. The mass demonstrations they had organized in Turin, Genoa, Alessandria, and other cities had been undoubtedly effective in convincing the wavering Charles Albert not to resist "that kind of occult or at least illegal government which [had] taken hold of the active populace" in his major cities.[26] The importance of this democratic victory became apparent in the 1850s. If the Sardinian *Statuto* survived the years of reaction whereas other documents of 1848 did not, it was not only because Victor Emmanuel II renewed his father's pledge or because the liberals needed to legitimize their successful penetration of the state structures. It was also because the democrats of the late 1840s had developed, at least in the major cities, large networks among the middle and lower classes, whose interests they represented in Parliament and whom they could mobilize again in time of crisis.[27]

Thus, in the Kingdom of Sardinia the lines of battle between liberals and democrats were drawn even before the emergence of more dramatic issues, such as the military defeat of August 1848 and the repression of a popular uprising in Genoa the following spring. In neighboring Lombardy the uneasy alliance between the democratic networks and the liberal notables of the capital held longer, because of the need for a united front against the Habsburg government's increasingly repressive policies. But the hidden tensions surfaced as soon as the leaders of the glorious Five Days began to discuss how to defend and institutionalize the freedom they had unexpectedly won.[28]

The successful popular uprising of March 18-22 against the Habsburg army created a major dilemma for the liberal notables of Milan. Much as they had looked forward to the end of Austrian rule, they were not ready to fill the power vacuum left by the departure of the foreign overlords. Moreover, having learned during the insurrection not to underestimate the political militancy and the patriotic sentiments of the urban artisans and workers, they worried about the connections between this group and democratic intellectuals such as Cattaneo, Macchi, and Maestri. From the liberals' point of view, it was imperative to fill the power vacuum before further political initiatives were taken from below and before the leaders of the various democratic networks had a chance to exploit their newly acquired popularity.

Like their adversaries, the Milanese liberals heretofore had focused their attention on local or regional issues, primarily on various attempts to reform and to Italianize the Habsburg administration. But now they had to look beyond to the creation of a new political order. The relative strength of Milanese democracy and the absence of a legitimate and credible candidate to head the sort of government the liberals preferred — a constitutional monarchy — placed them in a vulnerable position. There was no guarantee that the advocates of democratic republicanism would continue to defer to the authority of a liberal municipal government no longer backed by a central administration and defended by a regular army. Under the circumstances, the Milanese liberals would have sought an ally even if they had not been worried about an Austrian counteroffensive.

Their appeal to Charles Albert of Savoy, however, had some unintended consequences. His military intervention in Lombardy, although entirely consistent with long-standing policies of his House, had to be justified on higher grounds than territorial ambition. Whether out of genuine conviction or out of a need to justify the intervention vis-à-vis his own Parliament and the population of Lombardy, Charles Albert waged war in the name of Italian independence. His statements in this regard certainly took some wind out of the sails of the Milanese democrats, particularly the followers of Mazzini. But they also established a new political climate favorable to interaction and exchange between the democratic networks of Lombardy and those of Piedmont and other regions. There were two obvious reasons why democrats from every corner of Italy flocked to Milan and then to Venice in the late spring of 1848. First, they had a chance to fight for Italian independence. Second (and this set them apart from volunteers with different political views), they had a chance to observe and perhaps to influence the political future of the only part of Italy where a complete break with the Old Regime had occurred and where democratic republicanism did not seem just a farfetched dream. Their high expectations were not realized; nonetheless, the experiences of these volunteers marked a significant turning point in the history of Risorgimento democracy. Bixio, Montanelli, Pisacane, and many others who had been active in local or regional networks found themselves sharing the dangers of war and the excitement of political struggles. Without the bond of this revolutionary experience, which laid the foundation of a national network, they could never have attempted the subsequent experiments in republican and democratic government.

6

Experiments in Democratic Leadership, 1848–1849

For the Risorgimento democrats, the period from the beginning of the Lombard campaign against Austria in April 1848 to the fall of the Venetian Republic in August 1849 was one of dramatic and unexpected ascendancy followed by traumatic defeat. It left an indelible mark upon their political and personal lives.

The experiences of those months shaped the development of the democratic movement in at least three ways. First, the Lombard campaign, the proclamation of the Roman Republic, and the defense of Venice brought together prominent members of local and regional networks, shaping among them a deeper political consciousness of common problems and aspirations. Second, those events thrust several leaders of the movement into unprecedented prominence and gave them the opportunity to play political roles quite different from the old familiar ones of propagandists and conspirators. And third, those events created in Italy, for the first time since the 1790s, conditions favorable to radical experiments in government and in social and cultural reform.

The older men, survivors of the abortive revolutions of earlier decades, had dreamed of such opportunities; to a limited extent, they were prepared to take advantage of them. But in the early months of 1848 they did not actively seek new leadership roles. Indeed, the collapse of the neo-Guelf movement in the spring of 1848 and the crisis of moderate liberalism that followed came too soon from their point of view. As for the younger men, born in the 1820s, they were not conditioned by memories of past failures; but neither did they have any concrete experience of revolution. Eager to seek fame and glory on the barricades, they were ill-prepared for the responsibility of power and for the years of psychological and physical suffering that were to follow a few months of freedom.

The uneasy alliance between moderate liberals and democrats was shattered by the papal allocution of April 29, 1848, concerning the war in northern Italy. As volunteers from every part of Italy, including the Papal States, flocked to the Po Valley, Pius IX could no longer delay drawing a sharp line between his aspirations as an Italian and his responsibilities as head of the Roman Catholic Church.[1]

The pope's inevitable and indeed overdue refusal to endorse a patriotic war against Austria had no impact on those democrats who had always been hostile to the neo-Guelf idea. Ferrari, for instance, having refused to sing the pope's praises in 1847, saw no reason to blame him a year later because others had mistaken Gioberti's medieval reveries for the road to progress.[2] But De Boni, Montanelli, Levi, and others who had helped create the myth of the patriot pope were quite shaken. Not a few democrats who had previously refrained from criticizing the pope and the teachings of the Church, even while attacking the temporal power, hereafter adopted intransigently anti-Catholic positions. Among them was Casimiro De Lieto, who voiced his indignation and his concern for the future in a letter to his wife:

> I cannot predict the future course of events here in Rome. With an encyclical issued the other day Pius IX refused to declare war on Austria just as Roman troops, having crossed the Po, were beginning to fight in Lombardy and Venetia for the sublime cause of Italian liberty and independence . . . This impolitic pronouncement on the part of a pope who had raised such beautiful hopes for the future of Italy has exasperated everyone, but particularly those families who have given their sons for the defense of the fatherland.[3]

The papal allocution of April 29 probably marked a step in the evolution of democratic ideology toward a clear commitment to the secularization of Italian politics. It was certainly a turning point in the development of democratic political strategies. Until then the democrats had supported — or at least had not interfered with — the efforts of the moderate liberal leadership to bring about meaningful constitutional reforms in the Italian states. In Lombardy and Venetia they had gone along, albeit reluctantly, with the moderates' argument that issues of political reform would best be dealt with after a definitive military victory against Austria. But the pope's refusal to endorse an Italian national crusade against a Catholic power introduced a significant new element into the political picture. As all Italian revolutionaries feared, the pope's pronouncement made it easy for the other Italian rulers to deny their support to the king of Sardinia. Even more important from the democrats' point of view, it legitimized their efforts to prevent or to curb the departure from their territories of more volunteers for the war against Austria. In fact, although motivated by ecclesiastical concerns, the pope's move had immediate political consequences: in a few days it accomplished what all of Gioberti's critics had not been able to accomplish in a decade. But the collapse of neo-Guelfism posed new challenges for both moderate liberals and democrats.

In Lombardy the political consequences of Pius IX's new posture intensified the latent struggle between the two groups. The participation of volunteers from all regions of Italy in the war against Austria was not, perhaps, of great military significance, and it was viewed with suspicion by the professionals in Charles Albert's army. To the end, they were unwilling to share military secrets and weapons even with guerrilla leaders like Pisacane, who had graduated from a prestigious military academy. Yet the presence of the volunteers distinguished this campaign from all the previous ones fought in northern Italy by members of the House of Savoy. Democratic members and supporters of the Milanese and of other provisional governments had made this point very clearly upon Charles Albert's intervention. And Mazzini himself, emphasizing the national dimension of the struggle against the Austrian armies, had urged his followers to cooperate with the moderates until victory was achieved.[4] But in May and June of 1848 the democrats' willingness to cooperate diminished as the flow of volunteers, particularly from Tuscany and the Papal States, gradually came to a halt, and the patriotic *guerra di popolo* proclaimed during the Five Days of Milan threatened to turn into just another dynastic war.

A second event that broke the patriotic truce, leaving the moderate liberals adrift and driving the democrats to more extreme political positions, was the May 15 affair in Naples. Ferdinand II of Bourbon, the first Italian ruler to be pressured into granting a constitution, had been uncomfortable with his new role from the very beginning. His misgivings were deepened by the fall of the July Monarchy and by the Sicilian Parliament's decision on April 13, 1848, to proclaim the end of Bourbon rule on the island. Thus, he was particularly pleased and heartened by Pius IX's apparent determination to put an end to liberal reforms in the Papal States and to flirtations with Italian nationalism.[5] But Ferdinand's desire to stem a revolutionary tide that had already engulfed half his kingdom conflicted with the aims of the Neapolitan Parliament elected in the latter part of April 1848. Progressive liberals and democrats held a majority in that assembly, and they were determined not to take the loyalty oath unless it contained specific references to the need to liberalize the existing constitution. This crisis took place against the background of severe social unrest both in the capital and in the nearby Cilento area. Fear that this unrest might get out of control prompted the king on May 15 to order the deployment of more troops in and around Naples. This in turn led to the building of barricades and to several days of bloody street fighting.

La Cecilia, Petruccelli, Ricciardi, the young Morelli, and other democrats distinguished themselves in those days in the defense of constitutional liberties; and they learned some new political lessons. First, the king was never again to be trusted. Second, it was unwise to put all of one's political eggs in the basket of parliamentary politics and constitutional reform. Thus, after May 15 the leading southern democrats shifted their attention away from the political intrigues of the capital, where they were in any event unwelcome, to the provincial towns. Albini and Petruccelli in the Basilicata, Giuseppe Libertini in Lecce, and Nicola Mignogna in the Taranto area, for example, already enjoyed some following, thanks to their professional reputation or to their families' status in their native communities. In the latter part of 1848 they tried to capitalize on those assets by organizing democratic clubs with a strong republican bias and with various programs of social reform. But a few democratic activists who lacked a political base in the provinces, and who had reason to fear arrest if they remained in Naples, chose to join revolutionary groups in other states. The ever restless La Cecilia, for instance, a veteran of the May 15 street fighting, returned to Tuscany, where he had previously lived as an exile, and joined the left-wing clubs of Livorno.[6]

By the late spring of 1848, the diminished flow of volunteers to northern Italy and the apparent fragmentation of the democratic networks in the South threatened to undermine the consolidation of a national democratic movement. But the defeat of Charles Albert's army in August once again changed the political situation and the prospects of the democrats. First, Lombard democrats such as Maestri played a major role in a desperate attempt to organize the defense of Milan. They stayed on and reassured their fellow citizens, if only for a few days, while the liberal provisional government fled to Turin. Their courage could not save the city, but it assured them visibility and lasting personal prestige. Second, the Austrian reconquest of Lombardy and much of Venetia forced many democrats who had fought there to seek refuge in other states. The Grand Duchy of Tuscany was their first choice: It offered sympathetic friends (the young men who had fought with Montanelli at Curtatone and Montanara) and a fluid political climate still amenable to republican and democratic ideas.

Tuscan Democracy: Problems and Possibilities

In Tuscany as in Piedmont the initial success of the revolutionary movement was attributable to liberal notables who dominated the new constitutional government for several months. But they could not have succeeded without the democratic networks, particularly in Florence, Pisa, and Livorno. Democratic intellectuals and artisans organized street demonstrations and launched a press campaign in favor of reform; later on they pressured the reluctant Ridolfi government into sending troops to Lombardy. Their contribution was rewarded by a very liberal press law and by an electoral law that enfranchised most literate artisans, shopkeepers, and intellectuals.[7]

After the elections, the Tuscan democrats focused their efforts on two issues: the war in northern Italy and the creation of Circoli popolari ("People's Clubs") for the political and social education of the lower classes. Until the end of July 1848, the war issue, about which the Tuscans felt strongly, masked the dissension that existed among the democrats on a whole range of economic and social questions. Above all, it masked real differences among them on the purpose of the Circoli popolari and, more generally, on the relationship between the democratic leadership and the masses. Inevitably, these differences came out into the open in August 1848.

Large demonstrations in Florence and Livorno followed the announcement of Charles Albert's defeat. Blaming all of the Italian governments, their own included, for the disastrous outcome of the war against Austria, Montanelli and other democratic intellectuals called for an Italian constituent assembly that might generate patriotic enthusiasm and take on the responsibility for a new military effort. Montanelli's proposal was immediately endorsed by several exiles from other states; and it generated enough interest among the public to bring down two moderate governments in less than three months. Yet not all the Tuscan democratic leaders supported the proposal. Some simply thought it unrealistic to resume the war before far-reaching political changes had occurred in Tuscany itself and in Rome, the logical place for an Italian Assembly to meet. Cironi, for instance, having heard that Mazzini too had called for the renewal of the war, observed, "[Our] cause is just, and it will be vindicated. But the kings have betrayed it and the people . . . are just beginning to grasp its greatness."[8] But other democrats had an even more fundamental objection to the proposed constituent assembly. Although they supported it in principle, they wanted that assembly to act on questions of political and social reform within the various member states before it dealt with the issues of Italian independence and unity. In the meantime, they intended to devote all their energies to the creation of more Circoli popolari and to the establishment of stronger links with the masses, especially in rural areas. Such was the state of affairs in Tuscany at the end of October 1848 when Leopold II asked Montanelli to form a new government.

Although short-lived (October 27, 1848 to February 8, 1849), this government marked an important phase in the development of Risorgimento democracy. An analysis of its composition and policies, of its supporters and detractors, and of its strengths and weaknesses offers many clues to the nature of the democratic movement in Tuscany and many opportunities for comparisons with similar governments that followed.

In regard to its social composition, the most interesting feature of this government — the first of its kind in the history of modern Italy — was its antiaristocratic character. In contrast to all advisory councils of preconstitutional days and to the Ridolfi and Capponi ministries of 1847–48, the Montanelli government was dominated by men from the middle classes who had proclaimed often and loudly the superiority of intellectual merit over aristocratic birth and of hard work over inherited privilege. The one exception was the Neapolitan exile Mariano D'Ayala, who had fallen upon hard times. He was not, in any event, identified with the traditional Florentine oligarchy from which the grand duke had previously chosen his advisors and ministers.

In contrast to the old elite, the authority of these democratic ministers did not rest upon tradition or even property ownership per se, but upon special qualifications for political office and upon some personal following which they had built up over the years and which enabled them to mobilize large crowds. Premier and Foreign Minister Montanelli counted on his reputation as a member of the Tuscan intellectual and academic elite. But perhaps equally important to his rise to political power were his advocacy of a reformed Catholicism cleansed of the temporal power and his inspiring performance as commander of the Tuscan students' brigade in northern Italy. His colleague and chief rival, the fiery Minister of the Interior Guerrazzi, boasted among his qualifications for office his relatively humble family background, his record of arrests for having defied reactionary press laws, and his considerable popularity among the artisans, shopkeepers, and sailors of his native Livorno. Finally, two other important members of this government, Giuseppe Mazzoni of Prato and Pietro Augusto Adami of Livorno, represented those successful industrial and commercial families who supported the democratic movement at least in part as a protest against the predominantly agrarian outlook of the Florentine patriciate.[9]

Montanelli and his colleagues could rightly claim that this first democratic government marked the beginning of a new era in Tuscan and Italian politics. Yet they could not ignore that merit alone did not account for their political success. The failure of the moderate governments and the grand duke's decision to try a ministry of the Left had resulted in no small measure from the political work of Tuscan militants such as Montazio, Dolfi, and the brothers Sgarallino and of ambitious, experienced outsiders like La Cecilia. The ability of those men to organize mass demonstrations helped the more moderate elements in the democratic movement to attain power, and it remained perhaps their most important bargaining chip. Guerrazzi, in particular, used it openly and with a good deal of demagogic cynicism. Preparing for a showdown with the moderate liberals in late October 1848, for instance, he wrote to La Cecilia, "I need a massive demonstration by tomorrow; the *Corriere [livornese]* must incite it; the intrigues and cabals of the moderates are beyond belief; we must squelch them with fear."[10]

Once the democratic ministry had become well established, however, its leaders (Guerrazzi included) made it clear to their more radical colleagues that they no longer welcomed this kind of outside help. La Cecilia and other extremists were not allowed to share power; they had to be content to air their views on economic and social issues through the pages of lively but ephemeral publications such as *Il proletario*. Thus, for all practical purposes, by the end of the year the Tuscan revolution came to be directed and controlled by moderate elements of the democratic networks, well-known men with strong ties to the professional and commercial middle classes. But other protagonists of the underground opposition of the 1840s — radical intellectuals of modest means and uncertain social status, as well as lower-class leaders of neighborhood groups and trade associations — were gradually denied the opportunity to participate and even repressed. The journalist Montazio spoke out for these people when he warned the government "to recognize that its very existence [depended] upon the will of the sovereign people, to remember . . . its onerous obligations and its inescapable responsibilities to the sovereign people."[11]

Of the democratic leaders who came to power in 1848–49, only the Tuscans were able to govern for a significant period of time without the participation and the support of extremist elements clamoring for republican constitutions and social justice. And they did so even though it was precisely those elements that had helped them to attain power. Indeed, from about December 1848 until the spring of 1849, Montanelli and his colleagues expended more energy in fending off threats from the Left in their own movement than they did in confrontations with their old political adversaries.

It is true, of course, that differences and cleavages among democratic leaders appeared everywhere, perhaps inevitably, during the revolution. But in other regions such differences were caused, or at least exacerbated, by external events such as Charles Albert's defeat in Lombardy or the French intervention against the Roman Republic. In Tuscany, however, external pressures were not an important factor; and precisely for that reason the Tuscan case is the most useful for an analysis of the movement's internal dynamics during the revolution.

In some ways, the moderate character of the Montanelli government proved beneficial to the development of the Tuscan democratic movement. The democratic ministers were known to have republican sympathies, yet they proved willing to serve the grand duke as long as he respected the constitution. Despite their anticlerical views, they refrained from attacks against the clergy and ecclesiastical property. More important still, they resisted pressures from fellow democrats for the immediate introduction of radical social legislation in response to strikes by peasants and dockworkers. This display of democratic moderation, which continued even after the departure of the grand duke in February 1849, assuaged the worst fears of the clergy and of the propertied classes. By so doing, it gave the democratic ministers a degree of political legitimacy that they had not enjoyed before 1848 and that survived the failure of the revolution. Moreover, by their moderate posture Montanelli and his colleagues secured the support of large segments of public opinion for an Italian constituent assembly. For they regarded their own success in Tuscan politics as merely a prelude to a democratic revolution on a national scale. Thus, Montanelli wrote, "[My political faith] is National, because I regard the various Italian states as parts of a whole, like the limbs of one body. The good of one is worth little if it does not coincide with the common good of the Nation . . . The Italian Revolution is motivated above all by the need for National identity."[12]

But a price had to be paid for legitimacy within the Tuscan political system and for support of the national goals of the revolution. That price was a breakdown of the democratic networks such as they had developed before 1848. In the place of loosely organized groups that cut across socioeconomic lines and municipal rivalries there emerged by 1849 two fairly distinct and antagonistic factions: the members and supporters of the Montanelli government, on the one hand, and a coalition of radical intellectuals and *capipopolo*, that is, of neighborhood and craft leaders, on the other. The debate between the two factions, carried out in the press and in the Circoli popolari, illustrates many of the problems that nineteenth-century Italian democrats had to face from 1849 on.

Before the revolution the Tuscan democrats had agreed on one important goal, the need to break the aristocratic oligarchy's near monopoly of political power. In this they succeeded more easily than their counterparts in other regions. The next step was to be, in Montanelli's words, the establishment of political institutions suitable to "the era of the people . . . of collective welfare." But how these new institutions were to be defined, how soon they could be introduced, and above all, the meaning of "collective welfare" remained to be seen.

Although only a few had personal ties with Mazzini, the best-known leaders of Tuscan democracy defined their political goals in terms not very different from his. Criticizing the prerevolutionary political institutions because they favored "inherited privilege," they argued that it was possible and desirable to replace those institutions with a representative system responsive to and supported by all social classes. A democratic political system was one in which men (and perhaps also women) of all social classes would have a chance to rise from the ranks of the plebs to the status of responsible citizens. What distinguished *il popolo*, the responsible citizens entitled to positions of leadership, from the plebs? Guerrazzi put it this way to a skeptical aristocratic friend: "If a blacksmith, say, can write verses or prose, is a fine son, husband, and father, has genuine love for his country, abhors any kind of tryanny, and shuns idiotic superstitions, he is no longer plebs, but *popolo*."[13] Citizens such as these, he argued, would speak for their social class, community, or occupational group within elected assemblies. But they would also have the wisdom, as the plebs did not, to realize that the common welfare required compromises between their own particular goals and the interests of others. Tuscan society had already produced many such responsible citizens from diverse backgrounds, yet many more were needed before it could truly be called a democratic society. Civic consciousness, patriotism, love of liberty, and enlightenment were the prerequisites for the functioning of a democratic polity, and the plebs lacked all of those qualities. It was the responsibility of the democratic leaders, especially now that they were in power, to help the plebs become the sovereign people. But for this transformation of consciousness to occur it was necessary to create appropriate educational institutions. Until a system of free public elementary schools could be introduced — something not likely to happen during the revolution — the Circoli popolari would have to perform that function.

The statute of the Florentine Circolo founded by Guerrazzi and Pigli, to cite but one example, reflected these concerns of the democratic ministers and of their supporters. After stating that its members were drawn from all social classes and were devoted to the cause of Italian independence and liberty, the Circolo's founders thus spelled out their objectives: "(1) to instruct the people of their rights and duties; (2) to promote discussion of national and political questions; (3) to influence public opinion by whatever means are deemed appropriate; [and] (4) to keep in touch with other democratic Circoli in Italy and abroad."[14] This Florentine document was duplicated with only minor variations in other Tuscan cities. Its emphasis on "instructing" the people revealed the intellectual origins and the leadership aspirations of its authors. And its statement about the need to keep in touch with similar groups outside of Tuscany reflected their increasingly frequent contacts with fellow democrats from other regions and countries. The revolution was obviously breaking down the relative isolation in which regional and local networks had previously operated. Indeed, outsiders like De Boni and Cernuschi were invited to address the Florentine Circolo. But perhaps the most significant point of this democratic program was its distinction between "national" and "political" questions. In the reality of 1848 and in the outlook of the Tuscan democrats the two sets of questions were, of course, closely related; but they were also distinct, and their relationship was the subject of much controversy in the democratic press as well as in the Circoli.

Despite occasional protestations to the contrary, the democratic ministers and their supporters placed the solution of the national questions at the top of their political agenda. By national questions they generally meant the expulsion of the Austrian armies from Italy, the convocation of a national assembly, and the termination of the temporal power. Although they had never actually played a political role outside the boundaries of their native region, they were now envisioning that possibility, and they needed political supporters from all social classes who understood the national dimension of the revolution.[15]

Dissident democrats, however, felt that it was more important and more urgent to educate the masses to an understanding of domestic political questions. Those questions, they argued, would not be solved by the attainment of national independence, much less by the political unification advocated by Mazzini. Before the Tuscan masses could participate fully and responsibly in a larger revolutionary movement they would have to feel that they had a real voice in their own revolution. They could not have a sense of participation and commitment as long as their leaders postponed to an undetermined and uncertain future any plans, for instance, for reform of the agrarian contracts.[16]

That this debate within the democratic leadership revolved around concrete issues and not merely around ideological abstractions was demonstrated, for instance, by the peasant riots during Lent in 1849. Thousands of peasants converged on the Tuscan capital demanding refoms in the patterns of land tenure for sharecropping families and relief for salaried farmhands. They clamored for the "republican" provisional government which had taken power after the departure of Leopold II to take action. But the action they got was not the action they had asked for. Frightened by the riots, the democratic ministry sent out the National Guard, which consisted of middle-class men and urban astisans not likely to fraternize with the demonstrators. The Mazzinian Andrea Giannelli, then a very young guardsman, was a willing participant in this police action, for he believed the government's assertion that reactionary enemies of the revolution stood behind the riots. Later on, he came to realize that he had unconsciously acted out the prejudices of a literate city dweller against illiterate and unsophisticated people from the countryside. Then he confessed, "Our treatment of the peasants we took into custody was anything but urbane . . . we did not stop to think that they were only very poor people brainwashed by country priests working hand in hand with the leaders of reaction in Florence."[17] Even while he made this contrite statement, however, Giannelli remained firm in his conviction that the peasant demonstrators had been the dupes of counterrevolutionary elements. Anyone who threatened the stability of the democratic ministry amidst the perils and uncertainties of 1849, he thought, could only be looking backward. But in this he was probably wrong. His social background, his Mazzinian nationalism, and his admiration for men like Guerrazzi blinded him and other urban democrats to the complexity of the revolution. He was, in fact, applying to the social unrest of 1849 the historical lessons of the 1790s, when Tuscan peasants led by reactionary clergymen had made life difficult for liberal and Jacobin political figures.

Given the family background of many democrats, it is not surprising that memories of those difficult days were still alive in the 1840s. Yet in 1849 those memories stood in the way of what the Tuscan democrats had set out to do. Even democratic leaders like Vannucci, who had grown up in poor peasant communities and were sympathetic to the economic plight of the peasantry, could not overcome their distrust of a protest movement that threatened to turn the propertied classes against the national goals of the revolution. Although they had been until recently sincere advocates of social reform, they now remained silent or actually condemned the peasant movement. Their conviction that a counterrevolutionary cabal stood behind the protests was based less on hard evidence than on their own paternalistic view of the lower classes in general and of the peasantry in particular. Knowing that they did not control the peasant movement themselves, they took it for granted that someone else did. Thus, mutual distrust and confrontations occurred where dialogue and cooperation might have been expected.

Urban social protest was a different matter. The leading figures of Tuscan democracy had well-established links with artisans, shopkeepers, and sailors. In fact, seven of the seventeen Tuscans under discussion came from such backgrounds themselves. And democrats of higher social standing, such as Cattani-Cavalcanti, Mazzoni, and Pigli, sought the support of such groups against the conservatives and the moderate liberals in their respective cities. Regardless of their social background, before the revolution the democrats had found it much easier to establish a rapport with the urban lower classes than with the peasantry. The higher rate of literacy in urban centers accounted in part for this difference, for democratic intellectuals had relied heavily on broadsides and newspapers, legal or illegal, to spread their ideas. But other factors had been important too, such as the lack of those negative historical precedents that conditioned the democrats' attitude toward the peasantry, and the geographical concentration of potential urban recruits in particular neighborhoods of a handful of towns. At the beginning of the revolution, the Tuscan democrats had counted on and received the support of the urban *capipopolo*, especially in Florence and Livorno. The advent of the democratic ministry in the fall of 1848 and the subsequent drift of Tuscan politics in a republican direction should have strengthened this alliance. Instead, those events had the opposite effect; and by the spring of 1849 a serious cleavage had developed between the new political leaders and their erstwhile supporters.

Precisely because their own *capipopolo* now had direct access to the government, dockworkers in Livorno, textile workers in Prato, and others thought that the time was right to press their economic demands. To the dismay of the democratic ministers, an outbreak of strikes disrupted production at a time when the Tuscan economy had not yet recovered from the general economic crisis of 1846–47. Moreover, the strikes were often accompanied by threats of violence against all property owners. *Capipopolo* such as Dolfi and Andrea Sgarallino disapproved of these threats, and they appealed unsuccessfully for unity behind the beleaguered democratic government. It would have been difficult under any circumstances to direct and to control a protest movement that lacked a central organization and a specific focus. In this case it was impossible because the urban protesters, unlike the peasants, were asking for political equality and for social justice in the language characteristic of the democratic press. Thus, the political leaders could condemn the protesters' occasional excesses, but they could neither reject their demands nor claim that they had been duped by reactionaries. Montazio was well aware of this when he addressed the Tuscan Provisional Government: "Do not denigrate our people when they do not respond to your appeals. Is this country in their hands? No . . . until now you have given them nothing but promises."[18]

By March 1849 the democrats in the provisional governments were in serious difficulties. They were being attacked by the Right for lacking constitutional legitimacy in the absence of a monarch, by the Left for their reluctance to proclaim a republic. And they were losing credibility among the lower classes who had looked to them for major changes in their conditions. Frightened by social unrest yet unable to control it, the democrats had to choose between two equally risky options: to establish a republic of a Jacobin or socialist type, as the dissidents urged, or to reassert the primacy of national questions over political ones, a solution preferred by the moderate liberals. The men of the provisional government did not miss the significance of this turning point for the future of the democratic movement. Unable to leave Prato, Mazzoni, for instance, pleaded with his childhood friend Diego Martelli to attend political meetings in Florence because the future of the country was at stake and "[the democratic leaders] would be judged by the decisions [they] took."[19]

Reluctantly, Mazzoni and his colleagues chose to focus on national questions even if it meant ignoring or repressing social protests. In the context of 1849, this was a difficult but seemingly expedient choice. Like their counterparts in other regions, the Tuscan democrats expected that the national questions would soon be resolved by the patriots from all regions already assembled in Rome. There would be time later, they thought, to turn to political questions. Unfortunately for them, this proved to be a false assumption. By April 1849, Austrian troops entered Tuscany with the half-hearted approval of Leopold II. Except in Livorno, where Pigli, the Sgarallino brothers, and others led a fierce popular resistance to the Austrians, the democrats were not in the position to mobilize the masses in defense of the revolution. Victims of circumstances but also of their own political choices, they were forced to abandon this first experiment in democratic government.

The Roman Republic

Although Tuscany provided the opportunity for the first experiment in democratic government, it was in the Papal States that the Risorgimento democrats had a chance to upstage their moderate liberal colleagues in a dramatic break both with the vestiges of the old order and with the fledgling constitutional regime of Pius IX.

From the beginning of the revolution the democratic leaders in the Papal States played a more important role than did their colleagues in Tuscany. This was particularly true of such seasoned revolutionaries as Mattioli, Saffi, Rusconi, and Grazia in the Legations. And even in Rome itself and in the political backwaters of Umbria and the Marches, men like Montecchi, Pianciani, Eugenio Brizi, and Giuseppe Fratellini participated actively in demonstrations and in the founding of Circoli popolari. Between the election of Pius IX and his allocution of April 29, 1848, however, their activities did not clash with those of the moderate liberals, but rather complemented them. There certainly were moments of tension between the two groups, particularly when prominent moderates accused *capipopolo* like Angelo Masina of Bologna and Montecchi and Salvatore Piccioni of Rome of using the newly granted freedom of the press to spread dangerous social theories. But on the whole, the first months of the revolution were a period of cooperation on the one issue that both groups regarded as paramount, the declericalization of political and cultural institutions. Both groups were frustrated by the slow pace of progress, yet reluctant to challenge the pope's authority.[20]

The papal allocution of April 29 had ominous implications for the Giobertian program and, more generally, for the reform movement in the Papal States. One of its unintended consequences was the first serious rift between the supporters of a constitutional monarchy and the advocates of a democratic republic. At issue was not the pope's pronouncement, of which both groups disapproved, but how best to respond to it and to the new political situation emerging from it.

Although they continued secretly to subsidize the papal troops still fighting in northern Italy, Mamiani, Minghetti, and other prominent liberals turned their attention to domestic questions. Realizing that they could not pressure the pope into being the standard-bearer of Italian independence, they were determined at least to see him behave as a true constitutional monarch. This meant respecting the constitution that he had granted, but also opening up more positions of responsibility to laymen. As usual, there was noticeably less consensus among the democrats. Those from the Legations, where a strong republican tradition was thriving, argued that the time had come for a coup against the papal government and for the proclamation of a republic. This was no idle talk. Masina, for instance, was certainly involved in a major outbreak of riots in Bologna; and in the smaller towns of the Romagna members of the Mazzinian networks were arming themselves. But cooler heads prevailed in Rome, despite unrest in the popular sections. Democrats close to government circles, like the aristocratic Pianciani, feared that a coup by extremists might endanger painfully won liberties and precipitate a reaction.[21]

Pianciani's fears were well founded. All through the summer of 1848 the liberals labored steadily and persistently to transform the institutions of the Papal States. Their task had been difficult from the start, and it became more so after the May 15 affair in Naples and the defeat of Charles Albert in August. More than fellow liberals elsewhere, Mamiani and his colleagues needed a favorable political climate outside their own state to achieve their goals. Because of the pope's impressionable character and the reactionary views of the men in his inner circle, particularly the cardinal secretary of state, Giacomo Antonelli, it was especially important that the liberals in the Papal States be able to point to successful political reforms elsewhere, in order to claim that they were part of an irresistible national movement. Inevitably, therefore, the failure of political reform in the Kingdom of Naples and the return of the Austrians to Milan hindered their cause. And major outbreaks of social unrest in the Legations compounded their difficulties.

Mamiani, whose impeccable record of liberalism and of political exile commanded respect in the democratic camp, failed twice to obtain the pope's approval for truly representative institutions. In the fall of 1848, he was replaced by Pellegrino Rossi, the former ambassador to France and the last hope of the liberals. Rossi had completed his political apprenticeship in the France of Louis Philippe, and he was a confirmed believer in the politics of the *juste milieu*. Although he was said to have been a Carbonaro, he could expect little support from democratic quarters, and he knew it. Indeed, when he took office rumors began to fly in Rome that his former brethren intended to carry out a vendetta against him. There was some truth to those rumors; he was assassinated on November 15, apparently at the behest of Luigi Brunetti, son of the prominent Roman *capopopolo* Angelo Brunetti, known as Ciceruacchio.[22]

Rossi's tragic death marked the end of the pope's short-lived and reluctant experiment with liberal government. Worried by increasing unrest in the capital, Pius IX was determined to reverse the course on which he had embarked shortly after his election. Not surprisingly, he sought refuge on the territory of the one Italian ruler who had most successfully fought the revolutionary tide. Ferdinand II welcomed the pope to Gaeta and promised to help with the restoration of order in the Papal States.

For the liberals in Rome, the pope's flight was a mixed blessing at best. On the positive side, it became possible for them at last to proclaim a Roman constituent assembly, while resuming previously inconclusive negotiations with the governments of Tuscany and Venice for an Italian constituent assembly. On the negative side, Pius IX's decision undermined the premises on which their political strategy was built. Moreover, popular pressure forced them to share political power and bureaucratic appointments with democratic leaders. By contrast, most democrats were elated with this turn of events. Indeed, they began to indulge in wishful thinking and to overestimate the importance of the pope's departure. Mazzini more than anyone welcomed the news with a characteristic outburst of optimism. He wrote to a follower in the Papal States,

"Pius IX has fled; his flight is tantamount to an abdication; as an elective prince, he leaves behind no dynasty to carry on. Hence you are now a de facto republic, for there is among you no source of authority except the people."[23] Mazzini's enthusiasm was understandable, if excessive. For nearly twenty years he and other democrats had preached and conspired to bring about the downfall of the temporal power. They were now confident that Pius IX would never be able to reclaim that power. Moreover, the pope had fled after three failed experiments in constitutional monarchy. The artisans and unemployed laborers who had kept Bologna teetering on the brink of class warfare for several months had made clear all along what they thought of the liberal ministries. And now even the Roman populace, traditionally loyal to the popes, was expressing its discontent and demanding a government more representative of all social classes and certainly more responsive to its economic grievances.

Among the most vocal demonstrators were hundreds of commercial artists and apprentices who had previously worked for the papal government itself and for the powerful families of the Roman court. Early in 1849 these men and their families were ready to cast their lot with a democratic government, and their support helped the Roman democrats to overcome the remaining opposition to a republic. But they were a most volatile element that under different circumstances could be manipulated by conservatives. Equally unpredictable, and more alien to the experience of the democratic leaders, were the peasants of the Campagna romana, who began to appear in the capital toward the end of 1848.[24]

In late November 1848 the moderate liberals were far from conceding Mazzini's point that the Papal States had become a de facto republic. Dismayed by that prospect, in fact, they made several attempts in conjunction with the ambassadors of conservative powers to persuade Pius IX to leave Gaeta. Even after the proclamation of a Roman constituent assembly the moderates were reluctant to take bold initiatives, preferring a wait-and-see policy in the absence of a legitimate ruler. A report of December 12 by the Venetian envoy G. B. Castellani summed up perceptively their precarious position and their anguish over a turn of events that undermined the legitimacy of the constitutional movement: "The words 'Provisional and Supreme State Junta' [adopted upon the pope's departure] have now been replaced by the formula 'Provisional Pontifical Government.' Less contradictory, but no less misguided. Here a sovereign [body] that recognizes the present institutions; in Gaeta, another sovereign who contests and protests those same institutions."[25] The contradiction underscored in Castellani's report became ever more apparent in the following weeks, as the members of the moderate provisional government began to reckon on the one hand with the *capipopolo* of the kingdom's major cities and, on the other, with democratic leaders from every part of Italy. By the end of the year their attempts to negotiate the return of Pius IX were met with his uncompromising hostility and, in the end, with an excommunication decree. Thus, the moderates were left with little choice but to find the requisite political legitimacy through some kind of compromise with their opponents.

The *capipopolo* of Rome, Bologna, and Ancona had strong ties with democratic intellectuals, particularly with members of Young Italy. Masina in Bologna and Grazia and Pacifico Pacifici in the Rimini-Ancona area, for instance, supported the idea of a united Italy with republican and democratic institutions. But for them these were rather distant if worthy goals; of more immediate concern were the economic and social grievances of the artisans and shopkeepers and the alarming growth of unemployment among the urban poor.

The provisional government responded in various ways to these concerns of the *capipopolo*, whose moral arguments were usually accompanied by warnings of popular uprisings and violence. The influence of the *capipopolo* was evident in the social legislation introduced by the provisional government. It was both more radical in spirit and more far-reaching in scope than any other proposed by the liberals during the Risorgimento. Three measures were particularly important in securing the support of the urban lower classes for the provisional government and for the republican one that followed. The first measure was a general program of public works, including much-needed railroad construction, for the unemployed. The second, especially popular in Rome and in the smaller towns of Umbria, was a series of competitive projects for the restoration and decoration of churches and other public buildings. It was designed to help unemployed artists and craftsmen. And finally, the provisional government virtually outlawed imprisonment and arrest for debts. This last measure was greeted with general enthusiasm; but it was especially popular among thousands of small merchants, street vendors, and innkeepers who had most frequently endured the indignities of that archaic law.

The social policy of the provisional government was clearly skewed in favor of the urban lower classes. Their interests were represented by articulate leaders, such as the shrewd, colorful Ciceruacchio, who commanded respect in their communities and who were not at all intimidated by the superior social standing and education of the men in power. The peasants had no comparable leadership, and because they were not as great a potential threat to public order, the provisional government showed less concern for their grievances. By lowering the price of salt and abolishing the grist tax, however, it did act in one area where the urban populace's desire for cheap bread coincided with the peasants' desire for tax relief. Yet this decision created problems for many poor local governments that had depended on that source of revenue and could find no short-term substitutes for it.

The eloquence of a few *capipopolo* and the dreaded prospect of urban riots were significant but not sufficient reasons why the provisional government adopted such progressive social legislation. At least as important in shaping their policy was the presence in Rome of many well-known democrats from other states. By the end of 1848, these outsiders wielded a political influence out of proportion to their small number. They controlled the democratic press and presided over most of the Circoli popolari in Rome and other cities. Moreover, they had direct access to the provisional government through two prominent native sons, the Roman physician Pietro Sterbini and Giuseppe Galletti, a lawyer from the Romagna. As ministers, respectively, of public works and of the interior, Sterbini and Galletti were responsible for areas of particular concern to their democratic friends. The Circolo popolare of Rome, of which Sterbini was president, was the main contact point between the policymakers and those trying to influence them in a democratic direction.

The outsiders came from every region of Italy. Divided over matters of political strategy and priorities, they were nevertheless conscious of common goals. The revolution had brought them together in military and political battles, and regional and other differences had paled before those experiences. And now, together, they faced the most important challenge: to found a modern, democratic state in the heart of an ancient theocracy. To this challenge they brought both their experiences of the past year and their hopes for the future.

From Piedmont came Lorenzo Valerio, seeking for himself and for his colleagues in Turin a source of new hope after the collapse of Charles Albert's second anti-Austrian campaign and after the defeat of Gioberti's left-of-center ministry. The Venetians Modena, De Boni, and Dall'Ongaro brought a message of solidarity from the one revolutionary government of 1848 that had dared call itself republican. And from the South, Musolino, Pisacane, and Ricciardi came to remind their brethren that in hundreds of small towns and villages democratic activists were resisting the counterrevolutionary efforts of King Ferdinand's supporters. Most visible and active of all was the Tuscan contingent. Geographical proximity and a democratic ministry in power in their own region made it easy for Cironi, Mazzoni, and others to go back and forth between Florence and Rome. Less tried by political tribulations in the 1840s, they were now more than ever in a favored position vis-à-vis their colleagues from other regions. Not surprisingly, they played a leading role in the movement for an Italian constituent assembly and in the organization of Circoli popolari.[26]

The presence of these men in the Papal States did not go unnoticed by the provisional government. Although it could do little to control the activities of local *capipopolo* and even less to turn public opinion against them, it did try to curb the influx of democratic activists from other states. By December 1848 it was evident that they represented a political force to be reckoned with. Their presence was bringing new life and vigor even to the small, unadventurous clubs in the capital. But the moderates were particularly concerned about the development of new political ties between the outsiders and the militantly republican Circoli popolari of the Romagna. Representatives of these Circoli did, in fact, meet in Forlì on December 13, 1848, to declare that the experiment in constitutional monarchy had ended with the pope's departure. Their statement was drafted by the Mazzinian Saffi, who was then in touch almost daily with the Roman Circolo.[27]

Fearful of a republican coup, Mamiani a few days later proposed legislation to extradite "dangerous foreigners" whose presence in Rome was a threat to public order. Although they shared his concern, a majority of the deputies of the Roman Assembly refused to approve the proposed legislation. It was too reminiscent of the political repression of which they had so recently been the victims themselves. Moreover, they asked, how could the government distinguish between "dangerous foreigners" and blameless patriots who had fled from persecution in their native regions?[28]

The full impact of the democratic presence in Rome became apparent during the debates of late December concerning the need for a new Roman Assembly. For the provisional government could not continue to function indefinitely on the basis of the *Charte octroyée* of March 14, 1848. A decree of December 29 calling for the election of a national (that is, statewide) assembly contained significant concessions to democratic sentiment. Providing as it did for the direct election of deputies by all male citizens over the age of twenty-one, for secret balloting, for the payment of per diem expenses to the deputies, and for electoral colleges based on population, it went well beyond similar documents issued elsewhere during the revolution.

Newly enfranchised citizens of the middle and lower classes flocked eagerly to the polls at the end of January 1849. Even though prospective voters and candidates alike were subject to excommunication, a turnout of 70 percent or more was reported by many electoral colleges. During the campaign there had been much speculation about whether the clergy would defy the pope and support the new political developments. The election widened the rift between upper and lower clergy that had developed during the pontificate of Gregory XVI and that had been only temporarily healed during Pius IX's honeymoon with the liberal movement. On the whole, the upper clergy stood aloof, while thousands of priests and members of the regular orders cast their votes for the new democratic constitution.

The open, democratic character of this election was reflected in the social and ideological composition of the national assembly. Of the 200 deputies, for instance, only 13.5 percent were of aristocratic background—about one-half the percentage in the previous assembly. And among the aristocratic minority were men like Saffi and the Bolognese social theorist Carlo Rusconi who had long records of militancy in the democratic movement. A substantial majority of the deputies (approximately 60 percent) came from the professional and commercial middle classes. Sixty-seven of the new deputies gave their occupation as *possidente;* but this category included estate managers and urban land speculators as well as landowners in the narrow sense of the term.

There was little continuity between the old assembly and the new; over two thirds of the new deputies had never before held elective office. This is not to say that they lacked political experience, however. Those who did not have a record as conspirators and rebels against the papal regime had at least served a valuable apprenticeship in the Circoli popolari of their respective districts or neighborhoods. Among the most experienced in this practical sense were some twelve *capipopolo* elected to the assembly. Other deputies, such as Dall'Ongaro, brought to their new position the benefit of experiences in the revolutionary governments or assemblies of their native regions. And finally, two formidable outsiders elected in absentia and known to police officials all over Europe—Mazzini and Garibaldi—embodied the international dimension of this Roman revolution.

The election was a clear victory for the democratic movement, which profited greatly from the pope's self-imposed exile and from the national reputation and stature of some of its leaders. For the moderates the election was an unmitigated disaster, however, not only because they lost control of the assembly but because they became hopelessly divided over matters of political strategy. Worried about the obvious republican inclinations of the new majority, some liberal notables abandoned altogether the cause of constitutional monarchism and sought the pope's forgiveness for their political sins.[29] But others, like Mamiani, were not willing to abjure their principles, and they had in any event gone much too far to expect forgiveness. They were determined to be heard in the assembly.

On February 5, 1849, Carlo Armellini, one of the grand old men of Roman jurisprudence, rose among his colleagues to summarize the events of the past two years. With the end of the temporal power, he observed, and with the failure of the experiment in constitutional monarchy, Italy and Europe were now looking to Rome to complete the process of revolutionary change initiated by Palermo and continued by Paris: "You [fellow deputies] are sitting between the tombs of two great epochs. On the one side are the ruins of imperial Italy, on the other the ruins of papal Italy; it is up to you to build a new edifice upon those ruins . . . may the flag of a democratic Italy fly proudly in the place of the Roman eagles and of the Vatican insignia."[30] Armellini's speech initiated a debate over the form of government most appropriate to the emerging secular state. As expected, most of the speakers urged the immediate proclamation of a Roman Republic. One of the most distinguished figures of the democratic movement in the Papal Legations, the philosopher Filopanti, proposed the decree that was approved on February 9, 1849. While offering the pope a firm guarantee of freedom to exercise his spiritual mission, the deputies emphatically announced the end of the temporal power and its replacement by "a pure democracy that will bear the glorious name of Roman Republic."[31] That republic was the high point of Risorgimento democracy, the achievement against which all subsequent experiments in democratic leadership were measured. Its principles, leaders, and institutions, if not its actual record, remained a source of inspiration for republican and democratic movements of various sorts well after the unification.

From an ideological point of view, the Roman Republic reflected nearly two decades of debate among democratic intellectuals about the aims of the national revolution and the means to carry it out. Discussions within the national assembly revealed the emergence of a broad consensus in the democratic camp concerning the need for an egalitarian, secular, and socially responsive political system for Rome and eventually for the whole of Italy. Although surrounded by enemies at birth and short-lived, the Roman Republic embodied more clearly these main principles of democratic ideology than any other revolutionary government of 1848–49.

Several actions by the assembly's democratic majority bespoke its commitment to political equality. The assembly upheld, first of all, the electoral law of December 1848. That law not only granted the right to vote to all male citizens over twenty-one years of age, but it also enabled those over the age of twenty-five to run for political office without regard to wealth, social background, and formal education. Moreover, the national assembly insisted on implementing the principle of ministerial responsibility to the legislative branch, a principle for which the liberal notables had in vain tried to gain the pope's approval.

Under pressure from *capipopolo* and democratic intellectuals, the provisional government had shown itself open to demands for social justice and responsive to the needs of the lower classes. The republican government continued this policy, moving somewhat away, however, from the urban bias of previous legislation. One of its first initiatives, for instance, was the founding of an agricultural credit bank (Monte Agricolo Nazionale), designed to assist small landowners who could not otherwise find credit to keep and improve their property.

Filopanti's decree, with its stinging indictment of the temporal power, underscored the conviction of its author and most of his fellow deputies that a new age of secular politics had begun. By their very defiance of the pope's spiritual authority and disregard for his wishes in temporal matters, the men of the Roman Republic took a clear stand in favor of secularization. They expressed their views not only in speeches and pamphlets but in their political practices as well. Two legislative measures were particularly significant expressions of the republic's secular character. One abolished episcopal control over curriculum and personnel in the public schools; another provided for the confiscation of certain ecclesiastical properties and their sale or conversion for public uses.[32]

Even while taking such measures, however, the leaders of the republic refrained from attacking the clergy and Roman Catholicism, and they often reiterated their commitment not to interfere with the spiritual mission of the papacy. Their efforts to promote the secularization of culture remained limited to the elimination of clerical censorship over press and performing arts and of clerical control over the educational system. For the Papal States these were radical innovations indeed; in the uncertain situation of 1849 it seemed dangerous and foolhardy to go any further. Particularly after the fall of the republic, intransigent secularists like Ferrari criticized the republican government for not having acted more decisively in this area.[33] But perhaps the critics missed the symbolic significance of this first secular government, which spoke not from St. Peter's but from the Roman Capitol. Of the constitutions of 1848–49 only the Roman one carried the principle of freedom of worship to its most logical and most extreme conclusion by eliminating any mention of a state religion.[34]

If the Roman Republic's constitution and policies reflected an emerging consensus in regard to democratic ideology, its leadership reflected the growth of a national democratic movement. There were differences and tensions between the democrats native to the Papal States and those from other parts of Italy. But they paled before the impressive display of national solidarity that characterized the political life of the republic, particularly when it was attacked by the French army.

Fifty of the 146 democrats who are the subject of this study spent the early part of 1849 in or near Rome and took active part in the affairs of the republic. At least as many others followed the unfolding of events in Rome from a distance, but with a sense of deep commitment and concern. This commitment was expressed in various ways, from the recruitment of volunteers for the republican cause to donations of money, weapons, and medical supplies to the writing of inspirational poems and songs.

Of the fifty men who became personally involved in this experiment in republican and democratic government, nineteen held public office as deputies, ministers, or commanders of republican armies. This group included, of course, the most prominent democratic activists of Lazio, Umbria, the Marches, and the Legations. But from the beginning these native sons shared power with experienced outsiders who had already made their mark in revolutionary situations elsewhere. With the exception of Mazzini, all of the outsiders in this group were veterans of the Lombard campaign of 1848. The two Lombards Bertani and Maestri put to the service of the Roman Republic both their political wisdom and their expertise in organizing army medical corps. The Tuscan Cironi contributed his considerable journalistic talents writing propaganda for the Circoli popolari as well as for Foreign Minister Rusconi. And Dall'Ongaro proved that poets, too, could do their part for the common cause. The Roman Republic, he wrote, embodied the patriotic and democratic ideals to which he had dedicated his *Stornelli italiani* of the 1840s.[35]

The thirty-one democrats who were active in Rome but did not hold public office played a variety of political roles. Several natives of the Papal States acted as liaison between the government in Rome and local revolutionary clubs or committees that had sprung up in the provinces, especially after the pope's flight to Gaeta. They struggled to defend local interests and autonomies while trying to discourage particularist and separatist tendencies in their communities. Their task was difficult if they happened to represent rural areas, where traditional piety remained strong.[36] It was more so if they came from the Legations where anti-Roman sentiment ran high in both democratic and liberal circles. For these spokesmen and the people they represented, the presense of outsiders in the republican government and in the Circoli popolari took on a special meaning. It signified the end of the hated Roman hegemony and the beginning of a new political order in which all regions and cities would be represented not according to feudal notions of status and privilege, but according to population size.[37]

Among the outsiders, the Calabrians De Lieto and Luigi Miceli were noteworthy for their efforts to counteract the antirepublican propaganda of Bourbon agents who had slipped quietly across the border with the support of papal loyalists. Despairing of their own networks' ability to survive the ongoing confrontation with conservative forces, De Lieto and Miceli looked to the success of the national democratic movement now centered in Rome for salvation. Similar hopes were expressed by two activists from Liguria, Federico Campanella and Antonio Ghiglione, who arrived in Rome in April 1849. They represented the militant democratic clubs of Genoa, which had been twice disappointed by their king's failure to drive the Austrians out of northern Italy. The clubs had risen on March 27 to protest the end of the campaign, triggering week-long riots that had required military intervention. With that unhappy experience behind them, Campanella and Ghiglione no longer believed that their own region could lead the movement for a free and democratic Italy, and they pinned their hopes on the Roman Republic.[38]

These men undoubtedly played an important liaison role between their own networks, those of other regions, and the government of the republic. The formal and informal ties established in Rome during the spring of 1849 survived the collapse of the republic and the end of the revolution. In October of that year, for instance, from exile in Genoa the Calabrian De Lieto appealed to the Piedmontese Valerio in the name of a friendship born in the days of the republic: "[King] Ferdinand's boundless rage will precipitate [my] unhappy homeland into such an abyss of barbarism that all of Italy will be affected. Embrace, I beg you, the cause of that forsaken land."[39] The outsiders also played another political role, less obvious and more difficult to assess. They appear to have been the driving force behind the Circoli popolari, especially in Rome. Most active in this capacity were the democrats from northern Italy, from Valerio to the Tuscans Cironi and Vannucci, from Fabrizi of Modena and Lamberti of Reggio Emilia to the "Venetian Trinity," Dall'Ongaro, De Boni, and Modena. Of the southerners present in Rome, only Musolino played a role of comparable importance in the Circoli. As the founder of the secret society Figliuoli della Giovine Italia and a member of two or three others, he had in common with the northern democrats a great deal of experience in the art of political recruitment, organization, and indoctrination.

This sort of experience, it seems, had been in short supply in Lazio and Umbria, probably because of the economic and social structure of those regions. Clerical domination of public life had resulted in few opportunities for laymen to acquire the skills appropriate to political leadership. Moreover, a backward economy had retarded, even in urban centers, the development of those literate, politically conscious commercial and professional groups from which many democratic leaders had come in other parts of Italy. Indigenous leaders, though undistinguished, had managed to organize and hold together democratic networks in 1847–48. But the situation in 1849 required more sophisticated political skills than they possessed. The task at hand was no longer one of resistance, survival, and clandestine propaganda or terrorism—the typical concerns of a militant revolutionary minority. Rather, it consisted of attracting and educating large groups of potential supporters of the republic in open competition with opposing interests and ideologies. Reluctantly, indigenous democrats left the direction of this larger task to the more experienced outsiders.[40] The situation was quite different in the Legations, however, where the Circoli were directed by distinguished local leaders such as Mattioli, Rusconi, and Savino Savini in Bologna and Saffi and Oreste Regnoli in the Romagna. Outsiders were welcome, but only in the role of advisors and observers.[41]

That the democratic-led Circoli were able to generate popular support for the republic may be inferred from the absence of any real internal threat to the revolutionary government during the very difficult spring of 1849. As early as mid-March the government's financial condition precluded the fulfillment of some promises made to the masses, such as additional tax relief for the peasantry and more sanitary housing for the urban poor. As for the propertied classes, they were seriously concerned about the continuing paralysis of trade and production, the imminent collapse of the republic's credit, and the declining value of government bonds even when backed by confiscated ecclesiastical property. But even among these classes, concern and fear did not translate into attempts to overthrow the government; when it was attacked from the outside, they rallied, on the whole, to its defense.

The democratic deputies and ministers as well as the activists of the Circoli spared no effort to prove themselves capable of governing efficiently and honestly. These efforts were in character with their political ethos, but they were also motivated by the practical need to establish a political reputation and to acquire legitimacy in the eyes of fellow citizens. Imitating the vastly popular Mazzini, some democrats adopted a downright ascetic posture. They saw themselves as the apostles of a new civil religion destined to replace Roman Catholicism. Their quest for republican virtue, however, was a frequent source of difficulties, especially in Rome. Efficiency was not an important goal in a city where the papal bureaucracy traditionally had been regarded as a major source of employment. And attempts to stem corruption were thwarted by those who regarded it as simply a means of survival.[42]

By the end of April 1849, in any event, the defense of the republic had to take predence over attempts to reform its institutions and reeducate its public servants. This task fell upon a revolutionary triumvirate which had the approval and the support of the assembly. Each of the triumvirs — Mazzini, Saffi, and Armellini — stood as a symbol of the political ideas and forces upon which the republic was to draw for survival. Mazzini, of course, symbolized national unity and devotion to the revolutionary cause, but also, as the most famous outsider, the national character of the democratic leadership. Saffi represented the democratic movement of the Papal States at its intellectual and practical best. Significantly, his political roots were in the Romagna, although he had spent several years in Rome before the revolution. And Armellini served as liaison to the moderate liberal leadership. In that he was nearly one generation older than the other two, he also symbolized the historical continuity between the present revolutionary government and the Jacobin Republic of 1799.

Because the democrats had seized the revolutionary initiative in the Papal States after the pope's departure, it was fitting and inevitable that in May and June of 1849 they should bear the brunt of the republic's defense. In fact, several of the democrats studied here, native sons as well as outsiders, distinguished themselves on the battlefield, in the organization of support services, and in various diplomatic missions on behalf of the republic. They were defeated, of course, for their enemies could count on a well-armed professional force and on the support of the major European powers which were eager to restore order to a troubled continent. The French attack snuffed out this great experiment in democratic government before it had run its full course. Its protagonists were left to wonder how much further it might have gone under different historical circumstances. Certainly they wished to resume it at the first opportunity, and they regarded it as a milestone in the Italian Revolution.[43]

For the democratic movement, the violent death of the Roman Republic at the hands of France was not without advantages, although these may not have been obvious in the summer of 1849 to men trying desperately to escape the clutches of the restored papal government. Having been ousted by an overwhelming external force, the democrats were spared criticism for missed opportunities to lead the revolution and for the betrayal of democratic ideals. They were, in fact, able to capitalize on their political achievements and their spirited defense of the revolution, until the golden myth of the Roman Republic began to eclipse in their own minds and in those of their contemporaries the promising yet uncertain reality of 1849.

Democracy and the Dead Weight of Tradition: The Case of Venice

Despite their limitations and their brief lives, the experiments in democratic leadership in both Tuscany and the Papal States marked a definite break with tradition. They were truly new beginnings in Italian political history. The Tuscan experiment demonstrated that the development of Italian society had produced a new political elite, recruited largely from the middle classes, which stood ready to share power with or to replace the old elite. The Roman Republic offered further evidence of that development, and it demonstrated as well the national character and ambitions of this new elite. Many democratic leaders involved in those experiments were convinced that success depended in large measure on their willingness to break with tradition, to chart a new course for Italy. That conviction, in fact, inspired criticisms of the Roman triumvirs for their caution in promoting social legislation and in attacking the Catholic Church. Furthermore, it was widely believed in democratic circles that republican government was a prerequisite for the democratic transformation of social and cultural institutions. This belief was expressed in Asproni's idealization of the United States and in Cattaneo's praise of Switzerland. During the revolution it was also expressed, for instance, by Tuscan democrats critical of Guerrazzi's reluctance to proclaim a republic in the spring of 1849.[44]

In Venice, however, the proclamation of a republic did not mark a break with the past, but the exact opposite; that is, a revival of glorious (and now probably irrelevant) local traditions. The Venetian episode ultimately illustrated how unwise it was for those aspiring to lead a democratic revolution to use institutions, symbols, and myths of a predemocratic age. Starting from a position of enviable strength, the Venetian democrats suffered a political defeat from which they never quite recovered.

At the outbreak of revolution, the Venetian leaders enjoyed distinct advantages over their counterparts in other regions. In contrast to Lombardy, where at least a portion of the upper class was devoted to the Habsburgs or at least to the monarchical stability they provided, the Venetians were united in their dislike of the masters imposed on them by the Congress of Vienna. Moreover, unlike Lombardy Venetia was a political backwater where political factions were ill defined and not very active. The common desire for independence from Austria virtually offset differences between moderate liberals and democrats, and in Venice itself republicanism was not associated with the Jacobin experience of the 1790s. Thus, the Venetian democrats could not claim, as their colleagues did elsewhere, to be the only true heirs to a radical republican political tradition.

Given these advantages, the Venetian revolution succeeded with less bloodshed and much less political infighting than the revolution in Lombardy. It was crowned by what seemed like a most natural outcome: the announcement on March 22, 1848, that the Republic of St. Mark was reborn. Yet, precisely this easy success and this determination to revive a cherished past in the belief that it was applicable to the Italian Revolution were major reasons for the failure of the Venetian movement.

After the Five Days of Milan, Mazzini and other democrats spoke against the proclamation of a republic, arguing that such a move was certain to divide the leaders of the Lombard revolution and to push the moderates more than ever into the arms of Charles Albert, or worse. Guerrazzi made much the same point the following year apropos of the situation in Tuscany. Then and later, he and Mazzini worried about the potential divisiveness of a form of government often identified with extremist, even violent politics. The democratic leaders of Venice had no such qualms. The enthusiasm with which the people of their city greeted the hoisting of St. Mark's golden lion was as predictable as the insults they hurled at Austrian patrols in the streets and the courage they displayed in the attack on the old arsenal. And the leadership of Daniele Manin, a half-Jewish lawyer who enjoyed the support of several *capipopolo*, of Mazzinian organizations, and of religious and ethnic minorities, augured well for the future. In the spring of 1848, in fact, Venice seemed destined to become one of the focal points of the democratic movement.[45]

Manin, the Mazzinian Giambattista Varè, and other democratic leaders initially envisioned a new regional constitution based upon universal manhood suffrage and a close alliance with fellow democrats in France and Lombardy. They took it for granted that their own initiatives in such matters, having received at least informal sanction by the people of the capital, would also be acceptable to the lesser cities of Venetia. But they were wrong. The proclamation of a Venetian Republic was not at all welcome in the provinces, where unpleasant memories of domination and even exploitation by the capital still lingered. As for the creation of a *democratic* Venetian Republic on the French model, the provincial committees, controlled by moderate liberals, wanted no part of it. Most of the provincial political leaders were landowners, and they may have feared the peasantry's response to suddenly enlarged political participation and an ideology of social justice. Whatever the reasons, they certainly drew a sigh of relief when the moderate liberals prevailed in the political struggles in Milan and appealed for the military intervention of Charles Albert.

In the spring and summer of 1848 Manin and his colleagues had two options: to water down their egalitarian program and to include more provincial notables in the government or else to ignore the provincial committees and appeal directly to the peasants for support of the democratic objectives. Manin did not find either option particularly attractive, and he received conflicting advice from the leading lights of Venetian democracy. But his reluctance to choose created a stalemate with serious consequences for his government and for the revolution. It precluded the organization of an all-Venetian army for the defense of the republic; and, therefore, military preparations against the returning Austrian armies were largely left up to local committees. Moreover, Manin's posture created suspicion and distrust among provincial democrats who had supported the anti-Austrian revolution. They were prepared to fight for the creation of a united Italian republic, but not for the resurgence of the *Serenissima*, even if she was now led by new men who claimed to speak for Venetian democracy. Among Manin's harshest critics was the *possidente* Angelo Giacomelli of Treviso, who remarked, "Although I was a follower of Mazzini, I found myself unable to support Manin's and Tommaseo's decision to push for a republican government at that particular point; I deemed their decision rash and unlikely to promote the unification of Italy . . . that was no more the time to come out in favor of a republic than it was the time to come out in favor of annexation to Piedmont."[46] Given these feelings about the republican government in Venice, it is not surprising that Giacomelli and other provincial leaders eventually accepted a merger of their region with insurgent Lombardy and with Piedmont. Although they faulted Manin for not making the best use of the manpower available in the capital, they were not eager to fight the Austrians alone either. Indeed, they came to regard Charles Albert's intervention at once as a prelude to Italian unification and as a necessary counterweight to the ambitions of the politicians in their own capital. When the euphoria of March 1848 gave way to the gloomy prospects of May and June, they came to see how foolish they had been to rely so heavily on the Piedmontese army. But by then the military situation was as much beyond repair as was the rift between capital and provinces.

During the spring the Manin government took one major initiative that should have had unanimous support in democratic circles throughout Venetia. It implemented relief measures for hatters, gondoliers, and domestic workers. These groups, already hard hit by the prerevolutionary economic recession, were in desperate straits because of the flight of many wealthy families to country estates on the mainland. The relief measurers were dictated as much by humanitarian concerns as by political or ideological considerations. Nonetheless, they were criticized even by democratic leaders like Modena, the Mazzinian propagandist par excellence, known for the social message of his dialogues and plays.

As a native of Treviso, Modena knew that Manin's social policy was likely to antagonize even those provincial notables who were otherwise committed to democratic political ideas. Yet he pleaded for unity: "As for you, provincial leaders . . . let those among you who have never erred be the first to cast stones at Venice."[47] But in the spring of 1848, his plea for understanding and unity went unheeded. Misunderstandings continued during the summer, even in the face of Austrian military successes. Indeed, the only real moment of unity among the democrats of Venetia came the following spring, when their cause was nearly lost.

Among the democrats who are the subject of this study, twelve participated from the beginning in the defense of Venetia from the invading troops of General Laval Nugent. In June and July they were joined by ten additional men who had fought in Rome against the French. The common danger and the revolutionary experiences in other regions changed the outlook of Venetians from the provinces, such as Modena and De Boni, who now fought side by side with members of the Manin government. Along with democrats from other regions, they distinguished themselves in this last-ditch attempt to keep the revolution alive. But their bravery and self-denial could not alter the failure of the democratic movement in Venetia to achieve even the limited goals it had achieved in Tuscany and in Rome. Its urban leaders had counted heavily on the enduring popularity of republican institutions in their region. They had not taken into account, it seems, that the Venetian tradition — oligarchical, centrist, and urban — could not be easily adapted to the needs of a movement that stood for political democracy and social justice. Only one dimension of the ancient Venetian republic — its independence from the Roman Catholic Church — was relevant to the goals of Risorgimento democracy. But this dimension alone was not sufficient to turn a historical liability into a political asset.

Democracy in the Two Sicilies: Diversity and Drama

The events of 1848–49 proved that the Bourbon state was quite appropriately named the Kingdom of the Two Sicilies. Naples and Sicily, in fact, followed different paths to revolution, and so did the political factions within each part of the kingdom. To the extent that unity of purpose and action developed between Neapolitan and Sicilian democrats, it was largely the result of King Ferdinand's policy. In the early phase of the revolution, the two groups worked quite independently of each other, even though leaders of the democratic networks in Reggio Calabria and Messina had cooperated closely in planning the anti-Bourbon uprising of 1847.[48]

Early in 1848 the distinguished Sicilian liberals who had initiated the revolution announced that their political program would be built upon the Constitution of 1812, "updated to take into account the progress of the modern era."[49] As the debates in the assembly gradually made clear, their primary concern was to limit the powers of the monarch. Like the French and Belgian liberals of 1830, they intended to find a royal prince, preferably an Italian, who was capable of strong leadership yet also willing to submit his policies to the scrutiny and approval of an elected assembly.

The democrats, too, revered the Constitution of 1812 as the

symbol of Sicilian identity and of resistance to Bourbon despotism. But they had a different view of how that document should be updated. Although very few of them argued for a republican form of government, the democrats in the Sicilian Assembly insisted on the adoption of a democratic electoral law and on the replacement of the appointive House of Lords *(Camera dei Pari)* with an elective senate. Several democratic activists, such as Saverio Friscia of Sciacca and Salvatore Calvino of Trapani, chose not to run or were defeated in elections to the assembly. They ignored the constitutional debates, preferring instead to organize Circoli popolari in the urban centers and to politicize the peasantry. They were generally more radical in outlook than their parliamentary colleagues and more concerned with social and economic than with strictly political issues. As in Tuscany, there was considerable tension between the democratic members of the assembly and the dissidents outside. Yet in a sense the two groups complemented and needed each other. When accused of extremism by the liberals, the democrats in the assembly argued that if their own suggestions were not heeded, more radical elements might mobilize the urban populace and perhaps even the peasantry against the new constitutional government. As for the extraparliamentary dissidents, they could not have carried out their political work among the lower classes without at least a few supporters who from time to time defended and justified their activities before a suspicious liberal government.[50]

The eloquence of a few parliamentary democrats such as Crispi and Gabriele Carnazza did not suffice, however, to sway the opinions of the moderate liberal majority on the major constitutional issues. What did ultimately make a difference was the May 15 affair in Naples. The king's confrontation with the newly elected Neapolitan Parliament over the issue of constitutional reform strengthened, of course, the Sicilians' determination never again to trust a Bourbon. But more important, that event created in the Sicilian Assembly a climate favorable to the political demands of the democratic minority. Sobered by the fate of their Neapolitan colleagues, the Sicilian liberals saw the wisdom of abolishing an appointive upper chamber that seemed likely to side with the monarch in a future constitutional crisis of this type. They also accepted the argument made by middle-class spokesmen like Carnazza that a viable constitutional monarchy could not be built without the participation of all enlightened citizens. Thus, the new constitution approved in July 1848 abolished property requirements for the right to vote but retained a literacy requirement. The electoral law of 1848 was a victory for the democrats in the assembly, even though it enfranchised only some 5 percent of the Sicilian population. But it remained a dead letter. By August the Sicilian revolutionaries, whatever their ideological orientation, had to set aside political ambitions and programs for the grim task of defending themselves from the returning Bourbon army.

The reconquest of Sicily and the political repression that followed forced nearly all the members of the assembly into exile. Sicilian liberalism suffered a lethal blow, despite the efforts of exiled leaders to keep it alive. Sicilian democracy did not share this destiny, however. Although those democrats who had served in the revolutionary assembly suffered the same fate as their liberal colleagues, several extraparliamentary dissidents escaped arrest by going underground. In their efforts to survive and do clandestine political work during the 1850s, the dissidents had experiences quite different from those of their exiled democratic colleagues. As the years went by, the cleavage that had already emerged within the Sicilian democratic leadership during the revolution became deeper, with consequences that were to be painfully obvious at the moment of unification.

Although the Sicilian democrats had considerable influence in the revolutionary government, they did not replace or even seriously challenge the leadership of the moderate liberals. The situation was different in the Kingdom of Naples, particularly after May 15, 1848. The incidents of that day brought about a serious split in the liberal camp. Some leaders argued for cooperation with the king in the defense of social stability, while others urged the adoption of a genuinely liberal constitution to replace the one granted by the king in March. By contrast, those same events prompted the democrats to close ranks. They refused to approve any royal tampering with the legislature duly elected in April, and like many progressive liberals they adopted a posture of intransigent opposition.[51]

In Sicily the burning question had been how best to update the Constitution of 1812. After May 15, the question in the Kingdom of Naples was how best to resist Ferdinand's barely veiled attempts to cripple the constitutional movement. Within a month most democratic leaders came to the conclusion that it was pointless to stay in Naples and try to influence a government dominated by right-wing liberals. Even Ricciardi and Dassi, who had a following among students and workers, despaired of accomplishing something in the capital. A few street clashes were enough to convince them that their supporters were neither militant nor numerous enough to take on the loyalist *lazzaroni* as well as the army. Realizing that resistance in the capital was impossible, Ricciardi then joined the Calabrian insurgents.[52]

For most Neapolitan democrats, in any event, the decision to
leave the capital was not difficult for their homes were in the provinces. In fact, of the thirty-one Neapolitans studied here only five
had been born in or had grown up in the capital. By returning to
their provincial hometowns, many democrats hoped at once to survive the predictable repression and to exercise the leadership role
that had eluded them in Naples. These hopes were fulfilled, however
briefly, during the summer of 1848. The experiments in democratic
leadership in the Kingdom of Naples were even more short-lived
than in Tuscany and in Rome. Yet they added up to the most interesting chapter in the movement's history during the revolution, a
chapter marked by diversity and high drama.

In Calabria, Basilicata, Apulia, and Cilento democratic activists
led rebellions against the dynasty and its supporters. In the summer
of 1848 some of these rebellions culminated in the proclamation of
provisional governments that were to hold power until a new constituent assembly could be elected for the kingdom as a whole. Aware
of promising political developments in Tuscany and Rome, Mazzinian democrats such as Libertini of Lecce and Mignogna of Taranto
hoped, in fact, to hold out against local conservative opponents and
against the royal army long enough to participate in an all-Italian
assembly. Whatever their ultimate goals, that such revolutionary
governments were established at all and that they were able to raise
revenues and volunteer troops in the face of overwhelming obstacles
and of nearly certain failure is a good indication of the Neapolitan
democrats' strength and standing in their communities.

Several factors accounted for that strength. Some democratic
activists had made their mark in the capital before the revolution as
gifted men of letters, capable lawyers, or shrewd businessmen. In
the days before mass emigration, few people left small towns such as
Lecce, Taranto, or Potenza, and fewer still succeeded in the world
outside. Thus, the intellectual or professional achievements of a distinguished native son were more important in these communities
than his background and certainly more important than his politics.
But if the democratic activists had relied only on personal
achievements, they would have enjoyed no advantage over those
moderate liberal rivals who favored compromise with the king. For
the moderate liberals often had equally impressive personal
achievements to their credit and in addition, they had the advantages of greater wealth or more privileged social backgrounds. The
democrats, however, did have another politically valuable asset: the
networks that they had built in the decade prior to the revolution.

Particularly in the provinces of Lecce, Potenza, and Cosenza,
democratic activists reaped the benefits of previous organizational

The Democratic Movement in Italy

and propaganda efforts. Those who had left their hometowns for the capital to attend the university or for other reasons were rewarded for having kept in touch with political friends at home. Libertini, for instance, could not have led a revolutionary government in his native province without the support of friends like the priest Enrico Maffei, who had managed during Libertini's absence to safeguard the conspiratorial network of the 1840s. Similarly, in the Potenza and Matera area, democrats like Giacinto Albini, a law student in Naples, and the exiled conspirator Petruccelli could not have returned to lead a revolutionary committee and to organize anti-Bourbon forces without the patient work of obscure local organizers such as Pasquale Ciccotti.[53]

The proclamations of these short-lived revolutionary governments were remarkably similar to those issued by democratic leaders in Venice, Tuscany, and Rome. The best-known figures of Neapolitan democracy, from Ricciardi to Petruccelli and Musolino, made no mystery of their republican sympathies. Yet they did not emphasize republicanism, stressing instead the need for unity against despotism and their own commitment to a broadly representative and secular government. In the midst of demonstrations, looting, and seizures of public lands by peasants in many communities, however, they were curiously vague on issues of social and economic change. Their cautious pronouncements have generally been interpreted as evidence of social conservatism, of a desire to skirt the thorniest issues of southern politics so as not to antagonize the propertied classes. But the role of the Neapolitan democrats in 1848 cannot be evaluated primarily on the basis of the official proclamations of the revolutionary governments or committees of public safety. Not only did southerners like Landi, Pisacane, and Musolino write about the land question and the plight of the peasantry; some of their colleagues actually led peasant groups in confrontations with landowners and tax officials and in armed clashes with royal troops. Had the Neapolitan democrats been as far removed from the peasant masses as most historians have depicted them to be, they would not have been able to organize guerrilla actions against Ferdinand's army. Furthermore, of the thirty-one Neapolitan democrats studied here, nine survived the most ferocious repression of the postrevolutionary decade by going underground in rural areas. It is difficult to see, for instance, how a well-known figure like Petruccelli could have managed to remain at large for fifteen months, despite a large bounty on his head, if the peasants of Basilicata had regarded him as an enemy.[54]

Reflecting on the revolution in the Two Sicilies, Ricciardi and

Crispi, two democrats who had played a major role in that revolution, agreed that the moderate liberals were to blame for its failure. To his statement that Italy's leaders had "feared the masses above everything else," however, Ricciardi added: "But it is equally true that the people, without whose arms neither revolutions nor wars of liberation can succeed, too often sat passively on the sidelines."[55] On the contrary, Crispi saw the common people as victims, duped and betrayed by the revolutionaries whom they had helped to seize power. He maintained that "the Sicilian revolution suffered the same fate as the French; the shrewdest elements of the bourgeoisie monopolized it for their own interests, then turned it against the very people who had put them in power and kept them at the helm of public affairs."[56]

These two interpretations reflected a fundamental difference of opinion and strategy that had developed among democratic leaders during the revolution. In the 1850s Ricciardi complained that the people had "sat passively on the sidelines"; yet he was one of several prominent democrats who had not welcomed popular involvement in the committees for the defense of the revolution. In June 1848, having given up the political struggle in Naples, he joined the Calabrian insurgents in the Cosenza area. Local democrats such as Mosciaro and Miceli were then recruiting soldiers for a revolutionary army. They enjoyed a substantial following, particularly in the Albanian communities. Yet they argued that the revolution could not succeed unless a large segment of the peasantry was won over by the implementation of long-delayed land reforms. Ricciardi clashed with them, not so much because he ignored the importance of economic issues, but because he was trying to build a political coalition of all anti-Bourbon elements.

Not all of Ricciardi's colleagues believed that such a coalition was possible, or indeed desirable. Those who were not afraid of taking socially divisive positions could be remarkably successful in building bases of political power among the lower classes. In some of the most backward areas of the South, in fact, democratic leaders played a political role very similar to that of the urban *capipopolo* in other parts of Italy. Perhaps the best example of this type of leadership was Costabile Carducci of Capaccio, a village in the remote and troubled Cilento area.

Because his family owned some land around Capaccio and because he himself had studied law in Naples, Carducci could be considered a member of the rural middle class or, in the language of his time and place, a man of "civil condition" *(di condizione civile)*. But contacts with revolutionary groups during his student days in

Naples sparked his interest in political issues. After his return to the Cilento he held a succession of jobs as innkeeper, surveyor, and mail delivery contractor that brought him in daily contact with the peasantry. Early in 1848, he and his brother Giovanni led demonstrations for more equitable taxation. And in the summer of that year they canvassed the countryside for guerrilla fighters willing to follow them to Calabria, the center of anti-Bourbon resistance in the Kingdom of Naples. Costabile Carducci made an unforgettable impression on the common people, who responded well to his revolutionary appeal. Mounted on a beautiful horse and dressed in a black coat, aquamarine trousers, white boots, and a large plumed hat, he would lead them to a local tax collector's office, where they would requisition funds "for military expenses to fight for the constitution and for Italian independence." Carducci died a hero's death, the victim of an ambush by a reactionary priest. The murderer, it was said, had cut off Carducci's head and sent it to King Ferdinand in Naples. With the passing of time more legends sprang up about Carducci's revolutionary heroism, as they did in Calabria and Basilicata about other democratic *capipopolo*. In the 1850s the common people mourned the deaths or involuntary absences of their *capipopolo*, while they waited for new leaders who cared about their problems and were willing to speak for them.[57]

The revolution offered unprecedented opportunities not only for political but for military leadership as well. Among the democrats studied here, Bixio, Pisacane, and Montanelli played a major role as leaders of volunteer forces in Lombardy, and Garibaldi designed the Roman Republic's defense. But only in the Kingdom of the Two Sicilies were many democratic activists able to lead truly autonomous guerrilla forces. Carducci led his Cilento volunteers, alongside Mosciaro's more experienced Albanian soldiers, in raids against the royal army. Other democrats distinguished themselves as leaders of a Sicilian force of some six hundred men that crossed the straits of Messina on June 12, 1848, to aid the Calabrian insurgents.[58]

The commander of this expedition was Ignazio Ribotti, a Piedmontese career officer and political exile who had fought in the Spanish civil war. But on several occasions during the fighting, Sicilian democratic activists such as Calvino, Francesco Campo, and Landi stole the limelight. And it was they rather than Ribotti who made most of the contacts with revolutionary forces on the mainland. So eager were they to show their patriotic zeal and to see action on the battlefield that they frequently disregarded the commander's plans. Indeed, the lack of effective discipline and coordination at the top was a major flaw of the expedition and one of the principal reasons why it ended in disaster. But even so, the expedition marked an important development in the history of the democratic movement. Like the defense of the Roman Republic, it showed that militants from various parts of Italy were capable of working together on the basis of shared ideals. It also showed that at least some democratic activists were able to build a following among the lower classes and lead them into guerrilla actions. They experimented with precisely the kind of *guerra per bande* that the military theoretician Carlo Bianco di Saint-Jorioz and Mazzini himself had long regarded as a prerequisite for a successful Italian revolution.

Yet, as many participants acknowledged later, more had to be done to assure the future success of a revolutionary war. The peasants of Calabria and Basilicata had responded to the appeal of the democrats less because they hated the Bourbons than because they sought a way out of their degrading poverty. But, Campo observed, with regard to the revolutionary objectives of the democratic movement, the poverty of the southern masses was a double-edged sword. Inasmuch as it was a source of alienation and rebelliousness, it could serve the aims of revolutionary activists; it could also become a source of serious difficulties, however, if, as had happened in 1848, the inevitable disruption of normal activities produced by the revolution made life even harder for the masses.[59]

Reflecting on the same experience, Domenico Mauro concluded that the democratic leadership needed to concern itself more seriously with the political education of the masses, so that they would be prepared to face the hardships of revolution. Especially in the rural South, this task could not be accomplished by the same means (the underground press, the student organizations, the literary cafés and clubs) that had worked well among the middle classes. Yet without careful grass-roots work, the democrats could only look forward to other premature insurrections such as the ones of 1848.[60]

The liberal revolutionaries of 1848 fell far short of their goals to transform the Italian governments into genuine constitutional monarchies and to end the temporal power. But they could boast at least one lasting achievement: the preservation of constitutional government in the Kingdom of Sardinia, which became the symbol of their political faith and, for many, a haven from persecution. By contrast, for all their courage and dedication the democrats achieved neither Mazzini's goal of national unification nor the democratization of political and social structures within the existing states advocated by less ambitious leaders. Everywhere, even in Piedmont, their efforts had come to naught; or so it seemed in the summer of 1849, when the fall of Venice destroyed the last hope of the democrats. Why, despite some splendid moments, had success eluded them? What could be learned, if anything, from the experiments in revolutionary leadership? And, were those experiments going to be repeated in the future under different conditions? During the post-revolutionary decade the failed revolutionaries of 1848 had plenty of time to reflect upon and to debate these questions. Together with specific experiences of the 1850s, their analysis of the revolution shaped their expectations for Italy's future and determined where they stood at the moment of unification.

7

A Question of Survival: The Democratic Experience in the 1850s

ALL THINGS considered, political infighting and social unrest characterized the Italian Revolution of 1848–49 more than military actions or bloody clashes between revolutionaries and supporters of the old regimes. These characteristics of the Italian Revolution were reflected in the fate of the democratic leadership. The 146 democrats studied here were in the forefront of the war against Austria, of the movement to overthrow the Restoration governments, and of the defense of the Roman and Venetian Republics. Yet all but two of them survived the revolution, and only Costabile Carducci perished at the hands of political enemies.

For the democratic leaders the failure of the revolution was a major setback, but not a tragedy. They came out of it with substantial political experience, with unprecedented national visibility, and in many cases with enhanced personal reputations for having shown courage, patriotism, and a concern for the welfare of the masses. Even while they went to prison or fled into exile, the democrats in 1849–50 looked to the future with a certain optimism. They certainly expected to have a second chance, and they hoped to learn from their own mistakes as well as from those of the moderate liberals. They expected, above all, to preserve the political networks built in the 1840s and to build upon the experiences of the revolutionary biennium. From Lombardy to Calabria and from Genoa to Venice they had shown that they were able and ready to lead their country, that they were intellectually and politically equal to more established elite groups, and therefore equally entitled to govern.

During the revolution the Piedmontese journalist Costantino Reta spoke for many democrats when he broke his ties with Cavour's newspaper, *Il Risorgimento*. At that time he wrote to a friend: "[Cavour] flattered me [and] left it up to me to get the entire enterprise under way, at the cost of my health. Only then did he let it be known that I would not be given a responsible editorial position *parce que je n'avais pas une position sociale*. But now that the democratic element is taking the upper hand, he is biting his lips . . . but talent, not birth, not bank accounts, is the true measure of social position."[1]

In the eyes of the Risorgimento democrats, this emphasis on ability was the most important achievement of 1848. One of the great promises of the French Revolution—careers open to talent—was finally becoming a reality not only in the areas of education and employment but in the political sphere as well. Even in defeat the democrats were certain that there could be no turning back, that by proving their capacity for political and military leadership they had offset the social and economic advantages enjoyed by their liberal adversaries. But the expeiences of the 1850s were to destroy this self-confidence as well as the sense of democratic solidarity that had developed in the prerevolutionary decade. Men who had survived barricades and battlefields were destroyed by physical and emotional hardships. And those who were able to weather the storm emerged with a very different self-image and much lower political expectations.

Ironically, with the passing of time the survivors came to regard 1848 and 1849, the years of war and upheaval, as the halcyon days of their personal and political lives. Days and nights and endless reams of paper were devoted to recounting and reliving those years and preparing for new uprisings and for another war against Austria. Thus, when he announced to Fabrizi the publication of his *Programma rivoluzionario*, Milo Guggino expressed full confidence that a new revolution was imminent and that the democratic exiles would be its leaders.[2]

Apology and Analysis: The Democrats Look at the Revolution

Like all revolutions, successful or not, the Italian Revolution of 1848–49 produced a flood of memoirs, polemics, and popular accounts. The democrats studied here made more than a modest contribution to such literature. In the days of forced idleness and political isolation they remembered fondly the excitement and hopes of the revolutionary biennium. They relived it, discussed it, and tried to draw some useful lessons from it. Thirty-one of them wrote histories of the revolution or included substantial accounts of it in their autobiographies and memoirs. Some of those works were written long after the unification. They had primarily a didactic purpose, and thus they cannot be used to assess the attitudes of their authors at the close of the revolution. But the twenty-two accounts published between 1849 and 1853 offer excellent clues not only to the perceptions of the individual authors but also to the issues at stake and to the purposes of the literature itself.

Two themes, apology and analysis, stood out in the democrats' accounts. The first theme reflected their vulnerability at the close of the revolution. No sooner had Rome fallen to the French and had Venice settled down to a long siege than the leaders of the democratic movement came under attack. The moderate liberals who had initiated the revolution blamed the democrats for placing their republican inclinations ahead of their national patriotism, thus fostering dissension where unity was essential to success. And the conservatives returning to power held them primarily responsible for the social unrest that had accompanied the political upheaval in some regions. The democrats had to reply to those charges in the most forceful way possible, for if they failed to make a good case for their conduct in 1848–49, they might forfeit their claims to leadership of a future revolution.

Andreini, Carlo Cassola, and Dall'Ongaro who published their accounts in Cattaneo's series, *I documenti della guerra santa*, focused their self-defense on the heroic role that they and their colleagues had played in the war against Austria. Andreini described how a contingent of Romagna democrats led by Vincenzo Caldesi had forced the Austrian garrison at Comacchio to surrender in the spring of 1848. The republicans, he wrote, "historically have always been the first ones to fight, the last ones to argue." Yes, he added, Caldesi had defied the directives of the constitutional government of Bologna, but only because that government had too timidly pursued the attainment of national independence.[3] Like Cattaneo's *Dell'in-*

surrezione di Milano, Cassola's book on his native Brescia, the "lioness" of anti-Austrian resistance, and Dall'Ongaro's pamphlet on Venice emphasized the role of volunteer troops. Although they admitted that their own recruitment efforts and strategy had left much to be desired, these authors provided convincing evidence of Charles Albert's hostility to the volunteers and of the moderate liberals' unrealistic faith in his professional army. Yet, the strongest case against Charles Albert's generals was not made by disappointed Lombards or Venetians but by the Piedmontese social theorist Gentilini. Recounting his own efforts to reach out to the volunteer forces he wrote: "Intelligence and merit were shunted aside, were accused of republicanism . . . yet [the volunteers] were the only ones to grasp the real importance of the undertaking."[4]

The attention that these northern democrats devoted to military history and to the controversial issue of the volunteers reflected the paramount importance of the anti-Austrian campaign in the entire Po Valley. Democrats in other regions, such as Pianciani and Orsini in the Papal States and Campo in the South, proudly told of their military exploits; but their accounts focused primarily upon the internal political struggles that had occured during the revolution. If they were sometimes called upon to defend their words, they were almost always challenged to defend their actions. Not surprisingly, the former ministers and deputies of the Roman Republic came under the heaviest attack. It could be argued that their policies had been but a partial, mild, and very tentative implementation of democratic ideology. But even so, they had gone further than any other group during the revolution. And now from exile the democratic triumvirs Mazzini and Saffi claimed to speak for a democratic Italian nation with its capital in Rome. A historic precedent had been set, they wrote, and soon the representatives of the Italian nation were going to convene again on the Roman Capitol and again proclaim equality, secular government, and social justice.[5]

But the most spirited defense of the democrats' role in the founding of the Roman Republic was written by the Bolognese intellectuals Rusconi and Savini. As the former foreign minister of the defunct republic, Rusconi naturally stressed the attempts to secure for the republic international support and legitimacy, and he published diplomatic documents still in his possession. To counter moderate liberal charges, he emphasized the republic's cautious dealings with foreign governments, particularly with the Catholic powers alarmed by the flight of the pope and by the presence of Mazzini in Rome. He also defended the decision to proclaim a republican government, arguing that it had been a means of filling a power vacuum rather than a statement of democratic ideology. Many moderate liberals, he pointed out, had voted for the republic as the only viable alternative to anarchy after the demise of the temporal power. As a former member of the Roman Assembly and a founder of the Circolo popolare of Bologna, Savini was eminently qualified to defend his fellow democrats against charges that they had disrupted the social order. On the contrary, he observed, the social policies of the republic had instructed the people in their duties as well as their rights. Far from threatening the solution of the national questions, as the moderates claimed, those policies had made it possible for the common people to feel that they were part of the great struggle for independence and freedom. As proof of this achievement of democratic policy and propaganda, Savini cited the many popular tributes to the "outsider" Mazzini and the exceptional determination to resist the French shown by the people of lower-class Trastevere.[6]

Very similar arguments are found in the apologetic writings of the Tuscan dissidents Montazio, Cironi, and Pigli. They defended their ideas and conduct not so much against moderate liberal critics, but rather against the leading figures of the democratic ministry which they had opposed during the revolution. Montazio, whose revolutionary weapon had been above all the pen, resented charges that his pamphlets and his newspaper, *Il proletario*, had inflamed public opinion and turned it against the democratic ministry to the advantage of reactionaries. He answered, as did Savini apropos of the Roman Republic, that he had seen a tremendous and unfulfilled need for the political education of the masses. He was proud of his efforts to meet that need and argued that he deserved not a trial for treason and *lèse majesté* but rather the gratitude of the Tuscan upper classes. These were, of course, the self-serving arguments of a man seeking to avoid a harsh prison sentence or, as it happened, exile. Yet they were quite consistent with Montazio's writings and conduct during the revolution. Like many democratic revolutionaries of 1848, he viewed himself as a mediator between the disenfranchised and politically inarticulate masses, on the one hand, and the ruling elites on the other. His fellow dissidents Cironi and Pigli were attacked for supporting radical Livorno's defiance of the grand ducal government and later also of the democratic ministry. They, too, saw themselves as patriots who had aided the national cause by reaching out to the masses. Pigli, moreover, replied directly and tartly to Guerrazzi's charges that he had sabotaged the government's negotiations for the return of the grand duke and had schemed for a republican triumvirate. If he did not wish to apologize for his political conduct, neither was he willing to accept the blame for actions that nearly all democrats had favored in 1849.[7]

As these polemics indicate, the relative leniency of the Tuscan courts in the early 1850s created an atmosphere in which salvation was possible, and in that atmosphere the defeated democrats sometimes turned on one another. The situation was different in Lombardy-Venetia or in the Kingdom of the Two Sicilies, where polemics among the democrats usually revolved around substantive issues and where criticism of one's former comrades was not tainted by the desire to incur official favor. Indeed, among the democrats from those regions polemics, recriminations, and self-defense were frequently set aside for thoughtful historical and political analyses of the events. The most interesting and thoughtful by far came from the southern protagonists of the revolution, that is, from those who had fought the hardest and suffered the most. Their accounts were filled with references to social tensions and to the differential impact of the revolution on southern society. Despite their successes on the local level, they had not even come close to taking control of the Neapolitan state, and to the end they had played a subordinate role in Sicilian politics. Thus, more than their counterparts in other regions, they asked themselves why the revolution had failed and what they had to do to maximize their chances of success in the future.

Petruccelli came out of the revolutionary experience convinced that the ideological categories used by democratic intellectuals, himself included, in the 1840s were useless for understanding the events of 1848–49. To be sure, an analysis of the Neapolitan revolution revealed the existence of ideological cleavages, for instance, between monarchists and republicans, centralists and federalists, and so forth. But behind these lay much more fundamental divisions along social lines. Through an analysis of social structure he tried to identify those social groups that might have profited from a democratic revolution and that made logical targets for future propaganda and recruitment: "Women of all ages and social conditions, the proletariat, young people of every class, the generation born after 1820, that is, the generation least warped by Jesuit education under the threat of monarchical gallows and jails . . . these will be the soldiers of the revolution."[8]

Petruccelli was sensitive to the socioeconomic cleavages of Neapolitan society; yet he did not seek to define the future "soldiers of the revolution" along class lines in the narrow sense of the term. Rather, he sought his "soldiers" among all alienated and marginal elements of southern society, taking into account variables of sex and age as well as of income, occupation, and education. He proposed to appeal to the young of all social classes because he knew from personal experience that they had few opportunities for advancement and mobility. The "proletariat" of which he wrote consisted, of course, not of industrial workers but of the disinherited rural masses of his region. The ongoing transformation of the southern agricultural economy at the hands of new, profit-minded entrepreneurs, he wrote, was depriving the masses of communal resources and traditional rights essential to their survival. No longer able to count on a decadent and incompetent landed aristocracy or on the king for protection, the peasants desperately needed leadership. Despite their poor performance in 1848, Petruccelli still believed that democratic intellectuals and militants could provide that leadership. But they had to be willing to break with the economic interests and the cultural prejudices of their own class. An encouraging sign that this was happening was the clandestine work among the peasantry of some democratic militants of 1848 who had escaped prison and exile. Finally, Petruccelli made a strong case for the need to reach southern women of all social classes. Kept in "a condition of Oriental servitude," they were almost universally ignorant, submissive, and superstitious. But if made aware of their importance in society and of their servile condition, women might become an explosive force for revolution. Ultimately, Petruccelli concluded that in the past the democratic leadership had paid too much attention to the transformation or subversion of political institutions and hardly any attention to social problems. Thus, he urged his fellow democrats, particularly those who had remained in the kingdom, to reverse their priorities.

Musolino, Ricciardi, and Pisacane held a similar though more vaguely expressed interpretation. They agreed with Petruccelli on the wisdom of changing the movement's priorities, but they offered different suggestions on how to do so. In view of their disagreement over political strategy in 1848–49, it is ironic that Musolino and Ricciardi concurred that the democratization of southern society could be accomplished essentially by political means, through the introduction of universal suffrage, and free, secular public schools. Beginning with the artisans and lower middle class, the people had to be convinced first of all to demand those political rights, as they had in 1848, through mass meetings and demonstrations. Widespread agitation would bring about the collapse of the Bourbon monarchy even if the army remained loyal to it. In contrast to Petruccelli, however, Musolino and Ricciardi hesitated at the thought of trying to reach the peasantry. They did not fail to see the revolutionary potential in the dismal backwardness of the rural population, but they had learned during the revolution that the peasants were difficult to control once aroused. Ricciardi, in particular, had been greatly alarmed by episodes of land seizure and violence against property owners. He believed that the democratic leadership had to find a way of politicizing the middle and lower classes without risking a sudden collapse of the economic and social order, and without creating an atmosphere of class warfare. He was prepared to advocate political democracy and even a radical redistribution of wealth but not to identify with the most oppressed against his own social class.[9]

Pisacane agreed with Petruccelli that a choice, however painful, had to be made. The task of the democrats, as he saw it, was not to overthrow the existing conservative governments but to transform Italian society. The political revolution of 1848–49 had been initiated by the most progressive elements of the bourgeoisie (by which he meant the propertied classes generally). These elements could be counted on to resume their political struggle at the first opportunity because "they already [had] everything except political freedom." But after the bourgeoisie had modernized Italy's political institutions and possibly also achieved unification, the democratic intellectuals who themselves came from the propertied classes and knew their language, ethos, and tactics would have to make sure that political modernization did not become a new and more efficient tool for the social and economic oppression of the masses.[10]

Although southern protagonists of the revolution perceived it most clearly, this dilemma did not escape the attention of the Lombards Cattaneo and Ferrari, who wrote perhaps the most important analyses of the events of 1848–49. Both were critical of Mazzini for putting too much emphasis on the politicization of the Italian masses and on their moral as opposed to their material needs. Yet only Ferrari acknowledged the possibility that in order to attain power democratic leaders might have to choose between the interests of the propertied classes and those of the masses. Having seen the effects of the June Days of 1849 in Paris, he dismissed outright the notion that after an Italian "war of independence . . . without a revolution . . . philosophers and priests, nobles and bourgeois, the privileged and the disinherited [would] live together in harmony."[11] Cattaneo was fully aware of the importance of weaning the masses, especially the peasantry, away from their traditional loyalties and of protecting them from exploitation. Yet, unlike Ricciardi and Musolino, he was not at all confident that this could be accomplished by establishing a revolutionary democratic government. His experience during the political campaign for the merger of Lombardy with the Kingdom of Sardinia in 1848 had undermined his faith in democratic political reforms. When the political and social consciousness of the masses remained low, he wrote, even universal suffrage became but a tool for manipulation in the hands of those who held power. Yet, having made this rather cynical assessment of the situation in 1848, Cattaneo shied away from the extreme conclusions drawn by his friends Pisacane and Ferrari. Remaining intellectually close to the English free trade movement and the philosophical radicals, he urged fellow democrats in Italy to focus their efforts not on armed insurrection but on "attempts to influence opinions."[12]

Whether they saw themselves as déclassé intellectuals and militants hostile to the propertied classes or simply as moral and political mentors of the lower classes, the democrats studied here faced a common dilemma in the 1850s. They wanted to influence the masses; indeed, they feared that the movement they had established in the 1840s would wither away if they failed to do so. Yet the authors of this apologetic and analytical literature on 1848 were far away in exile, while other democrats who shared their views languished in prison. Paraphrasing his hero, Vittorio Alfieri, Ricciardi voiced their frustration: "I write because I am not allowed to act."[13] Action was not impossible, as Mazzini's followers demonstrated throughout the decade. But, of necessity, it could only consist of conspiracies and attempted insurrections by small, highly dedicated cadres. Such political weapons were hardly suitable for educating and attracting the masses. Moreover, the democrats in exile and in prison were often too preoccupied with sheer survival to devise more effective revolutionary weapons.

Broken Lives: The Psychological and Physical Impact of Defeat

Police harassment, economic deprivation, and homesickness were the lot of nearly all democratic leaders after 1848. Gradually these collective experiences sapped the vitality of the democratic movement to the point that its very survival was in doubt. But at least thirty of the democrats studied here endured crueler torments and faced greater dangers than their already benighted colleagues. They either lost their lives or they emerged from the postrevolutionary decade broken in spirit and in health.

Seventeen democrats did not live to see the liberation of their country from foreign rule. Orsini achieved international notoriety and was then executed for his attempt on the life of Napoleon III. Pisacane, a theorist of revolution and the movement's most gifted military strategist, perished in the attempt to resume a revolutionary war in his native Kingdom of Naples. De Cristoforis and Pilo died fighting for the liberation of their respective regions of Lombardy and Sicily in 1859–60. Giovanni Pezzotti, a stalwart of the Mazzinian network in Milan and Mantua, strangled himself in his prison cell for fear of breaking down under torture and of revealing the names of fellow conspirators. A member of the same network, the Mantuan priest Tazzoli, was spared the beatings sometimes used by the Austrian police to extract confessions and information from political suspects. But he was subjected to a psychological ordeal that was perhaps even more harrowing. Tazzoli was one of few democratic clergyman with a genuine pastoral vocation and a commitment to ecclesiastical obedience. Yet he was excommunicated and publicly stripped of his clerical garb by the bishop of Mantua. For him this was a fate infinitely worse than physical torture.[14] Indeed, had the Austrian courts not sentenced him to the gallows — along with the Venetians Angelo Scarsellini and Giovanni Paganoni — he might well have died of a broken heart. Nine others died of consumption or other illnesses aggravated by the hardships of jail and exile.

Pezzotti was the only democrat studied here who actually took his own life; but several other attempted or contemplated suicide in prison. For example, Giuseppe Finzi, one of the Mantuan conspirators arrested in 1851–52, served his prison sentence outside of Lombardy in the fortresses of Josephstadt and Theresienstadt. Conditions in those Habsburg prisons were not as harsh as those denounced by Silvio Pellico in the 1820s. Yet Finzi's sentence was severer than those meted out to other political offenders. Tazzoli's execution was intended as a warning to the Lombard clergy against political activism. Finzi's imprisonment so far from his family may have been intended as a similar warning to the Jewish community of Mantua. If it was a warning, it went unheeded. Finzi himself showed no signs of repentance; indeed, he expected "more bad straits and disruption." At the time of his arrest he had given his word not to take his own life. But in November 1853 he pleaded with his brother Moisè to release him from that promise, for he wished to "prepare [himself] for a courageous decision as long as [he had] the time and the opportunity." Finzi overcame his moment of despair at least in part because he had the means to bribe prison officials and because he was able to keep in touch with his family through a Czech business associate.[15] Other victims of Austrian repression were not so fortunate.

Francesco Siliprandi, for instance, never quite recovered from his ordeal in the Mantuan fortress of San Giorgio. After being kept awake and in solitary confinement for several days, he was severely beaten. But his tormentors could get nothing out of him: "I was unable to answer, for I was seized by terrible convulsions . . . and that was fortunate because I was saved from an act of cowardice . . . thus can moral and physical suffering overwhelm a man's reason."[16] For years thereafter he was obsessively afraid of being alone and guilt-ridden at the thought that he had, in fact, broken down, and that only a physical weakness (perhaps an epileptic seizure) had prevented him from betraying his fellow revolutionaries.

Siliprandi could at least find solace in the fact that his weakness had done no harm to others. The experience of the Veronese lawyer Giulio Faccioli illustrates the agony that awaited those who did talk. Arrested in 1852, Faccioli collapsed under threat of torture; his revelations led to other arrests, indeed, to the destruction of the Mazzinian network in his city. This was a serious blow to the democratic movement in northern Italy because Verona had been a major meeting point for activists from Lombardy and Venetia since the 1840s. Released on parole, Faccioli was—in the words of a local notable—"universally loathed, and when he died [after the liberation of Venetia] no one said so much as a compassionate word about him."[17] The unfortunate man tried in vain to defend himself from his critics; in his memoirs he gave a touching account of the terrifying circumstances of his arrest and interrogation. He asked for forgiveness, but he also wondered why so many who had been spared a similar ordeal now were pointing at him and proclaiming: "He should have resisted or else died."

Despite the social ostracism that Faccioli endured, his prison experience was not at all unusual. More hardened conspirators than he suffered mental breakdowns. Among them was Orsini, perhaps the most famous democratic militant ever to serve time in Mantua's San Giorgio prison and certainly its most wanted escapee. A daredevil by nature and a seasoned veteran of papal jails, Orsini was determined not to be broken by the Austrian police. But after days of interrogation he began to fear that the walls of his cell might close in on him. To mental stress was added the discomfort of malaria, a rampant disease within a prison that overlooked the Mantuan swamps. Although he eventually managed to escape, Orsini suffered from fever and hallucinations for the remainder of his life. In 1856 he wrote to a friend that he did not expect to live much longer.[18] He was certainly psychologically prepared for death when, two years later, he resolved to engage in a terrorist act that was tantamount to suicide.

Vigorous youth offered no better protection against these pressures than did the experience of previous arrests. Giovanni Nicotera, born in 1828, was a case in point. One of the youngest participants in the revolution and the son of Calabrian gentry, he was spared real hardship in the early 1850s. But in 1857 he joined Pisacane's ill-starred expedition to the South and was wounded and then captured by Bourbon troops. He served less than three years in prison, but his physical deterioration was such that upon his release in 1860 he looked middle-aged. And his unpredictable behavior and fits of temper betrayed the stresses that had driven him at least once to attempt suicide.

Nicotera was one of thirteen democrats who served time in the infamous prisons of the Kingdom of the Two Sicilies, which William Gladstone denounced as a blight on European civilization. Nowhere in Italy were conditions so primitive and brutal as those in Naples' medieval Sant'Elmo fortress, perched high on the hillside overlooking the bay, and in the Castel dell'Ovo, constantly battered by winds and often flooded at high tide. Worse, the Bourbon police used psychological and physical torture more frequently than their counterparts in Lombardy-Venetia or in the Papal States. Calvino and Campo, for instance, both of whom spent eighteen months to two years in the Sant'Elmo prison, were thrown into damp, vermin-infested cells already occupied by common criminals and were subjected to a variety of corporal punishments.[19]

Conditions were more tolerable in the penal colonies of Nisida and Ventotene. There, at least, the prisoners could see the sunshine and the ocean, and if they could afford it they could buy clean linens and fresh food from the guards. But escape was much more difficult than from the urban prisons, even if one could bribe the guards. Moreover, the colonies had more than their fair share of the criminally insane and of murderers, who often preyed upon the political prisoners; assaults and thefts were everyday occurrences which the guards could do little to prevent. The young Morelli, for instance, who spent nearly twelve years on the island of Ventotene, endured several beatings by other inmates.

Imprisonment in one of the provincial jails was no guarantee of more humane treatment. Francesco Angherà and his uncle Domenico, for instance, spent five months in the Catanzaro fortress, where they were kept in almost total darkness and periodically denied food. Frightened and worried about the fate of his wife and children, Francesco agreed to reveal the names of other Catanzaro conspirators. Later on, Domenico came to his nephew's defense, pointing out that he had not revealed anything the Bourbon police had not already known. But Francesco was obviously ashamed of his own weakness, and after his escape from prison he spared no effort to redeem himself in the eyes of his fellow revolutionaries. Thus, in 1855 as a member of the Anglo-Italian Legion that fought in the Crimean War, he tried to commandeer a British warship for action against the Bourbon fleet.[20]

Although many democrats were broken in prison, those who remained in hiding were not spared equally traumatic experiences. After the collapse of the revolution, for instance, Albini was able to continue his political work in and around his native Montemurro in the Basilicata. He did so by frequently moving in and out of the houses of relatives and trusted friends and by emerging from his hiding places only at night. When an earthquake hit Montemurro in 1852, Albini became trapped under the rubble of a friend's house. Although injured, he was afraid to reveal his presence. When friends found him at last, he was in shock and temporarily blind. After the tragic failure of Pisacane's expedition Albini was blamed for not having adequately prepared the ground for an insurrection in his province. His critics did not seem to realize that in 1857 he was no longer the vigorous man be had been in 1848. Although he was still quite capable of political leadership, after the accident he never quite regained the extraordinary stamina needed for clandestine work and for guerrilla fighting.[21]

Militants who had at first found safety in exile were not spared trauma either. In 1853, for instance, an abortive Mazzinian insurrection in Milan prompted the Austrian government to demand the expulsion of Italian exiles from nearby Canton Ticino; since 1848 the Lugano area had been the focal point of anti-Austrian propaganda and conspiracies. Among the democratic militants singled out for expulsion were Cassola and De Boni, both of whom were especially well known to the Austrian authorities. The former was a hero of the defense of Brescia against the returning Austrian armies; the latter, of course, had a long record of political militancy in republican and anticlerical circles. Both men defied the Swiss government's expulsion decree and went into hiding, expecting the crisis to blow over before long. For they knew that the Swiss public and the press were largely in favor of resisting Austrian demands. Events proved that their political intuition was correct; but this was of little comfort to De Boni, whose decision to stay in Switzerland ended in tragedy. In the fall and winter of 1853 he wandered in the mountain valleys above Berne, without work, food, or adequate clothing. At some point he found himself alone and snowbound for weeks in a shepherd's abandoned hut. He eventually turned up in Turin. Those who met him in the late 1850s described the once vigorous and handsome De Boni as a gaunt, sickly man plagued by hallucinations and, some said, addicted to strong drink.[22]

Some democrats were broken not by mistreatment in prison or by other physical hardships but by guilt at the thought of the suffering their political activism had visited upon their families. Such was the case, for instance, of Enrico Montazio. Upon his release from prison in 1850, he pleaded for permission to remain in Tuscany. But he was one of relatively few militants for whom a grand ducal pardon was out of the question at that time. Montazio's adolescent daughter, Elfrida, followed him into exile in France and later in England. Unable to care for her as he moved from one occasional job to another, he left her with friends. In Paris she may have been mistreated by her hosts; at any rate, she attempted suicide and on several occasions ran away. When she joined her father in England, he found a more suitable foster home for her, and the family who took her in also arranged for a doctor's care. But Elfrida did not improve. Indeed, her behavior became very strange, and at some point she joined or was lured into a prostitution ring. Through Pianciani, Montazio enlisted the help of British reformers. But the conduct of one man who dealt with Elfrida's case caused Montazio to comment bitterly on the motives behind the reformers' "interest in wayward girls." Convinced that his political activism had deprived his daughter of the opportunity for a happy life, Montazio never ceased to blame himself for Elfrida's mental problems. And he was denied a chance to make it up to her, for Elfrida died before they could return to Italy.[23]

Several of Montazio's colleagues had more reason than he to feel guilty vis-à-vis their families, whose problems were clearly a result of their actions. Such was the case, for instance, for Campo, whose parents and younger brothers were arrested after he had fled to Genoa. Likewise, the Calabrian Gaspare Marsico, who had found refuge in the Sila mountains, for nearly a decade was torn between his desire to remain at large, ready for a resumption of guerrilla warfare against the Bourbons, and his desire to turn himself in and thus to save his family from constant police harassment.[24]

Between 20 and 25 percent of the democrats studied here experienced severe traumas that had a direct bearing on their ability to continue their political work. The loss of such men would have weakened even the strongest of revolutionary movements; it was certainly serious for a movement still young in years, ideologically fragmented, and now more than ever forced to operate underground. Still, the loss might have ben offset — for instance, by the recruitment of younger militants — if the remaining 70 to 80 percent of the leadership had managed to hold its own in Italian society, to remain visible, and to preserve its political networks. But in fact, quite apart from the many individual tragedies, the democrats as a group experienced an erosion both of their socioeconomic position in Italian society and of the claims to political leadership established in 1848–49.

Unprofitable Martyrdom:
The Economic Consequences of Defeat

In the 1840s membership in a secret society or involvement with the underground press had provided activists and intellectuals from various social backgrounds and regions with common bonds. In the 1850s the common bond was the experience of exile. Of the 144 survivors of the revolution, 93 (64.6 percent) spent all or most of the postrevolutionary decade away from their native states. This number included eight Sardinian subjects who were heavily compromised in attempted insurrections and well known for their republican views. Even the constitutional government of Victor Emmanuel II regarded them as too dangerous for political leniency. Indeed, four of them (Mazzini, Campanella, Reta, and Antonio Mosto) had been sentenced to death in absentia. Not accidentally, six of the eight were Ligurians.

Despite its monarchical government, police surveillance, and censorship, however, the Kingdom of Sardinia was the mecca of political exiles from other states. Both personal and political reasons drove them to settle there. Those democrats who had not traveled much before the revolution found comfort in the knowledge that at least in Piedmont-Sardinia they would not encounter language difficulties. Others believed that it was going to be relatively easy to find employment there. More important, a concentration of democratic leaders in the one Italian state that had preserved constitutional government might permit the continuation of political debate and the strengthening of the national network of 1848–49. But only thirty-one of the democrats studied here were actually able to settle in Piedmont-Sardinia. In many cases, they were granted entry visas only in the mid- and late 1850s, after they had been expelled from foreign countries; and, even then, they frequently clashed with Sardinian authorities. Sixty-two of their colleagues spent the years of exile abroad, though rarely by choice. Ultimately the democrats' hopes for socioeconomic stability and for new political opportunities proved to be unrealistic. Many domestic and international factors worked against them, not the least the attitude of the Sardinian government and of its liberal allies from other states.

On July 3, 1849, a young protagonist of the Sicilian revolution, Rosolino Pilo, mailed to his brother a tear-stained request for money. He was in Marseilles but hoped to leave soon, "not wishing to remain in a country where all Italians, and Sicilians in particular, [were] held in contempt." His prayers were answered, and by the end of the month he wrote enthusiastically from Genoa, "where one [could] live in peace and liberty." As an afterthought, however, he added that he was a bit apprehensive about the influence of southern moderates on the Sardinian government. By early fall the thrill of being in an Italian-speaking country with constitutional government was already wearing off. As a scion of Sicilian feudal nobility, Pilo was ill equipped to earn a living in a modern commercial city. And his brother, who did not share his political views, was not generous with financial help. Pilo had no children of his own, but he had assumed the responsibility of raising the son of a cousin and close friend who had died in the revolution. Hence his growing concern when he was unable to find employment or to launch a business. By December 1849 he wrote: "Here we are doing very poorly, morally and physically . . . I hang around my place twenty-four hours a day, minding my own business and not seeing anyone."[25]

Pilo was undoubtedly handicapped in his quest for employment and social status by his lack of adequate education and of prior contacts in Genoa. But his plight was not much worse than that of other exiles who arrived with marketable skills and with letters of introduction to members of the local democratic networks. Cironi, for instance, to the chagrin of his Genoese brother-in-law who had secured an entry visa for him, was unable to find steady employment despite his demonstrated skill as a journalist. Nor was this problem limited to literati, of whom both Genoa and Turin had an amply supply. Enrico Guastalla, for instance, encountered similar difficulties, although he had worked as a salesman and accountant since adolescence. So did the lawyers Crispi and Luigi Zuppetta. In his native Apulia and in Naples the latter had achieved distinction as a jurist and a professor of law. Thus, he was stunned and dismayed to discover how little these achievements counted in Piedmont. "A righteous government such as this," he wrote with bitter irony, "has eyes only for meritorious men; and I have no merit in its eyes!"[26]

The experiences of these men, who either were expelled at some point or remained on the margin of Sardinian society, contrasted with those of a few more fortunate exiles. The milanese Gaetano Guttièrez, for instance, found a good job with an insurance company; and during his Piedmontese exile he developed a network of business contacts that proved extremely useful after Italy's unification. Others who became well integrated in Sardinian society included the Dalmatian Federico Seismit-Doda and Savini of Bologna. The latter found a mentor in the influential liberal exile Pasquale Stanislao Mancini, who recommended him for teaching positions and, more important, taught him the secret of a tranquil and stable life in the Kingdom of Sardinia. On November 14, 1851, Mancini urged his protégé to send for his wife and daughters and assured him that "the government's ill will [was] nothing to worry about." But a few weeks later, noting that he had again defended Savini from charges of republicanism, Mancini stressed in no uncertain terms the importance of "temperance, virtue, and political moderation."[27] Although Savini proved to be a somewhat recalcitrant pupil, Mancini's advice was basically very sound. Those were indeed the qualities necessary to achieve successful integration in Sardinian society and to avoid difficulties with the police.

In the eyes of the Sardinian government, an exile's regional origins mattered very little, although Crispi and others occasionally complained of antisouthern prejudice. Nor was the exile subject to discrimination or harassment by virtue of his social or political background. Guttièrez, for instance, had been a Mazzinian and a barricade fighter in Milan in March 1848, and the Habsburg government had sentenced him to death in absentia. Yet he was left alone, whereas fellow Lombards of similar background such as Acerbi and Sacchi were in and out of police headquarters. The main difference between these exiles was the extent and the nature of their involvement in current political issues. All applicants for an entry visa were required to pledge that they would not meddle in Sardinian politics or engage in activities harmful to the security of the host country. In practice this pledge meant little. Refugees were quite free to join political clubs and to write about political issues, provided that they did not challenge the policies and institutions of the liberal monarchy. Moreover, it was widely known among the exiles that letters of recommendation from influential moderate liberals such as the Bolognese Marco Minghetti and the Sicilians Filippo Cordova and Francesco Ferrara were the key to all but the most menial and precarious jobs. Such recommendations were not easy to come by for those democrats who were critical of liberal ideology or who had clashed with moderate liberal leaders during the revolution.[28]

Not surprisingly, the police tried to intercept the correspondence of exiles like Pilo, Pisacane, and Acerbi, who kept in touch with Mazzini to plan for the resumption of the revolution. But the strictest surveillance was reserved for those known to be close to democratic extremists within the Kingdom of Sardinia itself, such as Guastalla, editor of the radical newspaper *Libertà e associazione*, and Cironi and other contributors to the Mazzinian *L'Italia del popolo*. Among the native extremists with whom they associated were G. B. Tuveri, author of a treatise on the people's right to overthrow bad governments; Davide Levi and Nicolao Ferrari, both radical intellectuals; and B. F. Savi, a strong advocate of political rights for the lower classes. Although they were not forced to go into exile like their fellow democrats Campanella, Gentilini, Reta, and Mosto, these activists led semiclandestine lives. With the exception of Levi, whose family was well-to-do, they lived in abject poverty. For this reason they were much less able to help the exiles than were Valerio, Sineo, Brofferio, and others of more moderate views and of more secure position. Thus, by the mid-1850s a cleavage emerged among the democrats, whether Sardinian citizens or not. On the one side were those who refrained from attacks on the Sardinian monarchy and lived by the moderate liberals' code of conduct: temperance, virtue, and political moderation. On the other were the uncompromising advocates of political and in some cases of even social revolution.

A price had to be paid for ideological purity and intransigence. For some it meant life in dingy, cold rooms, meager communal meals, and endless appeals to the generosity of family and friends. For the fortunate few who were spared these daily indignities, it meant denied opportunities for professional advancement and for additional political experience. Many moderate liberal emigrés could and did hold political office, practice law and medicine, teach at the university, and frequent the best social circles. Democratic activists could do likewise, but only if they refrained from advocating republicanism, political equality, and social justice; that is, if they ceased to be democrats. Some of the democratic exiles were militant enough to sacrifice their careers, their families, and even their health to a political ideal that became more elusive with each passing year. But they had even fewer outlets for the dissemination of their ideas than they had had before the revolution. The diaspora of 1849 and the subsequent wave of arrests and political trials had disrupted the local and regional networks that had effectively prepared the ground for the revolution. One compensation was the greater freedom of expression allowed by the *Statuto* of 1848. But

Guastalla, Savi, Pisacane, and others soon discovered the limits of that freedom. Fines, confiscations, and contempt citations became part of their everyday lives. In times of severe political tension (for instance, after the Milanese uprising of February 1853 and after the discovery of a Mazzinian conspiracy in Genoa in 1857), these militants could expect arrest if they were Sardinian citizens, expulsion if they were not.[29]

Even with these limitations, however, the Kingdom of Sardinia was the only place where remnants of the national democratic network of 1848–49 continued to operate. Valerio, Sineo, Brofferio, Asproni, Agostino Depretis, and a few others spoke for that network in the Sardinian Parliament. By avoiding direct attacks on the monarchy these men, none of whom held radical views on social issues, gave the democratic movement visibility and respectability. At the same time they maintained close intellectual and personal ties with Sardinian activists and exiles of a more radical tinge. The main contact point, however, was not the Sardinian capital but the city of Genoa where the political and social climate was more hospitable to democratic ideas. By the mid-1850s Genoa was second only to Lugano as a center for the publication and dissemination of democratic newspapers and propaganda materials. And it was the only city in Italy where the democratic leaders of 1848–49 could still feel that they constituted a significant national force. Indeed, for several years after the unification Genoa continued to be the unofficial and informal headquarters of the democratic movement.

The experiences of the sixty-two democrats who went into exile abroad were quite different. Their social and economic positions varied considerably, depending upon the country where they found refuge, their skills and connections, and sheer luck. Some suffered dreadful hardships, whereas other did quite well in professional or business ventures. They all shared, however, a negative political experience, to wit, they found it even harder than their colleagues in Sardinia to preserve the prerevolutionary network of contacts. The one notable exception was a small group of militants whose devotion to Mazzini bordered on fanaticism. They followed *il Maestro* through Switzerland, France, and England without any thought of stable employment or normal family life. But for all their revolutionary zeal they, too, lost touch with their former supporters in their native cities or states. Other exiles wandered about Europe, not by choice but because no country would grant them political asylum. Gentilini eloquently expressed their plight to the Swiss gendarmes who arrested him in 1853: "Gentlemen, where do you expect me to go? In Piedmont they would hang me; France does not want me; Geneva drove me out. If the rest of Switzerland treats me with such humaneness, shall I have to jump in the lake?"[30]

At first sight, the literature of exile, to which the Risorgimento democrats contributed thousands of pathos-filled pages, seems to contradict the assertion that exile abroad was a negative political experience, that it disrupted the democratic networks. For even more than other exiles, the democrats studied here tended to cluster in relatively few cities (Marseilles, Paris, Brussels, London, Zurich, and Lugano) and there to live in the same neighborhoods where they patronized specific clubs and cafés. Nationality, language, and personal contacts made during the revolution drew them together. Indeed, to remain aloof from one's fellow exiles was regarded as a most deplorable form of eccentricity. Yet the interdependence and frequent intercourse that characterized the lives of the democratic exiles abroad did not generate solidarity and cooperation, but exactly the opposite. Having wandered about in exile since the early 1820s, La Cecilia understood the dynamics of these situations:

> Woe to him who distinguishes himself in a foreign land by virtue of his technical expertise or language proficiency, and who manages thereby to build a less squalid life for himself; he must endure the abuse and the importune demands of all those exiles who do not want to earn a decent living by their own work or who don't know how . . . Sons of the same lands, embittered by physical hardships, troubled by moral dilemmas, do not love one another, do not tolerate one another; on the contrary, they come to blows, they tear one another apart, they detest one another with a vengence.[31]

And indeed, by the mid-1850s the sixty-two democrats living abroad already fell into two groups roughly along the lines described by La Cecilia. Not only was there much animosity between haves and have-nots, but that animosity had obvious political implications. Mazzini was aware of this problem and tried his best to alleviate it. He warned that those who enjoyed security and stability in their adoptive lands should not forget their revolutionary goals; and that those suffering deprivation should not turn on fellow Italians but instead should appeal to their patriotism and generosity.[32]

Among the democrats in exile abroad no more than a dozen managed to avoid economic hardship and to keep up or to acquire business or professional skills that might be useful in normal times. This privileged group included the Lombards Giuseppe Ferrari, Frapolli, and De Cristoforis, who had professional training and also some independent means. The Ligurians Giovanni Battista Cuneo, Mosto, and Ghiglione, and the Livornese Lemmi and Andrea Sgarallino put to good use the commercial skills they had learned in their native port cities. But they were constantly on the move from the Middle East to England to the United States. If they did not go hungry, they were nevertheless periodically cut off from the main centers of political activity where fellow exiles continued with their work. The same was true of the fiery Bixio, whose only chance of avoiding both the Sardinian police and his creditors was to resume the seagoing life of his youth.

Exiles with the humanistic education but no specific skills tried desperately to get permanent teaching positions in the host countries. But even if they had the requisite language proficiency, the eager applicants found that it was nearly impossible to compete with qualified natives. Indeed, of the democrats studied here only two, Cattaneo and Saffi, were successful in the quest for permanent positions. The former became a highly regarded member of the faculty at the *liceo* of Lugano; the latter, thanks to his fluent English and appropriate social connections, taught Italian letters at Oxford University.

As La Cecilia observed, there were some exiles who might have earned a decent living by their own work but chose not to do so. Andreini was one such exile. He intermittently practiced medicine in Algeria, where his training was much in demand. But in March 1850, for instance, he was in Switzerland meeting with other revolutionaries. He wrote to a friend: "You know what a financial sacrifice is involved in my putting off my professional practice. But I swear to you that I would much rather die than abandon again the center of political events . . . which are imminent or at least not far away." Andreini deliberately chose to sacrifice his career and potential earnings to his political ideals partly because—as this letter indicates—he believed that a second European revolution was at hand.[33]

Both in France and in England the Roman Pianciani might have earned a living by applying the technical and managerial skills he acquired while helping his father and older brothers supervise the family's farms and textile mills in the Spoleto area. Instead, he devoted nearly all his time to political activities and to helping destitute fellow exiles. The allowance he received from his family was enough to cover his living expenses even after he married. To his father's dismay, for years he gave away or loaned what money he could spare. Two other democrats, Jacopo Sgarallino of Livorno and Angelo Usiglio of Modena (the "gentle Jew" of Mazzini's inner circle), were well versed in shipping and commerce; but they chose not to settle down to permanent jobs, working only when the wolf was at the door. Yet men like these, who became professional revolutionaries by choice abandoning or neglecting the pursuit of lucrative and respected careers, were the exception rather than the rule among the democrats studied here. At least fifty of the sixty-two men in exile abroad had no realistic prospects of steady employment and stable lives. They devoted all their energies and time to the revolution not only out of dedication but out of necessity. Only a second, successful Italian revolution could give them a chance to return to their homes and to live normal lives. Their predicament grew a little worse with each passing year, and their hopes for a favorable turn of the tide took on a messianic fervor.

From his room in a shabby Zurich boardinghouse De Boni thanked Mazzini, who had praised his revolutionary dedication: "Thank you for understanding the difference between myself and those [who preach] the cowardly line that revolutions are born spontaneously like mushrooms after a rain. Even if it were so, wouldn't the rain be necessary? I am forever a soldier of the revolution; of her I think, for her I work, for her I shall die . . . The revolution is a bride, and she does not allow divorce."[34] Statements like this appeared frequently in the correspondence of the democratic exiles abroad. They were usually made in good faith, but they were also rhetorical. De Boni's self-portrait as a soldier whose entire life was devoted to the revolution certainly corresponded to reality. But at the same time it was a convenient rationalization for the squalid aspects of that reality. It explained why he lived on the margin of Swiss society, without family or native friends and without a steady occupation. For De Boni as for many others, the reality of the 1850s was that they had nothing except their revolutionary enthusiasm to sustain them, to fill their days, to give them a sense of worth and purpose. What could this former seminarian and mediocre poet with a rudimentary knowledge of German offer Protestant, money-minded Zurich? The only jobs open to him, tutoring and translating, were hardly designed to facilitate his integration in Swiss society. For that matter, they were hardly sufficient to keep body and soul together. Similarly, Giuseppe Mazzoni found his formal education all but useless in Paris and concluded that it made no sense to try to survive by teaching Italian; he went to work for a winery instead. He was criticized, however, for this practical decision.[35]

Journalists, poets, and students whose education had been interrupted by the revolution, in addition to professional men unable to practice in a foreign country, competed with one another for lowly tutoring jobs and for an occasional book contract. In Lugano, Cattaneo enlisted several fellow exiles to work on the series *I documenti della guerra santa*, and he commissioned monographs on the revolution from a few others for the series *Archivio triennale delle cose d'Italia*. But his publishing company, the Tipografia Elvetica, was already in serious financial difficulties by 1853, when it was closed on government orders.

The exiles soon discovered that it was difficult to live by one's wits and that outside of Italy there was little interest in memoirs of the revolution. Thus, in June 1853 Quadrio informed a friend that he was "patiently mending the [Mazzinian] web" torn by the tragic events of February in Milan. But he was not sure that he would be able to stay in Neuchâtel: "I have looked for a job here, but haven't found one. Once in a while I write some damn thing for *L'Italia del popolo*, but I don't know yet whether it has been published . . . Someone suggested that I write a historical-critical history of the carbine; but the data on that subject are scattered through so many books that it would be impossible for me to consult them all, let alone buy them."[36] Other such literary plans foundered, and by 1854 Quadrio was again on the move and again writing home for money. In one Swiss village he slept in a room so cold that the water froze in his pitcher; during the day he was constantly surrounded by the numerous and noisy children of his host, who could afford to heat only one room. Yet difficult as his situation was, Quadrio at least had received help from his family throughout his long revolutionary career. Many of his colleagues were not so fortunate. Of the ninety-three democratic exiles studied here, Mazzini, Pianciani, Giuseppe Ferrari, Anelli, and perhaps two or three others received enough to cover their living expenses. But most democrats could not expect and did not receive that kind of help; indeed, given their modest social backgrounds, any amount they received entailed sacrifices on the part of relatives who had stayed in Italy. Thus, in September 1853 Crispi, by no means the poorest democratic exile, wrote from Malta that he was unable to leave "[that] accursed rock," having already spent the money his father had sent him. In November, although still stuck in Malta, he felt that he could no longer call on his family for help: "After such a long exile my fortune is exhausted; I have already asked too much of my family."[37]

Sometimes distance and suffering blinded the needy exiles to the sacrifices made on their behalf. Libertini, for instance, reproached his brother for not being generous enough even though the family had already incurred heavy expenses and debts during his trial in 1851–52. Most exiles experienced guilt more frequently than resentment, however, and they often went hungry rather than ask loved ones for yet more sacrifices.[38]

"No Hearth to Sit By": The Social Consequences of Defeat

Alone in a Lugano hotel room on New Year's Eve 1856, Cironi wrote: "Tonight everyone has a hearth by which to sit, a glass from which to drink, a hand to hold . . . here all is solitude and silence." He was one of many democrats separated from parents and siblings by the failure of revolution and denied a chance in the 1850s to marry and have a family of his own.[39]

At mid-nineteenth century, men from the middle and artisan classes, as most democrats were, achieved respectability and status vis-à-vis their kin and community first and foremost by finding gainful employment and, second, through stable family relationships, usually within the framework of marriage and child rearing. Before the revolution of 1848–49 as many as 20 percent of the democrats studied here departed from these accepted social norms. Their political interests and militancy resulted in interrupted education and careers and also in the disruption of family relationships because of arrest or exile. But in the 1850s what had previously happened only to the oldest and most conspicuous figures in the movement, such as Mazzini and Quadrio, became true of nearly all democrats, whether they were in prison, in hiding, or in exile.

The few exiles who had their families with them were the envy of their peers. But the emotional benefits they enjoyed were offset by the daily struggle for survival, made more difficult by the need to provide for wives and children. Even more trying was to be constantly reminded of their families' suffering. Having fled his native Piedmont, Reta complained, "I would not resent this unheard-of persecution if I were the only one to suffer. But to see my children's stunted growth and my wife's tears and pain puts me in a state of incredible anguish!"[40] Relationships between husbands and wives, already strained by the daily hardships, were made more difficult by the constant fear of unwanted births. Thus, announcing to Cattaneo that his common-law wife had given birth to a daughter, Pisacane mused, "For five years we managed to avoid making babies . . . but this time we really got ourselves into a bind!"[41]

If shared adversity led to tension within families, a long separation was also fraught with dangers. Inevitably, people and relationships became idealized and sometimes distorted through distance, time, and longing. Moreover, the distant exile was unable to perform his expected roles of husband and father, with consequences that could be most painful and disruptive. The experience of Savino Savini and his wife Teresa Mondini offers a good example of role changes and tensions brought on by prolonged separation. Although he was allowed to settle in Piedmont as early as 1851 and was able to find a teaching position there, Savini was unable to send for his family immediately. "Tisa" remained in Bologna with their daughters. At first she deferred to her husband in regard to the children's education and the management of family finances. But as time went on, she began to assert her independence. By 1853 she might have joined him in Piedmont, but she decided that it was better for the children not to leave Bologna. Although by all indications the Savinis had been very close before the revolution, they quarreled when she visited him in exile, and he found her neither as pretty nor as even-tempered as he had remembered her.[42]

Even in the absence of marital tension, many exiles wondered whether their children were receiving an adequate education and appropriate guidance. Giuseppe Mazzoni, lacking the means to send for his entire family, asked for his oldest child, Adele, "[whom he] wanted to get acquainted with." He did so not merely because he wanted the pleasure of her company, but "for the more important purpose of guiding her steps on the road to economic self-sufficiency."[43]

Whether in prison or in exile, the democrats seldom expressed doubts about the political education of their children. They trusted their spouses and relatives to instill in the younger generation the same values and pride that they had internalized themselves in the 1830s and 1840s. Rather, they worried about practical matters, as Mazzoni's remarks about his daughter's future suggest. They expected their children to do even better than they had done themselves; yet they knew that their families' prospects for economic and social advancement had been hurt by political defeat. Only a successful new phase of the revolution could redress the balance in their favor.

Unmarried exiles were free from such social pressures, but they were often desperately lonely. They became very susceptible to romantic involvements that usually ended in emotional disaster. Orsini and Cironi competed for the affections of the redoubtable Emma Herwegh; and Dall'Ongaro, after years of worshipping the memory of his beloved Giulia Dandolo, had a stormy affair with an actress. When she pressed for marriage and urged him to give up politics, he, too, invoked the imagery of the revolution as a jealous bride demanding absolute devotion: "Your reasoning would be perfect if we were both just beginning our [respective] careers. But I have a past that binds me. I cannot abandon my cause even in the wake of disastrous defeat. Neither you, nor Giulia, if she came back to life, nor a thousand Giulias could make me [do that]. Italy's soil has been stained by the blood of my two brothers and by my own. That spilled blood is a pact of death."[44] The feelings of those democrats who renounced the joys of the hearth and the pursuit of social respectability for the revolution's sake are expressed even more eloquently by Giovanni Ruffini's fictional alter ego in his novel *Doctor Antonio*. Reunited after many years with the aristocratic Englishwoman he loves and had once wanted to marry, Antonio is torn between his love for her and his commitment to the revolution. He decides at last: "Lucy, I love you . . . I shall love you to my grave. But my country has claims on me prior to yours . . . Let me redeem that pledge . . . help me to be worthy of you and myself."[45]

These were powerful statements of revolutionary self-denial reminiscent of the values Mazzini had espoused since youth. Without either denying their rhetorical effectiveness or impugning their sincerity, however, it must be said that such statements did not reflect the attitudes of most democratic leaders in the 1850s. In their correspondence and diaries, expressions of concern for their own survival and for the future of their families occur more often than heroic pronouncements à la Doctor Antonia. The democrats saw themselves as victims and martyrs, seldom as heroes. And although they were dedicated to the revolutionary transformation of Italian politics and society, they were not at all blind to the economic and social implications of revolutionary defeat. By the mid-1850s, the key questions for many of them were how to turn hardships and sacrifices into political assets and how to halt the deterioration of their social and economic position.

Democrats at the Crossroads, 1856–1859

In September 1855 one of the republican heroes of 1848, Daniele Manin, asked his friend Valerio, then editor of *Il diritto*, to publish the following statement: "The republican party, so cruelly slandered, once again gives evidence of self-abnegation and willingness to sacrifice for the national cause. Convinced that Italy must be made, that this is the most urgent and most important issue, it tells the House of Savoy: 'Make Italy, and I am with you; if not, not.' And it tells the moderate liberals: 'Think of making Italy, not of enlarging Piedmont; be Italians, not purveyors of municipalism, and I am with you; if not, not.'"[46] The "slander" to which Manin referred were the rumors of a Muratist conspiracy in the Kingdom of the Two Sicilies that were published in the French and British press. The replacement of the Bourbon dynasty by a constitutional monarchy under Prince Lucien Murat was actually the brainchild of the southern exile Aurelio Saliceti, who was once very close to Mazzini. But other democratic exiles in Paris, especially Ricciardi and Manin himself, had been mentioned in this connection as well. Defending himself from such allegations, Manin argued that if the political regeneration of Italy had to take place under the leadership of a king, that king could only be Victor Emmanuel II of Sardinia, who was independent of foreign powers and who had proved himself trustworthy as a constitutional ruler.

Manin's statement concerning the House of Savoy and its potential leadership role in Italy echoed the views of his friend Giorgio Pallavicino. Speaking for many moderate liberal exiles, that Lombard patrician had written as early as 1851: "[Italy] needs soldiers, not Mazzinian verbiage. Piedmont has soldiers and guns. Therefore, I am a Piedmontese. Piedmont is a monarchy by ancient tradition, by inclination, by duty. Therefore, I am not a republican."[47] Given Manin's reputation as a revolutionary leader and his impeccable (if perhaps outmoded) republican credentials, his acceptance of the moderate liberal program marked a significant development in the history of the democratic movement. His statement published in *Il diritto* brought into the public eye a controversy that had already taken shape among democratic leaders and that ultimately led to a cleavage between supporters of the "Piedmontese solution" and intransigent republicans.

From 1849 until the spring of 1853, nearly all the democrats studied here believed—as did Mazzini—that the restored Italian governments would not be able to maintain themselves in power and that mounting national unrest would paralyze the Habsburg Empire, making it impossible for its armies to intervene again in Italy. The democrats' task, as they saw it, was to help one another withstand defeat and repression and to keep in touch with their political bases in their respective towns and regions. In practice this proved extremely difficult to do, despite the founding of new propaganda organizations such as Mazzini's Italian National Committee and the gathering of money and weapons for a new revolutionary war. The diaspora of democratic leaders in the 1850s and the difficulties they encountered in Sardinia, if indeed they were allowed to enter her borders at all, undermined their efforts to preserve their political networks. Moreover, with the passing of time, prison and exile took their toll of even the most dedicated and energetic men.

By 1853 not a few militants felt that they were wasting their lives in poverty and idleness while their country remained under the heel of conservative governments and of a foreign power. Desperate to break the stalemate and to see action again, they took chances, and they failed. The most notable democratic failure was the Milanese uprising of February 1853. Despite Mazzini's misgivings, activists of every stripe and from every region flocked to Lombardy or to nearly Canton Ticino to take part in a replay, on a larger scale, of the Five Days of Milan. But the circumstances of the uprising were entirely different from those of March 1848. Men like Bertani, De Cristoforis, and Pezzotti who had mediated between their own social class and the lower-class insurgents in 1848 were now dead or in exile. Thus, the uprising never spread beyond the two or three popular quarters where Mazzinian propaganda had been particularly effective, and it was easily crushed.[48]

For a brief period in 1854–55, Giuseppe Ferrari and a few others placed their hopes for a European revolution in the ominous unfolding of the Near Eastern crisis. They hoped, above all, that Austria might become involved in that crisis and eventually go to war with France. By the spring of 1856, however, they realized that the revolutionary millennium was not at hand and that new approaches were needed to insure their individual and collective survival. Some concluded, as did Manin, that a renewed war against Austria could not be fought without a sanctuary and a well-equipped army. But if they wanted an alliance, even an informal one, with the government that controlled that sanctuary (Sardinia) and that army, they had to be prepared to pay a price. At the very least, they had to be prepared to renounce republican and egalitarian principles, which were anathema to Victor Emmanuel, and also to renounce their designs for social change, of which the moderate liberals were extremely suspicious.

Not counting the men of the Piedmontese parliamentary Left, who had already made their peace with the king and his liberal ministry, about twenty-five of the democrats studied here followed Manin's initiative between 1856 and 1858. During the latter part of 1858, as Cavour spun the diplomatic web that kept Austria on edge and set the stage for war, these men joined the Piedmontese army. If they could not join, they showed in other ways their willingness to accept as a necessary step toward unification what Cattaneo in 1848 had called "the royal war." Having thus shared with Cavour and the

Italian National Society the risk of failure in 1858–59, they were on hand in 1860 to share the fruits of success.

These democratic supporters of "the royal war," however, were outnumbered by fellow democrats who wanted no compromise with monarchy and moderate liberalism. From exile and prison, the militants urged instead renewed efforts to exploit the economic and social grievances of the lower classes and to overthrow the existing Italian governments through terrorism and armed insurrection. Their message was translated into action by Mario, Nicotera, and other exiles in Genoa, who in 1857 helped Pisacane organize a military expedition to the Kingdom of the Two Sicilies. Pisacane and his fellow conspirators hoped to take advantage of the democratic networks preserved in Naples by the clandestine efforts of Albini, Fanelli, Mosciaro, and others. These networks were to provide the backbone of an uprising in the Cilento, Basilicata, and Calabria, the areas of greatest democratic activity in 1848. Meanwhile, other militants were to incite popular rebellions in Tuscany and in Genoa.[49]

Named after the place where the insurgents clashed with Bourbon troops, the Sapri expedition epitomized the condition of the democratic movement in the late 1850s. The few militants who had managed to stay at large did have a following among the masses, but they needed weapons and supplies from the outside in order to attempt insurrection. When help came, however, they refused to follow the initiatives of the "outsiders" who provided it, even when these happened to be native sons like Pisacane and Nicotera who were returning from exile. As for those who returned, they sought positions of leadership at least in part as compensation for years of poverty and isolation. But they found it difficult to work with fellow militants who had remained on the scene during the 1850s. Even worse, they found that in only a few years the people of their cities or regions had forgotten them and cared but little about their political martyrdom.

By 1859 those who still refused to compromise with the liberal monarchy discovered that there were only two other alternatives for survival. One was to abandon political activity altogether and to try to recoup the losses of the 1850s in some other way. The second was to return home and resume the patient organizational work of the 1840s, with an eye to finding supporters for a future challenge to the moderate liberals. There was, however, a basic difference between the 1840s and the 1860s. In the late 1840s, Italians of all social classes and backgrounds had identified with the challenge to the Old Regime. But a challenge to the national and constitutional monarchy born in 1860 could only come from the most politically and economically disadvantaged groups in Italian society. To succeed, then, the democratic activists of the 1860s had to be prepared to do grass-root political work among these groups, both in the cities and in the countryside. At the long-awaited moment of national unification the democrats who had survived both the revolution and the ordeal of the 1850s examined these options and made their political choices.

8

Loyal Opposition: The Democratic Presence in the National Parliament, 1860–1876

OF THE democrats studied here, 127 survived the so-called decade of preparation preceding Italy's unification, and 122 of them lived long enough beyond 1860 to have postunification political careers. To these men fell the task of making new choices and redefining the goals of the democratic movement in the age of moderate liberal hegemony. It was a formidable task made more difficult by their individual and collective experiences of the 1850s. Yet it had to be faced because — as the democrats saw it — the revolution was unfinished. Moreover, renewed political activism in different forms and under different circumstances seemed the best and, for some, the only way to become reintegrated into the mainstream of Italian society. For those democrats who had supported Manin's statement and later cooperated with the moderate Italian National Society (SNI), reentry and adaptation presented few problems. By 1856–57 they had already subordinated their democratic ideals to the desire for national unity, and in 1860–61 they were content or resigned to work within political institutions shaped and dominated by their liberal adversaries. Most democrats, however, though they participated in the war of 1859 and led the liberation of southern Italy, had neither committed themselves to the goals of the SNI nor accepted the creation of a unified Italy as the concluding episode of the Italian Revolution. Reluctantly, they made their choices in the early 1860s.

In April 1860, immediately following elections to the first Italian Parliament, Giuseppe Ferrari urged his friend Cattaneo to leave Lugano and to take his seat among Italy's new leaders. Cattaneo's editorials were good, he added, but they could not substitute for "the legitimate, solemn, sovereign acts of sitting, speaking, and voting in Parliament."[1] Ferrari acknowledged that the new Parliament did not represent all regions of Italy, for Venetia remained under Habsburg rule and the presence of French troops in Rome assured the continued existence of the temporal power; and that it certainly did not represent the Italian people, even indirectly, for literacy, property requirements, and sex barriers denied suffrage to 98 percent of the population in national elections. But even if it was a far cry from a truly national, democratic assembly, Ferrari argued, the new Parliament was the only important forum for the discussion of national issues, if not for their resolution. Thus, a democratic presence there was very important even if it was destined to remain small.[2]

Most of the democrats studied here agreed with Ferrari's arguments and sought ways to contribute to that democratic presence by seeking election to Parliament. But they experienced considerable difficulties as a result of their radical ideas and of their isolation and poverty in the preceding decade. These difficulties were not obvious at the moment of unification; the democrats, in fact, did well in the elections of March 1860. Of the 122 men who survived beyond 1860, 65 were elected to the national Parliament, and an additional seven who had served in the Sardinian Parliament were reelected. Returning exiles and liberated prisoners jumped to hasty conclusions about their prospects. This initial success led them to believe that political careers might be built upon a record of revolutionary dedication and sacrifices, and that in the eyes of the electorate these might offset the radicalism of their ideas, their lack of wealth and social standing, and their legislative inexperience. However, the elections of 1861 — the first ones held after the annexation of the Bourbon Kingdom — dispelled such illusions.[3] Montanelli and seven others who had served in the Seventh Legislature were not reelected; and several democrats entering the contest for the first time were denied nomination or election. Ultimately, only 54

(44.3 percent) of the 122 democrats in question gained significant experience in parliamentary politics, meaning they served at least two
terms in the Chamber of Deputies between 1861 and 1876. Of these,
only 39 made more than a marginal contribution to the political
debates and legislation of that period. The remaining 68 democrats
either chose to leave the political arena altogether or formed a variety of extraparliamentary organizations. Differences between the
two groups became deeper with time, and there were moments of
tension that threatened the always precarious unity of Risorgimento
democracy. But there was also much interaction; at least a dozen
democrats moved back and forth with ease between terms in Parliament and leadership roles in the Società operaie or in the various
committees for the liberation of Rome and Venice. Moreover, in
1862, 1867, and 1870 several deputies left their posts to join
Garibaldi's guerrilla forces in defiance of the royal government. Indeed, until the liberation of Rome, and in some cases even later, the
democrats remained torn between a new role as "loyal opposition"
to the liberal governments and the old, familiar one as revolutionary
activists.

Democrats and the "Forced Labor" of Italian Politics

Ambivalence and uneasiness were the outstanding features of the
democrats' parliamentary behavior in the 1860s. Most of the fifty-
four democrats who had substantial parliamentary careers agreed
with Ferrari in theory on the importance of "sitting, speaking, and
voting" in the first elected assembly of united Italy. And most of
them were conscientious in the discharge of their duties toward the
districts that had elected them. In practice, though, personal and
political factors often combined to make them feel uncomfortable
with this new role. It was certainly not one for which their previous
experiences had prepared them.

Except for a few men of scholarly inclination like Ferrari and for
those who had served in the Sardinian legislature, the democrats
had developed a political style that was difficult to reconcile with
the requirements of parliamentary life. Socialized at an early age
within the milieu of secret societies, they had learned to be fiercely
loyal to fellow members and to subordinate their own interests to
higher collective goals. The were not psychologically prepared for
parliamentary politics which required constant give-and-take with
men of opposing views. Their tendency toward intransigent, even
dogmatic behavior was enhanced in the 1860s by their precarious
position as a small minority in Parliament. Those who had fought on

the barricades or headed revolutionary governments in 1848–49 found the routine of parliamentary debates, committee meetings, and caucuses unexciting by comparison. Moreover, their backgrounds and the experiences of the 1850s had not equipped them to deal with the complexities of the legislative process. Some democratic deputies discovered that even legal training per se was of little help in the absence of legislative or administrative experience.[4]

This difficult adjustment to parliamentary politics and to moderate liberal hegemony was often compounded by serious financial pressures. In an age when deputies were expected to serve without salaries or even expense accounts, a parliamentary career placed a considerable burden on all but the wealthiest men. Among the moderate liberal majority there were many deputies who sacrificed potential earnings and material comfort for the sake of politics; but the pressures and sacrifices were even greater for the men of the democratic minority, given their more modest socioeconomic conditions and the years they had spent in prison or exile.

Of the fifty-four democrats who served for two or more terms, at least thirty experienced serious economic difficulties. Acerbi was one of these men, having been disinherited by his father for his role in the revolution of 1848–49. Antonio Mordini, Crispi, Calvino, Mauro, and several others could no longer expect subsidies from their families, to whom they had turned all too often during the terrible 1850s. Like fellow democrats who had been born poor, they were forced now to live by their wits. The ideal solution for them was to combine a political career with compatible professional activities such as writing and newspaper editing, teaching, or a legal or medical practice. But this was easier said than done. Quite aside from the demands it made on a man's time and energy, a dual career could be pursued successfully only by those who had the requisite education and experience. Here again the democrats were handicapped by their political backgrounds. Men like Guerrazzi, for example, whose law practice had been erratic and frequently interrupted by political difficulties, could not easily compete with other professionals of more stable backgrounds and established reputations.[5]

Democrats who were basically men of letters were in an even less enviable situation. In the 1860s there was no dearth of outlets for their ideas and writing talents, for every major Italian city had democratic newspapers; and there was also a certain market for historical and autobiographical works. However, though political journalism and the writing of popular history were eminently compatible with a parliamentary career, they were hardly lucrative. To make matters worse, the democratic deputies who tried to earn a living at this sort of thing soon discovered that they were competing with one another and with fellow democrats outside of Parliament. Such was the case for fifteen democratic deputies whose economic plight was especially severe.

Poverty periodically forced Friscia, Zuppetta, and others to resign their mandate, but they ran again whenever their financial circumstances improved or when they found generous sponsors. This pattern made it more difficult for them to make an impact on their colleagues when they did serve in Parliament; it also made them less than effective in meeting the demands of their constituents. Even deputies who served their full terms were often absent from parliamentary sessions and caucus meetings because they could not afford the high rents in the postunification capitals. At least one democrat who could boast a better-than-average attendance record, Salvatore Morelli, solved this problem by sleeping in the first-class railroad cars in which, as a deputy, he was entitled to travel.[6] But Morelli was younger than most of his colleagues, and single. His spartan solution was hardly appropriate for middle-aged men whose health had been wrecked by war injuries or the hardships of the 1850s; and it was obviously impossible for those who wished to have their families with them.

In the early 1860s several of the democrats studied here were able to marry and have a family of their own, thus realizing aspirations suppressed and deferred in the years of revolutionary militancy. They typically married women much younger than themselves and therefore had young families to support. This was a problem for all those who remained politically active, but it was particularly true for the deputies. It was too expensive for many of them to find adequate lodgings for the entire family (they could manage in rented rooms or hotels when they were alone) and too difficult to live apart from loved ones for weeks and even months on end. Those who had suffered through years of loneliness and separation from their families were particularly reluctant to repeat the experience. In sum, for many democrats the need to earn a living and the desire to enjoy the long-denied pleasures of domesticity undermined a genuine desire to serve their country and to reap some rewards for the years of struggle and martyrdom.[7] But the democrats' ambivalence toward parliamentary politics went well beyond these personal factors. It was rooted in their assessment of Italy's domestic and international situation in the first decade after unification. This assessment influenced the behavior of nearly all the democratic deputies, including men like Ferrari and Cattani-

Cavalcanti who were not burdened by financial or family pressures.

First, the democrats were uneasy with the undemocratic character of the new political institutions. In many ways the national Parliament and the monarchical government of the 1860s did not match the expectations of even the most moderate among them. Although those who ran for Parliament clearly had made their peace with Cavour's foreign policy and with the monarchy, they maintained strong reservations about the system they had pledged to support.

The highly restricted franchise was, of course, a major source of difficulties for them. Whereas other countries in western Europe were moving perceptibly closer to universal manhood suffrage, united Italy started out with laws similar to those of Orleanist France or late-eighteenth-century England. Despite democratic efforts, there was no significant change until 1882. In the 1860s and early 1870s the democrats in Parliament would certainly have settled for a moderate reform of the existing laws. No more than half of them ever advocated the immediate introduction of universal manhood suffrage, and fewer still favored voting rights for women. Given their social backgrounds and philosophical convictions, they were, however, essentially united in opposition to the existing property requirements which the moderates deemed necessary to preserve social stability. Those requirements denied the vote to thousands of lower-class men who had proved their patriotism and political maturity during the struggle for Italian independence. The democrats were eager to change this state of affairs, not only because they regarded it as blatantly unjust but also because they expected to benefit from an expansion of the suffrage.[8]

Not expecting immediate results yet hoping for a long-range victory, the democratic deputies pursued a dual strategy. On the one hand, year after year they introduced suffrage reform bills in Parliament and sought the support of sympathetic liberals. On the other, they joined extraparliamentary colleagues in organizing rallies, petitions, and press campaigns aimed at sensitizing and arousing public opinion. The latter of these two approaches was the more fruitful even though it was a source of occasional disagreements between deputies and extraparliamentary activists. Participation in these political activities outside of Parliament placed a considerable burden on the deputies' time and energy, for they were expected to undertake speaking tours around the country and to produce an endless stream of articles and pamphlets.

Nor was this all that was expected of them. Ideological considerations as well as political expediency dictated that they behave like "deputies-at-large" of the disenfranchised majority of Italians. This meant, in a general sense, that they were expected to speak out against the class-bound social and economic policies of the ruling liberal elite. Specifically, it meant that year after year they were called upon to heed and, if possible, to help redress the grievances of hundreds of individuals, associations, and even municipalities. All deputies received such requests for help; but the democratic ones could least afford to ignore them, for they, and not their liberal colleagues, had gone on record defending the right of all citizens to participate in the life of the new state. Again, this need to be accessible and responsive to disenfranchised petitioners meant more work, especially for those who could not afford to hire a staff.

Other reasons for the democratic deputies' discomfort with the existing institutions were the liberals' socially unprogressive economic policy and an ecclesiastical policy generally perceived in the democratic camp as too timid and conciliatory. In these areas, too, the democratic deputies combined efforts to influence national legislation with activities designed to inform, persuade, and activate public opinion. The relative harmony of opinion that existed among them on these issues was undermined by a conflict, however— resolved only in 1870—between their desire to discharge their parliamentary duties responsibly and their conviction that an unfinished national revolution still held the promise of democratic victories. A democratic initiative led by one of the movement's most famous men had liberated the South in 1860. Similar initiatives, some argued, might be taken to liberate Venetia and Rome. This time, however, precautions would be taken to see that Garibaldi was not duped again by the liberals, to make sure that democratic initiatives and victories turned into long-lasting benefits for the movement. Not all democratic deputies subscribed to this point of view, but there was enough support for it to cause a series of political crises from 1862 to 1867 that divided the democratic minority and impaired its effectiveness.

Loyal Opposition versus Garibaldini

On August 1, 1862, the routine business of the Chamber of Deputies was interrupted by reports that three members of the democratic minority, Calvino, Fabrizi, and Mordini, had been arrested in Naples on extremely serious charges. According to the Rattazzi government then in office, the three had aided and abetted Garibaldi's plan to raise a revolutionary army and to march with it on Rome. The arrest immediately became a cause célèbre because all deputies understood its implications for the principle of parliamentary immunity. One of the Chamber's distinguished jurists, the liberal Mancini, demanded an investigation that eventually cleared his democratic colleagues. The three, who were respected in the democratic camp for their impeccable revolutionary credentials, had traveled to the South not to join Garibaldi but to urge him to beware of the king's and Urbano Rattazzi's apparent willingness to look the other way while he conquered Rome.[9]

For the Rattazzi government the investigation led to political disaster, not only because it was shown to have violated parliamentary immunity and arrested innocent men but also because its previous dealings with Garibaldi were exposed. Nevertheless, the government did have a case. If the three deputies in question were innocent of any wrongdoing, the same could not be said of Garibaldi himself and of other democrats in the Chamber. They had indeed surrendered, not for the last time, to the lure of a continuing revolution. The discredited Rattazzi was hardly in a position to bring them to task. Instead, this unpleasant but necessary chore fell upon the leaders of the democratic minority in the Chamber, especially Crispi and Ferrari.

Named after the Calabrian mountainside where royal troops stopped Garibaldi, the Aspromonte affair forced the parliamentary democrats to debate and reconsider their position. A major speech by Ferrari set the framework for the debate. The democratic deputies, he argued, could not have it both ways. They could not remain conspirators and rebels and still be effective and responsible legislators, "deputies-at-large" of the Italian masses, and future ministers. In 1859–60 Ferrari had greeted with enthusiasm the participation of volunteer units in the Lombard campaign and in Garibaldi's daring expedition. At that time he had hoped that the popularity of Garibaldi himself and of other democratic leaders might offset the undeniable political and diplomatic achievements of Cavour and his supporters. This had not happened, and Italy was created in the liberals' image. The democrats were under no obligation to approve of the existing institutions, however. Indeed, many forms of political activity could be carried on outside of and in opposition to those institutions, for instance, educating Italian workers to republican and egalitarian principles through the Società operaie. There was, Ferrari thought, a fundamental difference between those democratic activists who had chosen to work through extraparliamentary institutions and those, like himself, who had taken their seats in the national Parliament. Having accepted the parliamentary mandate and sworn to respect the monarchical constitution, the democratic deputies were now bound to work within the existing institutions. Again, this did not mean approval or even supine acceptance of the status quo. Institutions and policies could, after all, be changed, even if the only appropriate role for the democratic deputies was that of loyal opposition to the king's government. This point of view was lucidly expressed by Ferrari's friend Angelo Bargoni, who wrote to a fellow democrat, "Mazzini, as usual, confuses the moderate party which is now in power with the form of government per se. The former we can oppose and try our damnedest to overthrow; but the latter we must respect as the expression of that original will that emerged from the plebiscites proposed and advocated by Garibaldi and by ourselves."[10] Bargoni and Ferrari conceded that they and their fellow democrats were unaccustomed to the role of the loyal opposition; yet they insisted that it was the only role compatible with the parliamentary mandate. For the remainder of the decade they distinguished themselves both as severe critics of the liberal governments and as the chief proponents of the concept of loyal opposition among their fellow democrats. They had the support of two leftist groups in the Chamber, about thirty colleagues altogether. Among these were several deputies who had previously served in the Sardinian legislature, as well as the chief contributors to Bargoni's reformist newspaper, *Il diritto*. But Bargoni and Ferrari were never able to bring all of the democratic deputies around to their point of view.

Again and again several democratic deputies were lured away from their seats by the prospect of successful revolutionary coups de main. Participation in rallies, demonstrations, and plans for future insurrections in Italy and the Balkans led them to neglect their duties to their constituents and to miss important committee meetings and debates in the Chamber. Many factors accounted for this ambivalent attitude toward the parliamentary mandate. Not the least of these was the political style of several democrats which had been shaped by past experiences of conspiracy and even terrorism. But democratic solidarity also played a part in the divided loyalties of some deputies on the Left. Resignation or the threat of it, absences from the Chamber, and neglect of committee assignments—in short, all the actions Ferrari described as irresponsible—on close inspection often turned out to be forms of protest against the treatment accorded to fellow democrats outside of Parliament. Thus, for instance, a conscientious and effective deputy like Bertani resorted to resignation in December 1863 only after several unsuccessful appeals to the government to stop harassing members of the Genoese democratic club Solidarietà democratica.

The organizers of this club, republicans like Bertani himself, had helped him and other exiles during the 1850s, and thus he felt a special obligation to them.[11]

Garibaldi's charismatic personality was another powerful influence on the behavior of the parliamentary democrats. In the 1860s Garibaldi replaced Mazzini as the symbol of democratic ideology and the fountainhead of democratic initiatives. Modest to a fault and conscious of his own intellectual limitations, Garibaldi did not seek this honor. It was thrust upon him almost inevitably by his memorable deeds of 1860 and also by the continued absence from Italy of Mazzini, whose youthful rebellion against the House of Savoy had been neither forgotten nor forgiven. Although he served in the national Parliament, Garibaldi had mixed feelings about it from the beginning; he did not think it capable of completing Italy's territorial unification, much less of establishing a truly secular and democratic society. Moreover, he nursed a personal grudge against Cavour and his successors for having ceded his beloved Nice to France in 1860. Whenever he attacked the liberals or expressed skepticism about the existing political institutions, his speeches were reported in the democratic press and discussed at every street corner. And, conversely, whenever the country faced a crisis a thousand voices called for the Lion of Caprera once again to take the bold initiatives that the liberal governments were unable or unwilling to take. Those democrats who were themselves reluctant deputies, or whose seats were not secure, were too easily tempted to join (and perhaps also to manipulate) the popular enthusiasm for and trust in Garibaldi. Indeed, so great was the appeal of this unconventional hero to fellow democrats that in the 1860s the proponents of loyal opposition pleaded with him from time to time to respect the existing institutions and to become a symbol of democratic unity and responsibility instead of a catalyst for divisions and adventurism.[12] Their arguments, though, fell largely on deaf ears. Throughout the decade Garibaldi remained at the center of all attempts to resume a revolutionary war and, in general, of discontent and agitation against the liberal regime. He exercised a leadership of sorts, but his leadership generally had a negative effect on parliamentary democracy. One democrat who understood only too well Garibaldi's limitations as a political leader, yet continued to follow him, thus explained the situation:

> The Italian [national] movement . . . lacks a revolutionary ideology; this country is conscious neither of its rights nor of its duties; a vague idea of unity inspires it, but it is not ac-

companied by any other principles. All it knows how to do is
to personalize principles. Not all that long ago Bonaparte
embodied its principles; yesterday it was Cavour's turn; today it is Garibaldi's. Should [the Italian movement] lose
Garibaldi, it would lose its principles; then it might find
them again in Bonaparte or in one of his lackeys. As long as
this goes on Garibaldi is indispensable. And we, who would
much prefer to put in his place the whole people as the em-
bodiment [of the national movement], are forced for lack of
anything better to hang on to his coattails.[13]

By the end of 1863 even the most zealous *garibaldini* had to
agree with Ferrari that the democratic group in Parliament had
been lamentably ineffective. Possible remedies for this problem were
debated at length in a series of caucus meetings in November and
December 1863. While Ferrari, Bargoni, Gaspare Marsico, and
others hammered away at the need for responsible legislative
behavior and constructive counterproposals to the government's
program, twelve of their colleagues introduced a motion calling for
the resignation en masse of the democratic minority. Frustrated by
their inability to modify the government's policy of harsh repression
in the South and by what they viewed as a too timid foreign policy,
these mavericks argued that the cause of Italian democracy could
best be served by mass agitation outside of Parliament. To buttress
their argument, they cited the success of recent democrat-sponsored
mass rallies, such as the one in support of the Polish insurrection
against Russia. Attendance at such rallies had been very good; hundreds of people turned out to hear prominent democrats like Cairoli
and Ferrari and contributed money for the Polish cause. Moreover,
the young Bergamo democrat Francesco Nullo had organized a
volunteer force to fight in Poland. His death on the plains of eastern Europe had provided just the example demcratic orators needed
to contrast the international and heroic dimensions of their movement with the seemingly prosaic and narrow concerns of the liberals.[14]

These events and the success of the Società operaie in several
regions suggested that the democratic leadership had a much larger
potential following than its token presence in the national Parliament indicated. Thus, it seemed logical to try to tap that potential
and to use it as leverage to obtain major institutional reforms, beginning with more democratic electoral laws. A motion sponsored by
Ferrari and Bargoni ("The Left shall not desert its post") defeated
others that called for mass resignation. But even so, the Chamber

lost such well-known democratic leaders as Garibaldi, Bertani, Mario, Friscia, and Luigi La Porta.

Whether or not the defection of these frustrated deputies helped the work of extraparliamentary activists was a matter of considerable debate at the time, and its effect remains unclear. There can be little doubt, however, that the resignations weakened the democratic position in Parliament at a time when such critical national issues were being discussed as the repression of peasant unrest and banditry in the South, and the transfer of the capital from Turin to Florence. Bertani, an advocate of mass resignation in 1863, wrote two years later that he regretted his participation in the democratic schism, and he added, "Amidst shifting factions and conflicting ideas, it is easy to agree that nowadays a democratic nucleus, firm in its beliefs and bold in its initiatives, can hardly be in a more favorable position to help the country than to sit in the new Parliament representing the people, despite the restricted suffrage."[15]

Three or four years ealier Bargoni and Ferrari had presented precisely the same arguments; but despite Bertani's "conversion," not until the end of the decade did some of those who had resigned even attempt to return to the fold. On the whole, from the Aspromonte affair to the liberation of Rome, the democratic deputies were divided in their evaluation of parliamentary politics as an effective vehicle for change. What was worse, they were often unable to develop well-coordinated strategies around issues on which an ideological consensus obviously existed. One example illustrates particularly well these characteristics of democratic political behavior in the 1860s.

In 1862–63 democratic deputies distinguished themselves in the attempt to understand the phenomenon of banditry as an expression of the social and economic realities of the South instead of dismissing it as a result of bad administrations or, even more simplistically, of Bourbon loyalist machinations. Northern democrats like Saffi and Sirtori, who had once believed in that great Risorgimento myth of a prosperous South badly governed by corrupt despots, were disabused of such illusions by the first-hand observations of their colleagues Bixio, Mordini, and Ferrari. The major contribution the northern democrats made to the analysis of the problem contrasted, however, with their almost total lack of suggestions for solutions. The liberals' reply to banditry was the Pica Bill, passed in August 1863, which imposed a virtual state of siege on some southern regions. The democrats unanimously condemned repression as an inadequate response to the crisis; indeed, they saw it as a probable catalyst of further violence. Consistent with this position, Mordini introduced a major amendment to the bill that tied the implementation of repressive measures to the allocation of funds for public works. Modest though this proposal was, it might have altered the bill significantly and set a precedent for a more enlightened policy in areas where disaffection against the new state ran high. But Mordini's colleagues, already torn by the debate over resignation, failed to rally behind him. Their failure to act in this instance created the impression — as false as it was harmful to them — that the democratic deputies cared no more than the liberals about the poor and the oppressed. Embittered and worried about possible political repercussions, Mordini attributed this state of affairs to the waning of democratic solidarity. His former comrades in revolution, he observed, no longer seemed to remember the shared dreams and dangers of earlier years.[16]

Other opportunities to live up to democratic ideology were missed in similar fashion during annual debates on fiscal policy, on the disposal of ecclesiastical lands, and on education. These were the issues that most affected the lives of the disenfranchised masses in the 1860s. They were also issues on which the parliamentary democrats generally agreed. Yet ideological consensus was seldom translated into tactical agreements.

Personal animosities and lack of legislative experience were responsible in part for such self-defeating behavior. The inevitable pessimism that came from being faced with almost certain defeat contributed as well. Above all, though, the democrats often failed to act together in responding to liberal policies or in taking legislative initiatives because the members of the loyal opposition felt that they could not trust those colleagues infected with "the disease of Garibaldism," as Ferrari called it. That disease, which introduced a note of drama and excitement to the otherwise drab world of parliamentary politics, flared up in 1866 when some democratic deputies left their seats to aid Garibaldi's attempt to liberate the Trentino, and again in 1867 when they joined his last attempt to take Rome. Those deputies who distrusted the *garibaldini* in their midst hoped that the completed territorial unification would put an end to the ambivalent, even irresponsible behavior of the parliamentary Left. Although to some extent their hopes were fulfilled, "Garibaldism" remained a force in democratic politics long after Garibaldi's death.

Antidotes for Garibaldism

Throughout the early 1860s the proponents of loyal opposition realized that the "Garibaldian disease" could not be fought only with impassioned speeches on the floor of the Chamber or appeals to personal friends. Strategies and structures had to be devised for that purpose, and they were. In the process of trying to achieve unity and discipline, the members of the loyal opposition took significant steps toward the creation of a modern political party. They obtained only modest results in the immediate postunification years, but they set a significant example and precedent for the post-Risorgimento generation of leftist politicians.

The democratic caucus which met almost daily when the Chamber was in session was created by and critically important to the loyal opposition. In the 1860s it was also convened between sessions whenever some major issue required discussion and action. No minutes of these meetings have survived, and in all likelihood none were kept. The meetings took place in the offices of the best-known deputies of the Left or occasionally in private homes. The number of deputies present varied from day to day, but it is clear that attendance was expected. Indeed, the organizers of the caucus regarded a colleague's attendance record as a fair indication of his commitment to the parliamentary mandate. Attempts were made to persuade recalcitrant colleagues to participate. When persuasion did not work, the caucus leaders were able in some cases to bring political pressure to bear. They could, for instance, refuse to support a colleague's candidacy in the next elections, or they might use their influence with some ministry to see that he or his constituents were denied favors. But the effectiveness of the caucus in the elaboration of coherent positions on political issues depended more on the attitude of its individual members than on their numbers. At its worst, the caucus was merely a debating society or social club for deputies of roughly similar views; at its best, however, it was a forum for new ideas and also a stage where attacks on liberal policies were planned and rehearsed. The caucus clearly served this function in 1868–69 when democratic deputies, in a rare moment of tactical unity, planned an all-out effort against the unpopular and regressive grist tax. The caucus chose the keynote speakers from among many willing candidates, and it sketched the outline of the arguments they were to present on its behalf.[17]

Not surprisingly, in the early 1860s the democratic caucus was led by Piedmontese deputies like Depretis and Sineo who had served in the Sardinian Parliament before 1860, or by men from other regions who had been closely associated with them during the years of exile. Among the deputies in the latter group were Seismit-Doda, who became the parliamentary Left's outstanding financial expert, Giovanni Cadolini, an expert on public works and defense, and

Bargoni, who acted as liaison between the parliamentary loyal opposition and the reformist segment of the democratic press. Experienced in the practice of parliamentary politics, these men became role models for those with different political backgrounds. Thus, theorists like Ferrari learned from them the art of making political deals and of writing or amending legislation. And former conspirators and rebels like Crispi learned indispensable lessons about the need for compromise and conciliation. In sum, the caucus became a training ground for potential leaders of the parliamentary Left. That the most prominent politicians of the Left in the 1870s and 1880s shared this experience might be taken as an indication of how effectively the caucus functioned in this capacity. Finally, the democratic caucus at times became a rudimentary electoral machine. As such it played a crucial role in the career of several democratic deputies, and ultimately it may have kept the democratic contingent from getting even smaller.

For the democrats studied here, winning a seat in the national Parliament was an arduous task even if they were determined to succeed and were free of ambivalence toward the existing institutions. Before the age of mass politics and well-defined parties, deputies were elected because their views on major issues were (or appeared to be) compatible with those of their electors. On this score the democrats of the 1860s and 1870s were obviously at a disadvantage. An electorate consisting largely of mature, well-educated, male property owners was fairly responsive to the secular character of democratic ideology but generally unsympathetic to its egalitarian and socialist themes. Aware of this, democrats who wanted to succeed eschewed discussion of ideology or even of substantive political issues. They thought it more expedient to dwell on their patriotic record instead. Thus, during the electoral campaign of 1865 Bargoni reported to his political friends that a potentially dangerous adversary had appeared on the scene. The man was a professor at the University of Pavia, and he was known to harbor "advanced ideas." Bargoni observed that there was one bright spot in an otherwise dim situation: His rival had no patriotic credentials. By playing up his own record of barricade fighting, exile, and participation in the Sicilian Provisional Government of 1860, Bargoni won the nomination. But he was exceptionally lucky. The problem with trying to capitalize primarily on one's own political martyrdom was that liberal competitors often had equally valid claims.[18]

Like all other candidates, the democrats tried to run as favorite sons in towns or regions where their families were well known and respected. This approach worked well, for of the fifty-four democrats who had substantial parliamentary careers, forty-four ran at least initially as favorite sons. Thus, their success depended only in small part upon individual achievements or patriotic merit; rather, it was a reflection of the achievements or wealth or social standing of their families in the community. Democrats who did not enjoy such advantages were easily eliminated from the race. To his colleague Francesco Guglielmi, who had suffered this very fate, Asproni offered words of solace and hope: "You have a wife and children . . . Rejoice in the knowledge that you can leave to your descendants a rich and precious heritage of honor." The defeated candidate was not appeased, and for years thereafter he pleaded with fellow democrats for help in finding an administrative post.[19]

Because social and economic factors were so important to being elected, even successful democratic candidates were constantly looking over their shoulders. There was always a chance that the electors might shift their support to another native son who offered more compatible political views along with appropriate qualifications and social background. The few successful candidates who were not native sons ran all of these dangers, of course, and in addition they had to face the difficult search for a district. Occasionally a delegation of electors might approach a candidate known to be looking for a district. Garibaldi, for instance, was so approached in the 1860s by several delegations. Less famous men might also be asked if an outside candidacy seemed the only way to break a deadlock between two native contenders. Ferrari benefited from just such circumstances in 1860–61, when he was approached by the electors of Gavirate-Luino. This was a real stroke of luck for him because in Milan he had been unable to compete with better-known or less radical native sons.[20] But situations such as this were unusual. Among the democrats studied here Ferrari was one of only ten who did not stand for election as a native son. The other nine received no such invitations and had to shop around for a district from which to run. In the first two general elections, the search was conducted on an individual basis; but there is evidence that already by the mid-1860s the caucus of the parliamentary Left was trying to deal with this issue.

Certainly the most active deputies tried to help one another to survive politically. Some deputies had to find a new district every few years, either because they had run afoul of their electors or because poverty had forced them to resign. The caucus served as a clearinghouse for political intelligence for democratic deputies who were in trouble in their districts or for former deputies wishing to try again in a different setting. However, there were serious limitations—to the ability of the democrats to help one another. There were, of course, the inevitable rivalries that can be found in any such group and the differences of regional and social background. But in addition, the democrats were severely hampered because only a few districts were even moderately hospitable to their candidacies. Thus, it was not uncommon for two or more democrats to compete for nomination in the same district. In the mid-1860s, for instance, a bitter rivalry arose between Montecchi and Pianciani for the nomination in the Umbrian district of Poggio Mirteto. Local democratic electors leaned toward Pianciani, whom they regarded as more likely to win because he was less closely identified with Mazzinian radicalism and also because he had much higher social standing and visibility than Montecchi. But Montecchi's supporters pleaded with Pianciani to withdraw his name, for he had other options. They argued that unlike Montecchi, who was a native of Rome, Pianciani could run as a favorite son in the Spoleto area where his family was very influential; or else being much the wealthier of the two, he could try his luck in a district outside Umbria. Montecchi, who could not afford to travel, eventually won the argument and the seat.[21]

After several instances of such rivalries, not all of which were settled amicably, the parliamentary caucus tried to intervene and to bring some order out of chaos. To say that it established a smooth and rational method of engineering democratic candidacies would be an exaggeration. Throughout the 1860s responsibility for locating a promising district and for getting elected continued to lie with the candidate himself and with whatever political machine he was able to assemble in loco. But caucus members stood ready to help if they could, particularly when they found evidence that fellow democrats were being harassed by the prefects.[22] As an electoral machine the caucus never came close to matching the organizational resources available to the government's candidates, the so-called *ministeriali*. Yet without it, the loyal opposition, constantly torn between compromises with the dominant liberal elite and alliances with the extraparliamentary Left, might not have survived to see the electoral successes of 1874 and 1876.

The Legislative Record of the Loyal Opposition

The legislation that was significantly modified or initiated by the parliamentary Left during the period 1860–1876 deserves to be discussed for at least two reasons: It is a good indicator of the concerns of the parliamentary democrats and of the issues on which they reached a consensus; and it is useful for tracing the ideological and political antecedents of the contemporary Italian Left.

To the extent that it was able to develop a coherent strategy, the democratic minority in Parliament did not try to challenge the liberal governments at every turn and in every area of legislation. Instead, it focused on six or seven major issues. Several motives shaped this legislative behavior. First, for several years after the unification, the democrats in Parliament had to defend themselves against charges that they were patriots and not statesmen, ideologues and not practical men. There was a good deal of truth in these charges, as at least some of them realized. Most democrats lacked substantial legislative and administrative experience. As for the lessons learned during the revolution of 1848–49, they were not easily applicable to a peacetime constitutional government. In order to acquire the expertise they lacked, the parliamentary democrats tried whenever possible to concentrate on a few specific issues.

Second, the democrats' choice of issues reflected their self-image and in many instances their actual role as Italy's "deputies-at-large." They generally focused on those policies of the liberal governments that most affected the lower classes. In so doing they managed to remain remarkably true to their ideology while at the same time building a reservoir of good will among the potential beneficiaries of suffrage reform and social legislation.[23]

Third, the relatively narrow range of the democrats' legislative concerns also reflected the troublesome divisions within their ranks and the constant barrage of criticism that came from their extraparliamentary colleagues. After several failures, the leaders of the "loyal opposition" learned that individual attacks on the government were a waste of time. Yet collective attacks required a consensus that was only possible on a few selected issues. The least divisive of these were Italy's foreign policy and the domestic issues of public education, suffrage reform, women's rights, and fiscal policy.

All of the deputies in the national Parliament of the 1860s wished to see Italy's territorial unification completed and her borders secure. Yet calls for renewed war with Austria and for the occupation of Rome even at the price of a war with France came much more frequently from the Left than from the Right of the Chamber. A few dissidents, particularly Ferrari, complained that this bellicose, single-minded preoccupation with Rome and Venetia distracted the attention of the democratic opposition from more pressing domestic issues; but the agitation continued. White dyed-in-the-wool *garibaldini* plotted revolutionary coups de main, more moderate democrats reiterated at every opportunity the need for a strong standing army and for universal military service. Democratic thinkers as different from one another as Cattaneo, Mazzini, and Pisacane had advocated the concept of "the nation-in-arms." The parliamentary democrats wanted that concept to become a reality in Italian life, even though they knew it to be difficult to reconcile with the military tradition of the ruling dynasty. To that purpose, they led an unsuccessful fight to have Garibaldi's guerrilla units integrated into the national army.[24]

In the 1870s, with territorial unification completed, the proponents of "the nation-in-arms" turned their attention more generally to issues of foreign policy. They were often critical of the cautious, low-profile policy of Foreign Minister Emilio Visconti-Venosta. Northern deputies such as Bixio and Varè favored a more active presence in the Balkans and closer ties with Germany, and southerners such as Crispi and Musolino began to show an interest in Africa. The latter, in fact, revived his old plan for a new balance of power in the Mediterranean that was to protect Italian interests from ever more threatening French competition. The plan hinged on the creation under British protection of a Jewish state along the banks of the Suez Canal. Italy, Musolino argued, stood to gain both by a more secure access to Asia and by the stronger presence of a friendly power with whom she was not competing economically. There was an element of adventurism in such plans that eventually led the youngest democrats studied here, such as Musolino's own nephew Giovanni Nicotera and the ardent *garibaldini* Guastalla and Elia, to support irredentist or imperialist causes, or both.[25]

On major domestic issues the democrats were generally less interested in proposing radical alternatives to the liberal program than they were in broadening its scope or speeding up its implementation. In the area of education, for instance, there was a consensus on the need for a massive literacy campaign and for the secularization of the existing schools. When the democrats took issue with the Casati Education Law, it was not because they opposed it in principle but rather because they felt that it did not go far enough. Thus, Macchi expressed concern over the unequal allocation of funds to men's and women's schools. It was important, he argued, that students of both sexes learn to be self-supporting and responsible citizens. Others voiced the fear that ignorance, clerical influence, and poverty might interfere with the implementation of the Casati law precisely in those backward areas where the need for schools was greatest; for the law required that the communes themselves open and staff elementary schools.[26]

On the issue of suffrage reform and the related matters of women's rights and salaries for deputies, there were more substantive differences between liberal governments and democratic opposition. For both ideological and practical reasons the democrats favored the immediate abolition of property requirements for the right to vote, although they generally saw the wisdom of literacy tests. The question of women's suffrage—hotly debated before the approval of the Civil Code of 1865—was not raised exclusively by democrats. The liberal Mancini, for instance, who was married to a women of uncommon intellectual gifts, distinguished himself for his efforts in that area. But the democrats Macchi, Bertani, Ricciardi, Regnoli, and Morelli played an even more important role, both as sponsors of bills to enfranchise women and to reform the patriarchal character of Italian family law and as honorary members of several women's political and educational associations.[27]

Each of these men dealt with those aspects of "the woman question" which were closest to his intellectual and professional formation and to other political and social issues in which he had become involved over the years. Thus, the physician Bertani fought against legalized prostitution in the context of a larger struggle for human rights and improved public health. Morelli, whose primary concern was advertised in the title of the newspaper he edited, *Il suffragio universale*, became the paladin in Parliament of women's political rights. Macchi and Ricciardi, both strong advocates of women's education, also fought several unsuccessful battles for divorce legislation. As was his custom, Ricciardi wrote a pamphlet on this subject clearly designed to instruct the masses. Depicted there were noble characters victimized by the Catholic concept of marriage, one of whom clearly was Ricciardi's own "beloved Mauro" Macchi, who lived for many years with another man's wife.[28]

By far the most important democratic advocate of women's rights, however, was the lawyer Oreste Regnoli. A strong proponent of women's legal emancipation and of civil marriage, this former subject of the papal government was disappointed with the conservative character of the Civil Code of 1865 in the area of family legislation. Thus, he gave his support to the educational and political campaigns of such women activists as the Mazzinian Anna Maria Mozzoni and Gualberta Alaide Beccari, the editor of *La donna*.[29]

For Regnoli, Morelli, and other democratic deputies, the fight for women's political rights was always carried out within the context of a larger struggle for the democratization of all political and social institutions. This also held true for their interest in the issue of paid parliamentary service. That proposals for the payment of a salary to deputies should come from the democratic minority in the Chamber was to be expected, for several among them had severe financial problems. Moreover, the democrats knew of able colleagues who had declined the nomination or resigned their seats because they could not afford the expenses that went with the parliamentary mandate.[30] Deputies like Ferrari and Ricciardi, who were not poor themselves, presented the strongest arguments in favor of paid service. Ferrari pointed out the temptations and pressures to which his less affluent colleagues were constantly subjected by powerful individuals and interest groups. And Ricciardi argued that unless paid service was adopted the national Parliament would forever be the preserve of *possidenti*, bureaucrats, and professional men. Such a state of affairs deprived the nation of fresh ideas and new leaders and made a mockery of the oft-stated sovereignty of the people. Wishing to impress this point on as many people as possible outside the Parliament, Ricciardi wrote a play "inspired by the desire to expose and to arouse indignation against the corruption that [plagued] the elections, and the dishonorable intentions of many of those who [vied] for the honor of representing the people." His hero was an honorable but poor patriot fearful of losing the election to a wealthy opponent, yet reluctant to accept money from lawyers and journalists whom he knew to be agents of powerful special interests.[31]

Last but not least, the parliamentary democrats fought against the fiscal policies of the liberal governments. Their legislative behavior in matters of taxation differed from their approach to issues of suffrage reform and education. On the subjects of educational policy, paid service, and even women's rights, the democratic deputies were able to present broadly conceived policy alternatives, most of which were in fact adopted after the "parliamentary revolution" of 1876. They were not able to do so in regard to fiscal policy. The democrats argued against indirect taxes that fell heavily on lower-income groups and on basic commodities, discouraging their consumption. Yet for the most part they approved of the economic policy of the liberals with its heavy expenditures to service the cumulative debt of the preunification states, to build railroads and a navy, to prepare for another war against Austria, and so forth. Hence the criticism — largely justified — that the democrats' sympathy for the overburdened poor was an exercise in cheap demagogy. For it was true that the critics of the grist tax, the salt tax, the tobacco monopoly, and other regressive aspects of the liberal regime failed, on the whole, to suggest alternative sources of revenue. And those few who did so proposed alternatives that had no chance at all of passing. Such was the case, for instance, with Ferrari's pet scheme to restrict private ownership of land and to abolish inheritance rights, and of Giuseppe Romano's inflationary proposal of 1868 for an expansion of the money supply.[32]

If it was rather inconsistent and demagogic, however, the parliamentary democrats' critique of regressive taxation, especially of the grist tax, established a useful precedent for future leaders with fewer qualms about a drastic rearrangement of the nation's priorities. The same held true for the democrats' attempts to introduce social legislation on behalf of the lower classes. Except for issues that evoked widespread humanitarian concern, such as child labor, the bills drafted by Macchi, Morelli, and others in the 1860s and early 1870s were never even brought to the full Chamber for discussion. Yet they are noteworthy, not only because they set a precedent for the legislation of the 1880s and 1890s, but because they reveal the values and attitudes of their authors. As was the case with taxation, the democrats proposed to protect the Italian workers without questioning the basic relations of production, the distribution of wealth, and the inherently undemocratic character of the existing agrarian contracts and of factory organization. It is significant, too, that the deputies most active in this area were urban men with urban constituencies. Like Mazzini thirty years before, they had little to say that was applicable to the large majority of Italy's laboring poor, the peasantry. The problem was not that they were out of touch with working people. At the very least, extraparliamentary colleagues such as Dolfi in Tuscany and Dassi in Naples provided them with information and with potential supporters. Rather, the problem was that the working people whose conditions they knew best and to whom they listened were not very representative of Italian workers. The members of the Società operaie were particularly atypical, insofar as they were literate, politically articulate, and generally anti-Catholic. In the 1860s the leaders of the extraparliamentary wing of the movement, however, did make an effort to reach the illiterate, politically inarticulate Catholic masses. But those efforts, whether successful or not, left little trace in the records of the Italian Parliament.

9

Dropouts and Deviants: Extraparliamentary Democracy, 1860–1876

THE importance of the democratic presence in the first Italian Parliament cannot be underestimated. Although it remained small during the period 1860–1876, it could boast intellectually distinguished spokesmen like Ferrari as well as activists like Macchi who had solid ties with the nonvoting masses. If the parliamentary democrats were never strong enough to alter significantly the social and economic policies of the liberals, they did, however, develop political positions and tactics that served as models for later generations of bourgeois radicals and socialists. Their self-perception as "deputies-at-large" of all disenfranchised Italians caught the popular imagination. Thus, a precedent was set for a political role that remained characteristic of the parliamentary Left (and at the turn of the century also of Christian democracy) until the Giolittian suffrage reform of 1912. Moreover, the caucus of the democratic "loyal opposition" represented the first attempt to achieve a semblance of party discipline and professionalism in a legislative body otherwise dominated by fluid factions of notables.

Despite its importance, however, the parliamentary wing of the movement only included about one half of the democrats studied here. Of the remaining democrats, about 20 percent abandoned the political arena in the 1860s, and an additional 30 percent engaged primarily or exclusively in extraparliamentary activities. An analysis of both these groups offers additional insights into the difficult predicament of many democrats after the unification and into various means by which they attempted to carry on the unfinished Italian Revolution.

Although the democrats were put to severe tests during two decades of clandestine political activity and persecution, only 25 of them abandoned politics after the unification. Of the 122 who survived beyond the early 1860s, four (Gavazzi, Landi, Milo Guggino, and Piccioni) remained in the countries that had granted them political asylum. Landi did return to his native Messina in the early 1870s, but the experience of the Paris Commune had destroyed his faith in democratic government. Seven others had skills that were particularly valuable to the development of united Italy. Easily coopted by the moderate governments, they became — publicly at least — technocrats of neutral political views. They included four revolutionaries of 1848 (Angherà, Campo, Antonio Morici, and Francesco Pigozzi) who ended up with commissions in the Sardinian and then in the Italian army. The other technocrats were Maestri and Cesare Mazzoni, both economists and statisticians, and Guttièrez, who had learned business management during his exile in Piedmont. Except for Milo Guggino, so poor by 1860 that he may have been ashamed to return to Sicily and begin a new phase of his public life, the other democrats in this group chose to abandon politics for perhaps more satisfactory and certainly more lucrative activities. Franchi and La Cecilia may also have voluntarily retired from politics. The former had established enough of a reputation as a philosopher that he certainly could have found a district willing to nominate him for national office, but he preferred teaching and writing. The latter, nearly sixty years old by the time of unification and in poor health, felt that he had time left for little else than the memoirs of an unusually adventurous career.

It is clear, however, that at least a dozen of the democrats studied here abandoned politics not by choice but by necessity. Men who had devoted the best years of their lives to the Italian Revolution and who in the past had given evidence of political ambitions now felt that they had no real chance of a public life.

Only two of the "dropouts," Faccioli and Mattioli, were denied political careers of any sort because they had disgraced themselves in the eyes of their colleagues during the revolution. Several others had impeccable revolutionary and patriotic credentials, yet they found themselves in a most awkward situation that all but squelched their political ambitions. They were too poor to consider a parliamentary career and not sufficiently well known at the national level to attract powerful sponsors. At the same time they were not comfortable in extraparliamentary circles because their ideas, particulary on social issues, were not quite radical enough or because they were not influential enough at the local level to help parliamentary colleagues win elections or to protect extraparliamentary militants against the prefects. Among the democrats who fell into this sort of political limbo in the 1860s were Dall'Ongaro, a major protagonist of the revolution of 1848, whose native Venetia remained under Austrian rule until 1866, and two longtime leaders of Piedmontese democracy, Govean and Guglielmi.

For democrats who were better known, more politically savvy, or less hard-pressed economically, extraparliamentary activism could be very appealing indeed. About forty democrats found personal fulfillment and in some cases even lasting fame in the pursuit of one or more of the following activities: local politics, journalism, and the political organization and indoctrination of the lower classes.

Despite the argument made by Ferrari and other democratic deputies that the national Parliament was the only significant forum for the discussion of political issues, several democrats found that challenging and rewarding public lives could be built outside of it. True, local political struggles and journalism lacked the prestige of a seat in the national Parliament. Grass-roots political organizing among workers and peasants was taxing and occasionally even dangerous, but these extraparliamentary activities offered advantages as well. The most obvious was that the extraparliamentary activist could preserve his political independence and intellectual freedom more easily than the deputy. Another was that he could, if he so wished, state openly his belief that the Italian Revolution was unfinished and then act accordingly to change the existing institutions. Unlike his parliamentary colleagues, he could do so without being accused of inconsistency or worse. Such freedom and flexibility were especially important to Mazzini's most orthodox followers who clung to their republican convictions and to those democrats interested in the social dimensions of the national revolution. From their point of view the liberal kingdom proclaimed on March 17, 1861, was but a stepping-stone to a democratic Italy as yet to be attained.

Symbols and Substance: The Democratic Presence in Local Politics

Twenty-three of the democrats studied here held political office at the local or provincial level during the period 1861–1876. This small but significant group included men who never ran for national office as well as some who, for one reason or another, were elected to Parliament only once. Although most of them had not become nationally known political figures during the revolution, they had played important roles in it at the local or regional level. In the 1840s they had been members and leaders of underground democratic networks, an experience that proved valuable after the unification. In the fluid political situation of the 1860s and early 1870s they were able to perform a variety of interesting roles.

A few democratic protagonists of the national revolution were appointed to mayoral posts or to municipal and provincial councils because they were local heroes who simply could not be ignored, no matter how extreme their views or how limited their qualifications for such offices. How they used the opportunities grudgingly given by liberal ministers and prefects depended in good measure upon their past experience and personality. If they lacked political sophistication or had no genuine interest in the nuts and bolts of local government, they quickly became mere symbols of a democratic tradition to which everyone paid lip service in the interest of patriotic unity by which was no longer regarded as a force to reckon with. Nicola Mignogna of Taranto and Enrico Maffei of Potenza suffered such a fate.

An impressive-looking man with a flowing white beard and a booming voice, Mignogna was too well known a local figure to be ignored by the victorious liberals. Besides, more than three decades of revolutionary militancy and his role in Garibaldi's provisional government of 1860 obviously entitled him to some sort of reward. Thus he was appointed to several minor administrative posts, none of which, according to an otherwise admiring biographer, he filled with distinction. Like his fellow *garibaldini* in Parliament, he was rather bored by the routine aspects of peacetime government, and he became more impatient with advancing age. As time went by he became at once an object of veneration and ridicule, living proof that yesterday's heroism was of little use in solving united Italy's problems. But at least this old conspirator was fully aware of his own limitations, and he resisted pressure from his admirers to reach for higher goals. In 1863, for instance, he refused to run for Parliament on the grounds that he lacked appropriate educational qualifications (he had been a seminary dropout in his youth) and that he wanted to remain available for Garibaldi's future attempts to liberate Rome and Venetia. In sum, if Mignogna never became more than a token democratic presence in Apulian politics, at least he maintained his integrity and honor.

Maffei's postunification experience illustrates the perils faced by token democrats with a less realistic sense of their weakness vis-à-vis the liberal elite. With Libertini of Lecce, Maffei had been the leader of the democratic forces on the Adriatic side of the Kingdom of Naples in 1848. In the 1850s he had experienced political martyrdom in Bourbon prisons, and a brutal attack by a fellow inmate had done irreparable damage, it seems, to his mental faculties. In the 1860s, at any rate, he thirsted for the recognition and influence that his modest social origins and status as a small-town priest had denied him in the days of the Bourbons. According to a fellow revolutionary, "certain old lackeys of the fallen dynasty," having helped Maffei to get a seat on the Potenza municipal council and then on a board that regulated the price of staple foods (*Annona*), tried to use him to discredit other democrats. When he finally realized what was happening, Maffei protested bitterly. His would-be political friends then quickly abandoned him, and by the end of his life he was literally reduced to begging the royal government for a pension.[1]

These examples show that it was difficult for token democrats working at the local level amidst liberal majorities to maintain their political credibility and independence. Indeed, that difficulty was overcome only by three or four of the democrats studied here, men who were highly visible and respected in their communities and who were also endowed with unusual intellectual gifts. One such democrat was the Sardinian Tuveri, a contributor to the constitutional debates of 1848 and a councilman in his native commune of Forru.

Like Asproni, his better-known parliamentary colleague, Tuveri spoke for the shepherds and peasants of Sardinia whose ancient rights and traditional ways were being threatened by economic modernization. He was not opposed in principle to the development of capitalist enterprise for the exploitation, for instance, of the island's mineral wealth. But he was concerned about the impact on a backward rural society of the mixture of laissez-faire ideology and heavy taxation that was characteristic of Italian liberalism at the time. Tuveri's views did not receive as much publicity outside Sardinia as did Asproni's parliamentary speeches and articles in *Il popolo d'Italia*. Yet his personal prestige on the island was such that he did not suffer the fate of Mignogna or Maffei. On the contrary, by his opposition to economic policies that threatened to perpetuate Sardinia's quasi-colonial condition, he set a precedent that was followed by later generations of Sardinian intellectuals, including Antonio Gramsci.[2]

Other democrats, however, were more interested in practical matters than in the formulation of ideological positions or in the exercise of moral leadership. Those lucky enough to have a substantial local following or close ties with colleagues in Parliament tried to get more fellow democrats appointed or elected to public office and to maneuver for a share of political patronage. Among the democrats who devoted the postunification years to these efforts and who succeeded thereby in making a place in the sun for themselves were De Lieto in Reggio Calabria, and Carnazza and Giovanni Raffaele in Sicily. Success did not come easily. Despite their sterling patriotic credentials, when they returned home from exile or prison they often encountered some hostility. Not infrequently it was fomented by political rivals fearful that the returning heroes of the revolution would steal the limelight. Thus, Raffaele was the target of an anonymous threat in 1860: "If [Pasquale] Calvi, Raffaele, and others whose names I will not mention for now want a republic . . . let them be slaughtered and torn to pieces. Believe me, the great powers have admired us thus far; secretly they are on our side, and if we are content to demand our [Sicilian] constitution, our wish will be granted."[3] Raffaele's revolutionary record and his hair-raising experiences as a political prisoner of the Bourbon government were sufficient, it seems, to secure his election in 1861 to the Eighth Legislature, although at the local level they carried less weight. To establish himself first as a councilman in Messina, then as mayor of Palermo, he relied upon his prerevolutionary reputation as a physician and scientist. But above all he had to prove to the satisfaction of his anonymous critic and of the leaders of Sicilian liberalism that he was willing to work within the framework of constitutional monarchy. Supporting the liberals' economic policies, he gradually drifted toward moderate positions. Even as he changed his views on some issues of national importance, however, Raffaele in his capacity as a local official and political leader promoted reforms in the areas of public health and education that showed his concern for the lower classes. For example, he opposed a law designed to punish mothers who abandoned their unwanted babies at the doorstep of orphanages. He pointed out that the law, motivated by the desire to eliminate an ancient and barbaric custom and to save public moneys as well, did not address itself to the root causes of child abandonment. Among these he mentioned poverty, ignorance, laws that prevented women from initiating paternity suits and, finally, laws that prevented many men, especially soldiers, from marrying before the age of thirty. Raffaele had a ready answer for critics who accused him of having sold out to the liberals for the sake of his own political career: He maintained that his arguments were virtually identical with those presented in Parliament by such unimpeachable champions of women and the poor as Morelli and Macchi.[4]

Beyond being willing to compromise with the political victors of 1860, the candidate for success in local politics had to be finely attuned to the particular needs of his city or region. An accurate evaluation of those needs was not always easy to make, particularly if the candidate in question had been absent from the scene for several years. Perhaps nowhere in Italy was this task more difficult than in Sicily, where there was a long-standing distrust of continental leaders and the strong pull of the separatist tradition. Here again, Raffaele's experience provides insight into a problem that democrats elsewhere had to face in somewhat different form.

As mayor of Palermo, on several occasions he went on record defending the autonomy of municipal governments against encroachment by the central government. He did so primarily by asking prominent Sicilian liberals to practice what they had often preached in speeches and political writings about the blessings of self-government. His position was quite consistent with the views expressed in the 1860s by the leading theorists of the democratic movement, Mazzini included. Unfortunately, in the Sicilian context Raffaele's defense of local autonomy left him vulnerable to charges of collusion with separatists whose ultimate goal was not to strengthen democratic participation at the grass roots but rather to create an independent Sicily. While defending himself against these charges, he pleaded with Italy's national political leaders to consider that "municipal administrations [were] by their very nature autonomous, that unity [was] not undermined by their actions." There was a wide gap, he added, between those concerned with local autonomies and the "regionalists" who did not care about Italian unity. Thus, by intervening with a heavy hand in municipal affairs, the central government was actually strengthening its own enemies.[5]

These same concerns were expressed by other democrats who held local political office in the early 1860s. As time went by, however, they came to realize that the liberal ruling elite would not and indeed probably could not live up to its own philosophical ideals. The realities of Italy's military weakness, poverty, and regional diversity were pushing it increasingly in the direction of highly centralized authoritarian government. Democrats active in local politics responded to this national trend with a change of strategy. They continued to press for more autonomy for municipalities and provincial councils, yet at the same time they also became more concerned with strengthening the democratic opposition in the national Parliament. Their strategy consisted of seeking out and supporting candidates who showed promise, usually native sons with a background of democratic activism. If no suitable native candidates happened to be available, local democratic activists might undertake a search for such candidates outside their district. In either case it is noteworthy that nonvoters became actively involved in this process of scrutiny and selection. And that was undoubtedly an important reason why some parliamentary democrats could claim to be "deputies-at-large" of the Italian people.

In 1862–63, for instance, Dassi attempted to promote the candidacy of Giuseppe Ferrari in Naples. Dassi's primary motive was less the desire to see his native city represented by an outstanding democratic intellectual than the hope of personal gain. Ferrari was flattered and intrigued by the prospect of trading his safe but backward rural district in Lombardy for one in Italy's largest city. However, when he discovered to his chagrin that his charming and energetic sponsor planned to use him as a conduit to north Italian and French businessmen interested in southern lumber, the whole project fell through. Yet despite his hidden motives and less than candid relationship with the would-be candidate, Dassi's political strategy was fairly typical of extraparliamentary activists in those years.[6]

First, although Ferrari's candidacy was Dassi's idea, Dassi did not act alone. In fact, before approaching Ferrari he secured the approval and cooperation of artisan and student organizations with which he had been connected ever since the 1840s. That he did so suggests that these potential supporters, though for the most part excluded from the vote, had ways of approaching the electors and of influencing the nomination process and perhaps the election itself. The most obvious though not necessarily the most important way to accomplish this was for artisan and student groups to meet and endorse a candidate whose views they liked. These endorsements were politically valuable, it seems, even if those who issued them could not vote in a national election. Thus Ricciardi, the doyen of Neapolitan democracy, solicited formal endorsements from the local Società operaia, boasting before its members of his own patriotic credentials and progressive voting record on issues affecting the Italian workers.[7]

Second, Dassi and his counterparts in other districts served as resource people on local and even regional conditions and problems. In the case of the Ferrari candidacy, for instance, information concerning Naples and its environs was assembled even before negotiations with the prospective candidate had come to a close. This kind of resource network was useful to all candidates, but it was obviously more valuable to those who were not native sons. Local activists also kept an eye on how the press, especially the liberal and clerical newspapers, portrayed their candidate or deputy. If necessary, they wrote letters to the editors to protest biased reporting or unfair criticism. Again, these humble but very useful political chores could be performed by literate men who were perhaps too young or too poor to qualify for the vote. The wide range of activities that local democratic politicians undertook in the attempt to influence national policy became for such men an invaluable source of political experiences. The post-Risorgimento generation of radical and socialist politicians served its political apprenticeship under democrats like Raffaele and Dassi. From them it learned the art of political organizing, and through them it developed important ties to the democratic press.

Democratic Journalism

During the 1860s and early 1870s, democratic deputies made a major contribution to the press as regular or guest columnists and even as editors. For many years, for instance, Bargoni somehow juggled the parliamentary mandate and a legal practice along with the editorship of *Il diritto*. Mazzinian deputies like Saffi were regular contributors to *Il dovere*, and De Boni and Asproni were primarily responsible for the success of the Neapolitan *Il popolo d'Italia*. Yet the most interesting and politically significant aspect of the democratic press is that it provided an outlet for the energies and a forum for the ideas of extraparliamentary intellectuals and activists. Among them were loyal Mazzinians like Campanella, Quadrio, and Sacchi, but also men like Rusconi, Siliprandi, and Andreini who stood considerably to the left of Mazzini on issues of social reform and Church-State relations.

Nearly all the democrats studied here had made some contribution to the underground press of the 1840s or to the various revolutionary newspapers of 1848–49. But before the unification they generally had not tried to earn a living as political journalists. Partly for ideological and partly for financial and social reasons, however, quite a few democrats tried to do so in the 1860s. From an ideological point of view, all democrats, whether or not they liked to write, were committed to reaching the widest possible reading public. The press was the most important tool available to them for the task of mass political education, which in turn was the key to the transformation of Italian culture and society. Although not lucrative, journalism offered at least a chance to eke out a living to men of modest social origins who had forfeited more promising career opportunities during many years of political militancy. Despite its low status as a profession, journalism assured them a visible and potentially influential place in Italian society. However, there were more democrats interested in the full-time practice of this profession than there were available opportunities. Thus, extra-parliamentary intellectuals had to compete with one another in much the same way as the parliamentary democrats sometimes competed for nomination in the same district.

The character of the democratic press in this period reflectd ideological differences and personal rivalries among the men responsible for its growth and direction. With the exception of *Il diritto*, which was mostly the mouthpiece of the parliamentary "loyal opposition" and which avoided republican or extreme anti-Catholic pronouncements, no democratic periodical publication gained a nationwide readership. Even such well-known newspapers as *Il dovere*, whose contributors came from every part of Italy, remained primarily identified with one city or region, and their circulation ranged from a few hundred to three to four thousand. These low figures indicate subscribers, however, not readers. The number of readers was probably several times higher, for those who could afford the subscriptions presumably shared their newspapers with friends and relatives. More important, the Società operaie and other such organizations subscribed to the democratic press and made it available to their members. Thus, the various democratic newspapers together reached thousands of Italians who were otherwise excluded from the political process and had little access to political information. Even so, the fragmented character of the democratic press meant that no single newspaper in this period attained a large circulation or a national constituency. And none enjoyed even a modicum of financial health.[8]

During the 1860s at least a dozen democratic newspapers, including Cattaneo's reborn *Il politecnico* and Mario's promising *La nuova Europa*, went under for lack of adequate financing, even though many contributors worked without compensation and, particularly in Genoa and Florence, printers loyal to the movement provided their labor and the use of their equipment free of charge.

Publishers and editors spent much of their time devising ways to re-main solvent. The use of commercial advertising as a source of revenue was then just in its infancy; and in any event, daily or-weekly newspapers devoted primarily to political issues were of limited interest to potential advertisers. Hoping to attract a wider audience, however, Andreini of *Il corriere del popolo*, Ciccotti of *Il cittadino lucano*, and other democratic editors devoted space to human interest stories, fiction, or drama.

This material, which invariably contained not-so-subtle social or political messages, was usually provided by fellow democrats who had made a full-time career of writing fiction or plays. Among the most prolific contributors whose works were serialized in the demo-cratic press were Gaetano Tallinucci, author of polemical anti-moderate plays, Montazio, known for his mordant Tuscan wit, and Angelo Usiglio, who specialized in pathos-filled stories about women exploited and oppressed by an unjust society. Another popular writer, Antonio Ghiglione, capitalized on his adventures of the 1850s in the United States. His long poems, *Simone Kenton* and *Nelson Orr*, celebrated the freedom, the boundless resources, and the wide open spaces of that country in contrast to the author's homeland with its undemocratic government, poverty, and crowded cities.[9]

From the viewpoint of democratic editors, all of these works ac-complished a twofold purpose: They increased the level of ordinary citizens' political and social awareness and at the same time they provided inexpensive entertainment. All too often, however, the poor literary quality of these contributions gave away the authors' penchants for purple prose and their daily struggles to meet deadlines. And the content sometimes reflected their dissatisfaction with the marginal role that they seemed destined to play in Italian politics. That their contributions continued to be solicited, however, is an indication that they enjoyed a substantial following, and the appearance in the late 1870s and in the 1880s of bound editions of several works originally serialized in democratic newspapers is also evidence of a certain success.

Still, as a device to raise revenue the addition of literary pieces to news items and political editorials had definite limitations. One such drawback was that in most cases there was no direct relationship between an increase in readership and an increase in subscriptions. Another was that these authors usually wrote to keep body and soul together, and thus could not afford to offer their services gratis. Therefore, a better answer to the chronic deficits seemed to lie in finding wealthy and generous sponsors. Predictably, the few well-known democrats who had some means were bombarded with requests for donations.

Among those studied here, Adriano Lemmi above all became the financial patron saint of the democratic press. He was not only frequently called upon to contribute funds from his substantial income as a businessman but also to facilitate contacts between democratic journalists in Italy and their counterparts in other countries. Lemmi was ideally qualified for this task, and he enjoyed it, though he complained occasionally of excessive demands on his time. In the 1850s, in fact, he had traveled widely in Europe and the Middle East as a commercial agent and also as personal secretary to the Hungarian national hero Louis Kossuth. Having accompanied Kossuth on triumphal tours of the United States and England, Lemmi was well acquainted with radical, anticlerical, and Masonic circles in those countries.[10]

The *garibaldino* Giacinto Bruzzesi also subsidized the democratic press and sometimes secured contributions from abroad. Although less wealthy than Lemmi, he was equally well connected with businessmen throughout Italy and southeastern Europe. Some of his contacts had been established during the years of his exile; others developed in the 1860s after his marriage to Noerina Noè, the daughter of a wealthy and cultured Jewish merchant. Noerina herself contributed articles and photographs to the democratic press, particularly on women's issues. She and other young women of her social background found an ideal role model for such activities in the Mazzinian loyalist Sara Levi Nathan, whose entire family in one way or another had been involved in democratic politics from the beginning of the movement.[11]

For all the efforts of such loyal supporters, the democratic press in the 1860s and 1870s remained fragmented, underfinanced, and subject to frequent failures. This state of affairs obviously hindered the spread of democratic ideas and weakened the voice of the extraparliamentary opposition to the liberals. Aware of this problem, which dated back to the democratic press of Piedmont-Sardinia in the 1850s, several editors and supporters came up with suggestions for cooperation and even mergers. The most interesting and ambitious of these was Bertani's proposal for a nationwide consortium of democratic newspapers. As early as 1861 Bertani proposed to minimize competition among the existing newspapers and to maximize their chances of survival by establishing a common financial basis, common rates of compensation for contributors, and guidelines to prevent encroachment by one newspaper upon the geographical turf of another. However, the members of Bertani's proposed consortium were to retain their editorial independence.[12]

Although they acknowledged the practical merits of this proposal, Bargoni, Campanella, and other influential journalists refused to endorse it, and in the years that followed they remained generally cool to other suggestions along these lines. Their attitude, in some ways self-defeating, reflected more than a concern with intellectual independence. It also reflected the fears of some democrats who had taken up political journalism as a full-time occupation that consolidation might mean diminished opportunities for them. Moreover, militants like Carlo Mileti voiced the opinion that any attempts to create a centralized structure would play into the hands of government censors, who were always on the alert for excuses to muzzle the democratic press.

As editor of *Il popolo d'Italia*, the mouthpiece of the democratic movement in Naples in the 1860s, Mileti knew whereof he spoke. Like other democrats who worked in the same métier, he spent a considerable amount of time fending off official warnings by the local prefect, occasional confiscations, and even death threats from anonymous correspondents who objected to his newspaper's republican and socialist diatribes. As long as many democratic newspapers managed to stay in business, however, the effects of preventive censorship, intimidation, and even outright confiscations of issues or equipment were less severe than they might otherwise have been. As Mileti understood, the fragmented character of the democratic press could be a source of resilience.[13] And this was a most important quality in the constant tug-of-war between the democratic editors and the prefects, whose duty it was to strike a delicate balance between the constitutional guarantee of freedom of the press and the political demands of the elite in power.

Just as decentralization and fragmentation offered some protection against censorship, the predominantly local character of the democratic press perhaps enhanced its importance as a vehicle for mass political education. Even in the absence of reliable estimates one may assume that newspapers like *La plebe* of Lodi, *Il popolano* of Cremona, or *Il cittadino lucano* of Potenza with their bits of local news, their homegrown contributors, and their frequent lapses into the vernacular were more appealing to a semiliterate public than the more sophisticated *Il diritto* with its aspirations to national fame and political prestige.

Still it remains difficult to assess how effective the democratic press was as a vehicle for mass political education. It is clear, however, that it performed quite well as a training ground for future leaders of the Italian Left. The best-known figures of the post-Risorgimento radical and socialist movements, from Felice Cavallotti and Enrico Ferri to the anarchist Errico Malatesta, got their political start as contributors to democratic newspapers. To work for such newspapers, especially those with a strictly local readership, required more than literary ability and intellectual effort. It required familiarity with and often direct involvement in a myriad of activities. In the best Risorgimento tradition, the usual working day of the democratic journalist reflected unity of thought and action. He was expected not merely to think, observe, and report the reality around him but to help shape it and change it. Thus, working alongside activists who were less comfortable than he with paper and pen, the journalist learned to appreciate the importance of mass political organizations as he learned to analyze the policies of the ruling elite.

Democratic Leaders and the Masses

The 1860s and early 1870s were years of intense democratic activity at the level of the masses, particularly in urban centers among artisans and industrial workers. It was also a period of new conflicts among democratic leaders over goals and strategies. For the most part, the attitudes and approaches that had won the democrats a substantial following in the 1840s were of little value in the post-unification era. In the process of discarding those and developing new ones, the democrats became hopelessly divided. By the early 1870s some sought to lead the masses by means of an updated version of Mazzini's republicanism and of his social theory. Others, in a sharper break with the Risorgimento, looked for new prophets abroad and eventually flocked to Mikhail Bakunin's colors. The lines of battle were drawn not merely in the democratic press but in hundreds of grass-roots political and social organizations. The most important of these by far were the Società operaie, originally of Mazzinian inspiration but in the 1860s and 1870s open to other influences as well. The Risorgimento democrats counted heavily on the members of the Società, politically active during the revolution and mostly literate, for the survival and growth of their movement. Their confidence was not misplaced, although the Società sometimes developed goals quite different from and sometimes even alien to those of their democratic mentors.

Indeed, so important were the Società operaie to the post-unification development of the democratic movement that some twenty-seven of the democrats studied here worked with them virtually on a full-time basis. Several others, including all the distinguished names of parliamentary democracy, also became involved as patrons, honorary presidents, and occasional speakers. Mazzinian loyalists such as Campanella, Dolfi, Quadrio, and Saffi were particularly active in this area. They enjoyed an initial advantage over other members of the movement who were also eager to proselytize among the masses. Long before the unification the Master himself had defined both the raison d'être of the Società operaie and the role of the democratic activist in their midst. Basically, the Società were to be vehicles for the moral and political education of the lower classes. There Italy's workers were to learn first and foremost their collective responsibilities toward the fulfillment of their national mission. Second, they were to claim the rights and fulfill the duties of citizenship. The Società and other such groups could, of course, also function as mutual aid societies, social clubs, and political pressure groups at election time. But, as Mazzini saw it, these functions were trivial compared with that of moral and patriotic education. As for the democratic intellectual or organizer, his chief responsibility was to set a personal example of selfless patriotism and responsible citizenship. Only thus could he establish credibility in the absence of ascriptive or at least long-established claims to leadership. Once he had gained the respect and trust of the lower classes he could proceed to exercise his second most important responsibility, to interpret for them the principles of democratic ideology.[14]

Several democrats tried to live up to these Mazzinian definitions in their dealings with workers' and artisans' associations. The definitions, of course, had to be modified to fit the times. Men and women who had participated in the struggle for national independence and unity obviously no longer needed to have their patriotic consciousness raised. Thus, Mazzini's followers focused instead on raising their civic consciousness and their understanding of liberal institutions and democratic ideology. To these purposes the activists employed a variety of approaches and means, depending on regional conditions and on the level of literacy and political militancy of each association.

In areas where the Società operaie or other working-class associations were well entrenched and had a large and literate membership, democratic activists were highly visible in actual political struggles. Such was the case with Dolfi, who was the grand master of Fratellanza artigiana's twelve hundred members. An elite of Florentine journeymen, master artisans, and *capipopolo*, these men hardly needed paternalistic protection or ideological indoctrination. What they did ask of Dolfi, Giuseppe Mazzoni, and other

Tuscan democrats was the benefit of their political experience and connections as founders of democratic networks in the 1840s and chief protagonists of the revolution of 1848. Democratic activists and intellectuals provided, above all, the necessary links between the membership of Fratellanza artigiana, on the one hand, and democratic deputies and journalists on the other. Only through such links could these politically conscious and articulate but disenfranchised groups hope to influence national policy. In return for such assistance, for instance in regard to suffrage reform, Fratellanza artigiana endorsed democratic condidates for both local and national offices and occasionally staged street demostrations to show its support.[15]

Where the associations were smaller or of more recent origin, democratic activists contributed ideas and strategies to attract new members, perhaps drawing on their own youthful experiences in secret societies and student organizations. An important ingredient in the success of these efforts was the introduction of symbols and rituals with which the lower classes could easily identify. These were sometimes borrowed from local folklore but more often from the Catholic or Masonic traditions. The adaptation of Catholic or Masonic rites with their colorful pageantry and repetitive formulas was particularly useful for conveying political messages to semi-literate people accustomed to religious imagery. Among Mazzini's old followers Quadrio particularly distinguished himself for a fertile imagination in this regard. Although he showed the effects of old age and a strenuous life, in the 1860s he traveled frequently among a dozen associations of which he was an honorary president or member. Everywhere he impressed upon his associates the need to enrich otherwise drab political meetings with song, ritual, and good fellowship. Moreover, he wrote a much-imitated political catechism that summarized in brief and simple statements the main principles of democratic ideology. Not accidentally, his little manual closely resembled those used by parish priests to prepare the young for first communion or confirmation.[16]

On the whole, northern democrats such as Dolfi, Quadrio, and Macchi (who was very active in Turin), worked with vigorous and growing urban associations. Other democrats, however, labored in rather more difficult and precarious circumstances, particularly in the small towns of central and southern Italy. For both economic and cultural reasons workingmen's political associations were weak and small in those areas and in greater need of leadership than those in northern Italy. The associations that existed in economically backward regions at the time of unification typically had only a few dozen members, many of whom were illiterate and afraid of both government officials and powerful local notables. For such associations the participation of local democratic activists could make the difference between survival and demise. For example, the Società operaia of Potenza faltered until two well-known local democrats, Albini and Ciccotti, took an active interest in its future. Albini, who held honorary office in the Società for several years, was the less active of the two, at least on a day-to-day basis. But he was the scion of a well-regarded local family as well as a hero of the national revolution ("the Mazzini of Basilicata") and a member of the provisional government of 1860. As such, by his involvement he conferred an aura of patriotism and respectability upon an organization that was otherwise easily branded as subversive of the social order. Ciccotti, less famous though no less able, presided over meetings, traveled around the province to recruit new members, and wrote propaganda materials for the association. More important, as a practicing lawyer of some standing in his profession, he provided invaluable legal advice and defense whenever members of the association were charged with such offenses as endangering public order, illegal assembly, or insulting public officials.[17]

Albini's and Ciccotti's work in Potenza provides two examples of protective or defensive roles that the democrats played at times vis-à-vis lower-class associations. These were peaceful roles played entirely within the framework of the existing laws. But among the democrats studied here there were some with a more militant (desperate, perhaps) view of their responsibility in this regard. For example, in the Catanzaro area Raffaele Piccoli, a staunch republican to the end of his life, encouraged workers and peasants not to shy away from confrontations with local authorities. In 1870 he led a number of them in an unsuccessful uprising that sanctioned at once the proclamation of a democratic republic and the distribution of underutilized land to poor families. Militants like Piccoli tried to convince their lower-class followers that offense was the best defense. Yet because only small groups of people heeded their message, their revolutionary attempts failed and they themselves often came to a bad end.[18]

Among the leaders of Risorgimento democracy, men of Mazzinian background—whether moderate like Albini and Dolfi or militant like Piccoli—undoubtedly made the greatest contribution to the success of working-class associations in the 1860s. Even so, their leadership was frequently criticized. By the end of the decade the tide began to turn against them, and by the mid-1870s they were on the defensive, losing ground especially among the younger generation to indigenous anarchist leaders and to organizers of the First Workingmen's International.

As Gastone Manacorda has pointed out, in Piedmont-Sardinia in the 1850s and elsewhere in the early 1860s the struggle for leadership of the Società operaie was primarily one between Mazzinians and moderate liberals. The main issue at stake was whether and to what extent the Società operaie were to become invoved in the political process. Many moderates, at least in urban centers, supported efforts to promote literacy among the lower classes; they even looked forward to the day when Italian workingmen would cease to be plebs and become citizens in the full sense of the word. But they argued that for the time being it seemed inappropriate for the Società operaie to act as schools for political indoctrination or, worse, as political pressure groups. They could too easily fall prey to demagogues as they sometimes had during the revolution of 1848–49. Moreover, political involvement was sure to strain their limited resources. Thus, the liberals urged their lower-class allies and protégés to focus on more practical, short-term goals such as mutual aid, pension funds, evening and Sunday classes for their members, and the regulation of child labor. Mazzini's social theory, by contrast, placed the political education of the workers and their gradual involvement in concrete political issues far above such useful but limited practical functions.

The Mazzinians fared rather well in this debate. In the major Italian cities and in old republican strongholds like Forlì, Ravenna, and Ancona, artisans and workers rejected the limited role prescribed for them by liberal advisors. Instead they tried to influence nominations and elections, and they joined democratic intellectuals in the agitation for suffrage reform. Already at the Ninth Congress of the Società operaie in the fall of 1861 B. F. Savi defended their right to do these things on the grounds that "it [was] time for every social need to have an expression, for every category of citizens to be officially represented in the nation's legislative bodies." As for the liberal argument that the working classes were not ready for full political participation, he observed that "no one [had] ever learned to swim without first jumping into the water."[19] To remain within this metaphor, the real question for the Società operaie was not whether to jump into the water of Italian politics, but rather how to swim and in what direction.

Subsequent congresses held in Parma in 1863 and in Naples in 1864 revealed beyond doubt that the Mazzinian point of view had triumphed over the liberal one. With a Pact of Brotherhood (*Patto di fratellanza*) signed by representatives from every part of Italy, the

Società made a firm commitment to political action. This commitment, however, was made within the parameters of Mazzinian
ideology. Thus, national questions, particularly the liberation of
Rome and Venetia, were to be given precedence over institutional
ones. Further, the pact restated the Mazzinian commitment to cooperation among social classes.

The resolutions of the Parma and Naples congresses, however,
did not go unchallenged. Just as they were winning artisans and
workers away from the liberal point of view, the Mazzinians came
under attack from the Left. The full impact of the attack became
clear during the Twelfth Congress of the Società operaie held in
Rome in the fall of 1871. Horrified by the Paris Commune, Mazzinian loyalists asked for a renewed assertion of the need for class cooperation; but a significant minority of those present refused to con-
cur. The schism that then took place among the democratic intellectuals and organizers who worked with the Società operaie bore a
close resemblance to that which had occurred in 1848–49. During
the 1860s orthodox Mazzinians had been able to steer the Società in a
nationalist and associationist direction. But as soon as Italy's territorial unification had been completed, dissident democrats began
to call for a new and more aggressive political stance, not merely on
the issue of constitutional reform but also on the liberals' economic
and social policies.[20]

The Twelfth Congress brought out into the open differences of
opinion that had emerged during the late 1860s, thus casting a pall
over the last years of Mazzini's life. The problem — as he still perceived it — was the growing influence of the socialist concept of class
struggle and the proclivity of modern society to emphasize material
over moral concerns. He was especially saddened to see young men
who had once fought for Italian unity now inciting workers and
peasants to violence against fellow Italians. Of Attanasio Dramis,
for instance, he wrote that although "he [was] an excellent young
man," he was wrong to abandon Mazzinian principles in favor of
what he called "socialism." Dramis and others, Mazzini added, were
only copying those French socialists who had made possible the coup
d'état of 1851.[21]

For Mazzini himself and for those who remained loyal to his
teachings the defection of former supporters or sympathizers was
obviously hard to bear. It was made even worse by the presence in
Italy of the Russian anarchist Bakunin, who helped organize an
Italian branch of the First International. Among the democrats who
joined the International in the 1860s and early 1870s were young
dissidents like Dramis, but also such older stalwarts of the national

struggle as Fanelli, Friscia, and Giuseppe Mazzoni. With Mazzini ailing and living a semiclandestine life in Pisa, the task of fighting Bakunin's influence fell to Saffi and Quadrio within the Società operaie and to Campanella and Petroni in the democratic press. Under Petroni's editorship, *La Roma del popolo* became the mouthpiece of orthodox Mazzinianism, while other democratic newspapers remained open to a variety of ideological currents or else actually espoused the ideas of the International.

The importance of Bakunin's mission in Italy and his overall impact on the development of the Italian Left in the 1870s probably has been overrated. Certainly the crisis of Mazzinian leadership in the Società operaie preceded his arrival, and it may have been inevitable once Italy's unification was achieved. With the growth of literacy and of industry in some regions, it may also have been inevitable that the rank-and-file members of the Società began to push for more vigorous opposition to the existing political and social arrangements. Bakunin's presence nonetheless played a significant role in the history of Risorgimento democracy as the catalyst of a major schism.

It did not matter to the democrats that Bakunin was in many ways outside the mainstream of the European Left. Nor did it matter much that the First International was a faltering organization, torn by the rivalry between Bakunin and Marx. Bakunin's arrival in Italy, and later the reports from revolutionary Paris, pointed to the rise of new social forces that were changing the face of Europe. Italy could not for long remain untouched. Members of the parliamentary "loyal opposition," democratic activists working quietly at the local level, and Mazzinian leaders of the Società operaie took these as signs that Italy's as yet fragile political unity was in danger; and they responded by closing ranks with the liberals. By contrast, a militant minority abandoned their halfhearted attempts to continue the Italian Revolution by boring from within the existing institutions. They returned to the strategy outlined in the 1850s by their hero Pisacane, but with one major difference. Insofar as possible, they proposed to work hand in hand with other European revolutionaries. It seemed fitting, somehow, that among the democrats studied here Niccolò Lo Savio, a former Mazzinian, became the chief theorist of the militant minority and Giuseppe Fanelli, Pisacane's agent in 1856–57, became the architect of their ties with the International in Spain and other countries.[22]

Epilogue _____
Democrats in the Post-Risorgimento

Both within and without the national Parliament, the democratic presence in Italian politics after the unification was intellectually lively, occasionally significant, always interesting. This was in large part a result of the constant interaction between deputies committed to a reformist, gradualist outlook and extra-parliamentary activists committed to some form of continuing revolution.

The occupation of Rome in September 1870 eliminated the most serious weakness of parliamentary democracy, the constant tension between "loyal opposition" and *garibaldini.* Ironically, however, those same international events that marked the end of Italy's national revolution brought about parliamentary democracy's irreversible drift toward the moderate liberal camp. Just as the revolutionary failures of the 1850s had prompted some democrats to support the national program of the moderate liberals, so did the Paris Commune and the growth of socialist and anarchist groups persuade others to close ranks with their former rivals in the interest of Italy's internal stability and international security.

What the conquest of Rome and the Paris Commune were to the democratic deputies, Bakunin's influence in Italy and Mazzini's death in 1872 were to extraparliamentary intellectuals and activists. As their parliamentary colleagues came closer and closer to sharing power with and eventually replacing Cavour's successors, they gradually abandoned any hopes of changing Italy's institutions in the near future. Instead, through the democratic press and hundreds of working-class associations they concentrated on long-range goals of cultural and social change. The differences between these two groups were profound and fraught with important consequences for the development of future mass movements on the Left. Yet they were less significant than the growing chasm between those Risorgimento democrats who became primarily concerned with preserving the immediate results of the national revolution and those concerned above all with continuing it until its beneficial impact could be extended from a revolutionary elite to all Italians.

Fifty-six of the democrats studied here (38.4 percent of the original sample) had political careers that lasted well beyond the electoral victories of the "loyal opposition" in 1874–1876. On numerous occasions in the late 1870s they bemoaned the lack of a democratic united front in Italian politics. But in the last quarter of the nineteenth century a national network such as had existed before the unification had become impossible. Instead, the surviving democrats became the pivotal figures in two interlocking democratic networks, one centered around the parliamentary group that became known as the Sinistra storica, the other around the left-wing opposition group formed in 1877 and known as l'Estrema. Both of these networks retained some elements of democratic ideology and discarded or ignored others. In each of them, older men who had been initiated to revolutionary politics well before the unification served as role models and mentors for the post-Risorgimento generation. But whether old stalwarts or young recruits to the movement, the democrats in the late 1870s faced a common problem: how to adjust aspirations and strategies formulated in the heroic age of nation building to the unheroic age of state building. In the Umbertian era, Victor Emmanuel II and Cavour were fast becoming the principal deities of a national pantheon that had no place for patriots of republican or socialist inclinations. Although Garibaldi did figure prominently in that pantheon, alongside the king and Cavour, the official iconography of the period no longer reflected his past as a guerrilla in South America, his Mazzinian republicanism, or even his notoriously virulent anti-Catholicism. Rather, he was honored as the man who had conquered the Bourbon Kingdom "in the name of of Italy and Victor Emmanuel" and had then met the king at Teano to hand over the conquered territories.

Cattaneo, Ferrari, Pisacane, and other leading lights of Risorgimento democracy were altogether absent from the official pantheon and seldom mentioned in the official speeches of the Umbertian era. As for Mazzini, he was remembered not as the apostle of democratic and republican government, but only as the advocate of Italian unity, independence, and greatness. Italy's ruling elite, which by the late 1870s included not a few of his former disciples, forgot his vision of political and social democracy. Instead, it often emphasized his concept of a Third Rome, an Italy greater and more powerful than that of the Caesars and the popes.

Under certain conditions, the surviving democrats did find a place in the national pantheon of the late nineteenth century. A formal abjuration of republican or socialist principles was not required for admission, but some gesture of loyalty toward the constitutional monarchy was expected. It might be a statement, such as Crispi's "Monarchy unites us; a republic would divide us," or an action, such as Cairoli's brave attempt to shield the king from an assassin's bullets. At any rate, it was no accident that among the surviving democrats only those who demonstrated devotion to the constitutional monarchy held important government posts in the 1880s and 1890s. Among them were, of course, members of the parliamentary "loyal opposition" and their supporters outside Parliament. Together these men constituted the first of the two post-Risorgimento networks.

Of the twenty-four democrats in the Sinistra storica network, about one half were men of Crispi's generation, old if in most cases still vigorous by the time they came to power. Hardened by decades of struggle, they were determined to savor the fruits of political success that had eluded them after 1848–49. Although younger democrats such as Nicotera, Guastalla, and Elia were not denied opportunities for political apprenticeship, their older colleagues maintained control over this first post-Risorgimento network at least until the death of Depretis in 1887. Consistent with democratic ideology, these men fought successfully for suffrage reform and for fiscal policies less burdensome to the lower classes. Yet the results of their efforts were modest, as the more radical members of the movement pointed out. Although the electoral reform of 1882 roughly quadrupled the number of enfranchised adult males, it still left the electorate at only about 2 percent of the population, a very low figure by comparison with other western European countries. As for fiscal reform, it did not go beyond the much-publicized repeal of the grist tax, a popular gesture but hardly a major shift in the country's economic priorities.

There were several reasons why the democratic "loyal opposition," and particularly its oldest leaders, settled for such modest goals once they came to power. Not only were they divided among themselves concerning the scope and the timetable for reform of Italy's political and social institutions, they were also most anxious to avoid a return to the political wilderness. Thus, unwilling to risk electoral defeat on a program of pronounced democratic character, they worked instead for the broadest possible coalition. As they saw it, the Italian national interest required not two substantially different parties competing for electoral success and for power, but rather a consensus around important issues. This "transformist" view of Italian politics, although shared by moderate liberal leaders, was especially appropriate to the men of the emerging Sinistra storica. When those Risorgimento democrats who were still politically active in the Umbertian period came to power, they proved no more willing to work under a genuine two-party system than the leaders of the Destra storica had been a decade earlier. Indeed, the prospect of losing their hard-won majority was more threatening to the parliamentary democrats of the 1880s — full-time politicians, *faute de mieux* — than it had been to the liberal notables of the 1870s.

Trasformismo, however, was more than a protective device by which the surviving democrats in this network hoped to avoid new political setbacks. It was also a means by which they could legitimize their position and affirm their right to govern Italy under a monarchical constitution, despite their past record of revolutionary republicanism. A broad parliamentary coalition that included liberals of proven loyalty to the king as well as former democratic members of the Sardinian Parliament was convincing proof that yesterday's subversives had become responsible statesmen. Broad coalitions, however, could not be built easily around issues of constitutional reform, much less around social and economic ones. Hence Depretis and his colleagues needed to focus on new and popular issues that had not been at the center of political controversy during the Risorgimento. In the 1880s, in fact, issues of imperialism and irredentism became an important part of the program and strategy of the parliamentary democrats and their supporters.

During the Risorgimento several democrats had argued that Italy was destined to play a leading role in the Mediterranean and that, therefore, after the unification she would need a dynamic foreign policy and a viable navy. Among the most articulate prophets of Italy's great future overseas had been Bixio, Crispi, and Musolino. Bixio died at sea in 1873, but the two southerners lived

long enough to express their outrage at the eclipse of Italian interests
in Tunisia as well as their delight at the first Italian outposts on the
Red Sea. Democrats of their generation, however, were generally
careful to preserve a balance between the new preoccupation with
expansion and their movement's more traditional concern with
domestic issues. This was not always the case for younger members
of the network. Nicotera's foreign policy, for instance, although
ostensibly derived from those of elder statesmen of the movement, in
fact owed more to the increasing popularity of imported doctrines,
such as social Darwinism, than to the democratic nationalism of his
mentors. The difference became even more pronounced in the
1890s, when Crispi found greater support for an imperialist foreign
policy among democrats two or three generations younger than he
did among his own contemporaries.

Irredentism also proved occasionally useful to the Sinistra
storica as a building block for parliamentary coalitions. But it was
an issue that had to be handled with the greatest care. During the
Risorgimento, Mazzini, Cattaneo, and other democratic thinkers
had turned their attention to the Italian-speaking people of Trento,
Trieste, and Dalmatia. Emigrés from those areas, such as Seismit-
Doda, or men who had lived and worked there, such as Dall'Ongaro
and his brother-in-law Pacifico Valussi, had publicized (and often
exaggerated) the plight of Italian minorities surrounded by a sea of
Slavs or Germans. After the unification, however, the democratic
"loyal opposition" had focused on the liberation of Venetia, and little more had been said about other Italian-speaking areas of the
Habsburg Empire. The subsequent growth of irredentism and its
evolution into a form of armed struggle were determined much
more by the internal tensions of the Habsburg Empire than by the
actions of anti-Austrian groups within Italy or of the Italian government itself. Yet on several occasions in the 1880s and 1890s the parliamentary democrats were able to capitalize on the irredentist
cause and to present themselves as the true paladins of Italian national rights and honor. Young recruits to the movement, especially
Salvatore Barzilai from Trieste, then joined hands in the irredentist
campaign with such revered old stalwarts as Cairoli, Fabrizi, and
Saffi.

Although it was easier to reconcile with the traditions of Risorgimento democracy than was imperialism, irredentism at times
became a political liability for leaders who wished to cultivate the
friendship of the Austrian and German Empires. Crispi, in particular, was torn between his desire to use irredentism to bolster the
popular base of his government and his conviction that only an

alliance with the great powers of central Europe could protect Italy's economic and strategic interests from a hostile France. But even with these limitations, the Sinistra storica governed Italy for more than a decade. Between 1876 and 1887 the Sinistra storica established its legitimacy be defending the *Statuto* and the monarchy while at the same time taking some modest steps toward the democratization of Italian politics. Its historic mission, then, was to continue the political aspect of the Italian Revolution and to demonstrate that the goals of Risorgimento democracy could be pursued even in the context of nondemocratic institutions. In so doing they pushed from within for a gradual transformation of the liberal political system into one that was democratic.

In the 1890s, as the last Risorgimento democrats retired from politics or died, this task fell to younger men whose strategy combined genuine aspirations to political democracy with unquestionable loyalty to the institutions of the liberal state. Giovanni Giolitti epitomized more than any post-Risorgimento politician the synthesis of liberal and democratic ideas wrought by the men of the Sinistra storica. He was their rightful heir not only because he presided over a gradual democratization of the liberal state from within but also because, like most of them, he lived by and for the practice of parliamentary politics. Like them, throughout his long career he was criticized from the Left for opportunism and lack of vision. Until the turn of the century, most of this criticism came from the second post-Risorgimento democratic network, one that consisted of the parliamentary Estrema and of Mazzinian loyalists outside of Parliament. The evolution of parliamentary democracy from "loyal opposition" into the Sinistra storica gave Italy a kind of stability, unity, and continuity that were crucial to her survival as a new state. However, it also created a power vacuum on the Left of the political spectrum.

In Parliament the process of *trasformismo* stifled the lively political debates that had marked the early years of Italian unity, and it discouraged those who wished to offer meaningful alternatives to the existing institutions and policies. Moreover, the death or electoral defeat of men like Ferrari reduced the number of parliamentary democrats willing to play the role of "deputies-at-large" of the disenfranchised majority of Italians. Thus, despite the modest suffrage reform of 1882, the chasm between *paese legale* and *paese reale*, that is, between the liberal state and the Italian people, became perhaps even wider than it had been at the moment of the unification.

Already in the late 1870s several democrats expressed the view that this trend could not be allowed to continue. Bertani, for instance, warned his fellow deputies of the dangers that lay ahead for a ruling elite too exclusively preoccupied with parliamentary coalitions. Extraparliamentary democrats such as Mario feared that the democratic intellectuals, corrupted by the influence of *trasformismo*, were losing that ability to reach out to the masses which had been perhaps their greatest contribution to the Risorgimento. The growth of *trasformismo* in the 1880s proved that the misgivings of these democrats were justified and that it was indeed urgent to oppose the emerging Sinistra storica. Twenty-five of the democrats studied here took part in this effort. Those who were members of Parliament joined or supported l'Estrema, the radical Left of the Umbertian era. Others such as Campanella and Mario, who were already quite active in extraparliamentary groups, redoubled their efforts to prepare the lower classes to seek direct representation and participation in the political system.

As the "loyal opposition" of the 1860s gradually evolved into the Sinistra storica of the 1880s, the political vacuum on the Left was filled by the members of these two groups, which remained distinct although they worked toward similar goals. But the Estrema and its allies outside Parliament experienced considerable difficulties in establishing themselves as a legitimate opposition to the government coalition. For even more than Depretis, Crispi, Mordini, and other founders of the Sinistra storica, they came almost without exception from the ranks of Mazzinian republicanism. And despite their protestations of respect for the existing institutions, their political behavior often gave away their ambivalence and uneasiness. Even Cairoli, who had defended these radical colleagues against conspiracy charges in 1875, as prime minister in 1878 admonished them to clarify their position vis-à-vis the *Statuto* and the monarchy. Only thus, he argued, could they be effective in the role of "loyal opposition" which he and other democrats had played in the 1860s vis-à-vis Cavour's successors. Over the years this old *garibaldino* evidently had forgotten that he himself had regarded the original proponents of the concept of "loyal opposition" at best as ambitious opportunists, at worst as traitors to the democratic tradition of the Risorgimento. Yet Cairoli's point was well taken. Before the Estrema and its allies could fill the power vacuum created by the growth of *trasformismo*, they had to clarify both the ideological content and the pragmatic forms of their opposition.

With regard to ideology there was substantial agreement among those who aspired to become the new "loyal opposition" to the king's government. They supported the political goals of the Sinistra storica, particularly its persistent and successful efforts to legitimize the practice of ministerial responsibility to the Chamber. But they were impatient with the slow pace of social reforms, limited as these were in the 1880s to the repeal of the grist tax and the expansion of elementary education. The members of the second democratic network were divided, however, on questions of political strategy. Although they denied any desire to subvert the existing institutions, Mazzinian loyalists such as Mario, Campanella, Petroni, and Giannelli showed little faith in the effectiveness of parliamentary opposition. Mario did not seek elective office again after his much-publicized resignation in December 1863. As for his colleagues—prominent organizers and journalists all—they showed little inclination to take the oath of loyalty to the king that was required of all deputies. Instead, they continued to write for the democratic press and to work with the Società operaie, preaching democratic republicanism and training a new generation of leaders like themselves, educated, articulate, and relatively poor. Among the recruits to these extraparliamentary activities were the future labor leader Osvaldo Gnocchi-Viani, future spokesmen of the Radical party such as Carlo Romussi and Giuseppe Marcora and, finally, future leaders of the Socialist party like Ettore Sacchi and Leonida Bissolati.

Neither the surviving Risorgimento democrats nor the neophytes who joined them in the 1880s ever conspired to overthrow the constitutional monarchy or condoned any form of political violence. Although all were ardent republicans and some advocated radical changes in their country's economic and social institutions, their claim that they were not subversive is substantiated by the police records that have survived. (All the democrats in question were watched rather closely.) Their ideas may have been subversive, but their actions usually were not. The radical democrats of the Umbertian era carried on a political tradition established in the early 1860s by Ferrari and other members of the "loyal opposition," a tradition that has remained characteristic of mainstream groups of the Italian Left to this day. That is, they made a distinction between what was ideologically preferable (a democratic republic) and what was historically and politically possible. Their willingness to work within the laws of the liberal monarchy was not, however, motivated by mere expediency. They were convinced that the historical conditions for a democratic republic did not yet exist in Italy. To create those conditions it was not enough to establish political parties or even to introduce universal suffrage and education. Rather, it was necessary to change the ways in which Italians thought about themselves as citizens, about their society, about the state. Until such changes in consciousness occurred, it was imperative to make sure that the political ruling elite provided what it had promised in 1860: freedom of speech, assembly, and press.

Although they, too, did not hide their republican backgrounds, parliamentary opponents of the Sinistra storica such as Filopanti, Levi, and Morelli did not need to justify their claims to the role of "loyal opposition," for they had taken the oath of loyalty to the king. Unlike their extraparliamentary allies, they believed that significant social progress could be made within the existing political institutions. As they saw it, the key to success lay in parallel efforts to educate the masses, on the one hand, and on the other to convince the ruling classes of the urgent need for reform. Their standard-bearers were Bertani and Morelli, their most brilliant pupil the young Lombard journalist Felice Cavallotti. These men were the social conscience of the Italian Parliament of the 1880s as Ferrari had been until his death in 1876. Their speeches on the social question and the bills they introduced on issues ranging from the regulation of child labor to public health to the reform of agrarian contracts prepared the ground for the socialist deputies of the next two decades. Moreover, the radical democrats of the post-Risorgimento defended and carried on the tradition of secularism from which the Sinistra storica departed occasionally. Particularly in the early 1890s, they became the watchdogs of the government's ecclesiastical policy and the paladins of secular culture and religious minorities. For in the tense climate of those years they had reason to fear that even old anticlerical hands like Crispi might be ready for a compromise with the Catholic hierarchy in the interest of social stability.

In a creative antagonism, Sinistra storica and Estrema carried on and updated an important part of the democratic program of the Risorgimento. The national phase of the revolution was behind them (except perhaps for the *terre irredente*). Still, they knew that much remained to be done toward the fulfillment of its political and cultural aspects. They did not perceive the Italian Revolution as a failure, but they regarded it as unfinished. Their efforts to complete the great task of the Risorgimento, however, were made within the framework created by the moderate liberals in the early 1860s. To a significant extent, this was also true of the republicans working at the grass-root level. Their refusal to pay homage to the monarchy and their occasional slips into the rhetoric of class struggle did not alter the fact that, like most of their ideological mentors, they were social reformers rather than revolutionaries. They were not and they did not intend to be a threat to the existing social order. Instead, they aspired to see it function better.

In sum, most of the democrats who remained active after 1876 passed on to their disciples and admirers some of the passion for political equality, secular culture, and social justice that had guided their own actions during the Risorgimento. What they did not provide were role models of revolutionary activism, despite their own record of militancy and despite having had precisely such role models in their youth. Even in their old age they remained too active in a myriad of social and cultural activities to be dismissed as the stereotypical "tired radicals" of much social science literature. Rather, they seem to have feared that an overzealous younger generation in the pursuit of a better society might unwittingly jeopardize the achievements of the Risorgimento. They who had lived under despotic governments appreciated fully the liberties available to the citizens of united Italy. But younger men who might take those liberties for granted had to be taught to respect the existing institutions, even while seeking a more perfect democracy.

Although there can be no question that in the post-Risorgimento the democratic mainstream ran along the banks of constitutional orthodoxy and reformism, a small anarcho-socialist current branched off in the direction of revolution and armed struggle against the liberal state. In the 1860s and 1870s militants like Dramis and Friscia had generally supported the parliamentary "loyal opposition" and operated within the law, at least in part because they expected major political changes from the demise of the moderate liberals. But disappointment, and a certain amount of persecution at the hands of prefects and police, hardened their position in the late 1870s, until they broke completely with the mainstream of Italian democracy. They rejected not only the liberal state and the *trasformismo* of the Sinistra storica, but also the bourgeois radicalism of the Estrema. Intellectually, if not literally, they were the heirs of Pisacane and Landi, more noteworthy for their revolutionary dedication than for their political acumen and influence. In the 1880s and 1890s they built up a considerable following among rural laborers in some areas of the South and especially in the lower Po Valley, where they often supplanted older Mazzinian organizations. Yet for all their success among the poorest, most alienated elements of Umbertian society, they had but a small impact on the ideological and organizational character of the Left in the post-Risorgimento.

With the birth of modern working-class parties—the Partito operaio in 1882 and the Partito socialista in 1892—the teachings of Marx and Engels were grafted onto the existing body of democratic social theories. The resulting programs, with their emphasis on political equality, secular education, and social justice owed much more to Mazzini and the radical intellectuals of the Estrema than they did to the Internationalists. As for strategy, these parties never quite adopted the true anarchist posture of rejection of and withdrawal from the life of the state. Instead, following the example of the Mazzinian republicans, they distinguished between long-term and short-term goals. They chose to pursue short-term goals such as suffrage and economic reforms, for which they had the support of bourgeois radicals in Parliament. And like the Mazzinians, they made changes in popular consciousness their most important long-range goal. The main difference between the anarchist and early socialist militants on the one hand, and the more direct heirs to Risorgimento democracy on the other, lay in the militants' attitude toward the political uses of violence. Anarchists and early socialists resorted, if only occasionally, to the politics of confrontation and to terrorist acts. Though deplored by mainstream democrats, even these tactics were not alien to the Risorgimento tradition. That tradition was, thus, largely preserved for future generations of Italians. But different political groups, whose social base and interests became increasingly diverse with passage of time, carried on different aspects of that tradition. The fragmentation that began in the late 1870s explains in part why Italy's political culture has produced a myriad of intellectually lively non-Marxist democratic groups but no important secular democratic party with a social base in the middle classes.

Appendix

The Sample

Name	Region of Origin	Dates
Acerbi, Giovanni	Lombardy	1825–1869
Albini, Giacinto	Basilicata[a]	1821–1884
Andreini, Rinaldo	Romagna	1818–1890
Anelli, Luigi	Lombardy	1813–1889
Angherà, Francesco	Calabria	1820–1879
Asproni, Giorgio	Sardinia	1809–1876
Bacco, Giuseppe	Venetia	1821–1877
Barbetti, Eusebio	Romagna	1816–1848
Bargoni, Angelo	Lombardy	1829–1901
Bertani, Agostino	Lombardy	1812–1886
Bixio, Gerolamo (Nino)	Liguria	1821–1873
Brizi, Eugenio	Umbria	1812–1894
Brofferio, Angelo	Piedmont	1802–1866
Bruzzesi, Giacinto	Latium	1822–1900

Name	Region of Origin	Dates
Budini, Giuseppe	Romagna	1804–1877
Cadolini, Giovanni	Lombardy	1830–1917
Cairoli, Benedetto	Lombardy	1825–1889
Caldesi, Vincenzo	Romagna	1817–1870
Calvino, Salvatore	Sicily	1820–1883
Campanella, Federico	Liguria	1804–1884
Campo, Francesco	Sicily	1827–ca. 1892
Carducci, Costabile	Campania	1804–1849
Carnazza, Gabriele	Sicily	1809–1880
Cassola, Carlo	Lombardy	1814–1894
Cattaneo, Carlo	Lombardy	1801–1869
Cattani-Cavalcanti, Leopoldo	Tuscany	1813–1882
Cironi, Piero	Tuscany	1819–1862
Crispi, Francesco	Sicily	1818–1901
Cuneo, Giovanni Battista	Liguria	1809–1875
Dall'Ongaro, Francesco	Venetia	1808–1873
Dassi, Giuseppe	Campania	ca. 1825–1883
De Boni, Filippo	Venetia	1816–1870
De Cristoforis, Carlo	Lombardy	1824–1859
De Lieto, Casimiro	Calabria	1803–1874
De Luca, Francesco	Calabria	1811–1875
De Luigi, Attilio	Lombardy	1814–1854
Depretis, Agostino	Piedmont	1813–1887
Dolfi, Giuseppe	Tuscany	1818–1869
Dramis, Attanasio	Basilicata	1829–1911
Elia, Augusto	Marches	1829–1909
Fabrizi, Nicola	Emilia	1804–1885
Faccioli, Giulio	Venetia	1810–1864
Fanelli, Giuseppe	Apulia	1827–1877
Ferrari, Giuseppe	Lombardy	1811–1876
Ferrari, Nicolao	Liguria	1827–1855
Filopanti, Quirico	Emilia	1812–1894
Finzi, Giuseppe	Lombardy	1815–1886
Franchi, Ausonio	Liguria	1821–1895
Frapolli, Ludovico	Lombardy	1815–1878
Fratellini, Giuseppe	Umbria	1814–1899

Name	Region of Origin	Dates
Friscia, Saverio	Sicily	1818–1886
Garibaldi, Giuseppe	Nice[b]	1805–1882
Gavazzi, Alessandro	Emilia	1809–1889
Gentilini, Enrico	Piedmont	ca. 1810–1859
Ghiglione, (Carlo) Antonio	Liguria	1813–1872
Giacomelli, Angelo	Venetia	1821–1893
Giannelli, Andrea	Tuscany	1831–1914
Govean, Felice	Piedmont	1819–1898
Grazia, Massimiliano	Romagna	1817–1861
Guastalla, Enrico	Emilia	1826–1903
Guerrazzi, Francesco Domenico	Tuscany	1804–1873
Guglielmi, Francesco	Piedmont	1812–1878
Guttièrez, Gaetano	Lombardy	ca. 1825–1880
La Cecilia, Giovanni	Campania	1801–1880
Lamberti, Giuseppe	Emilia	1803–1851
Landi, Tommaso	Sicily	ca. 1820–1874
La Porta, Luigi	Sicily	1817–1894
Lemmi, Adriano	Tuscany	1822–1906
Levi, Davide	Piedmont	1816–1898
Libertini, Giuseppe	Apulia	1826–1873
Lo Savio, Niccolò	Apulia	1830–1911
Macchi, Mauro	Lombardy	1818–1880
Maestri, Pietro	Lombardy	1816–1871
Maffei, Enrico	Apulia	1809–1881
Mario, Alberto	Venetia	1825–1886
Marsico, Gaspare	Calabria	1813–1874
Mattioli, Giuseppe Camillo	Emilia	1817–1893
Mauro, Domenico	Calabria	1812–1873
Mazzini, Giuseppe	Liguria	1805–1872
Mazzoni, Cesare	Latium	ca. 1810–1869
Mazzoni, Giuseppe	Tuscany	1808–1880
Mellana, Filippo	Piedmont	1810–1874
Miceli, Luigi	Calabria	1824–1906
Mignogna, Nicola	Apulia	1808–1870
Mileti, Carlo	Calabria	ca. 1828–1880

Name	Region of Origin	Dates
Milo Guggino, Francesco	Sicily	ca. 1812–1867
Mini, Costantino	Tuscany	1823–1859
Modena, Gustavo	Venetia	1805–1861
Moja, Cristoforo	Piedmont	1811–1858
Montanelli, Giuseppe	Tuscany	1813–1862
Montazio, Enrico	Tuscany	1817–1886
Montecchi, Mattia	Latium	1816–1871
Mordini, Antonio	Tuscany	1819–1902
Morelli, Salvatore	Apulia	1830–1898
Morici, Antonio	Calabria	ca. 1828–1898
Mosciaro, Giovanni	Calabria	ca. 1825–1875
Mosto, Antonio	Liguria	1824–1890
Musolino, Benedetto	Calabria	1809–1885
Nicotera, Giovanni	Calabria	1828–1894
Nullo, Francesco	Lombardy	1826–1863
Orsini, Felice	Romagna	1819–1859
Pacifici, Pacifico	Marches	1823–1895
Pantaleo, Giovanni	Sicily	1830–1879
Petroni, Giuseppe	Latium	1812–1888
Petruccelli, Ferdinando	Basilicata	1815–1890
Pezzotti, Giovanni	Lombardy	1811–1852
Pianciani, Luigi	Umbria	1810–1890
Piccoli, Raffaele	Calabria	1819–1888
Pigli, Carlo	Tuscany	1802–1860
Pigozzi, Francesco	Emilia	1815–1891
Pilo, Rosalino	Sicily	1820–1860
Pisacane, Carlo	Campania	1815–1857
Pistrucci, Scipione	Latium	1811–1854
Quadrio, Maurizio	Lombardy	1800–1876
Raffaele, Giovanni	Sicily	1804–1882
Ragona, Vito	Sicily	ca. 1800–1875
Regnoli, Oreste	Romagna	1816–1896
Reta, Costantino	Piedmont	1816–1858
Ricciardi, Giuseppe	Campania	1808–1882
Romano, Giuseppe	Apulia	1809–1876
Rosa, Gabriele	Lombardy	1812–1897
Rubieri, Ermolao	Tuscany	1818–1879

Name	Region of Origin	Dates
Ruffini, Giovanni	Liguria	1807–1881
Rusconi, Carlo	Emilia	1819–1889
Sacchi, Achille	Lombardy	1827–1890
Saffi, (Marco) Aurelio	Romagna	1819–1890
Savi, Bartolomeo Francesco	Liguria	1820–1865
Savini, Savino	Emilia	1813–1859
Scarsellini, Angelo	Venetia	1820–1853
Seismit-Doda, Federico	Dalmatia[c]	1825–1893
Sgarallino, Andrea	Tuscany	1819–1887
Sgarallino, Jacopo	Tuscany	1823–1879
Siliprandi, Francesco	Lombardy	1816–1892
Sineo, Riccardo	Piedmont	1805–1876
Sirtori, Giuseppe	Lombardy	1813–1874
Tallinucci, Gaetano	Tuscany	1819–1879
Tazzoli, Enrico	Lombardy	1812–1853
Tuveri, Giovanni Battista	Sardinia	1815–1887
Ugdulena, Gregorio	Sicily	1815–1872
Usiglio, Angelo	Emilia	1803–1875
Usiglio, Emilio	Emilia	1813–1895
Valerio, Lorenzo	Piedmont	1810–1865
Vannucci, Atto	Tuscany	1810–1883
Varè, Giambattista	Venetia	1817–1884
Ventre, Aniello	Campania	1827–1874
Zuppetta, Luigi	Apulia	1810–1889

a. Called Lucania in the nineteenth century.

b. Ceded to France in 1860.

c. Culturally and politically a part of Venetia in the nineteenth century.

Abbreviations

ACMO	Archivio communale, Modena	ASPZ	Archivio di Stato, Potenza
ACS	Archivio centrale dello Stato, Rome	ASR	Archivio di Stato, Rome
AHR	*American Historical Review*	ASSA	Archivio di Stato, Salerno
APCD	*Atti parlamentari.* Camera dei Deputati	ASTO	Archivio di Stato, Turin
ASCS	Archivio di Stato, Cosenza	ASVE	Archivio di Stato, Venice
ASCZ	Archivio di Stato, Catanzaro	BABO	Biblioteca-Archivio dell'Archiginnasio, Bologna
ASMN	Archivio di Stato, Mantua	BAM	Biblioteca Ambrosiana, Milan
ASNA	Archivio di Stato, Naples	BCPA	Biblioteca comunale, Palermo
ASPA	Archivio di Stato, Palermo	BCRE	Biblioteca comunale, Reggio Emilia

BCVR	Biblioteca comunale, Verona	IMGE	Istituto mazziniano, Genoa
BDM	Biblioteca-Archivio della Domus mazziniana, Pisa	*JMH*	*Journal of Modern History*
BFPT	Biblioteca Forteguerriana, Pistoia	MNSMNA	Museo Nazionale San Martino, Naples
BIFM	Biblioteca dell'Istituto Giangiacomo Feltrinelli, Milan	MRF	Museo del Risorgimento, Florence
BISR	Biblioteca dell'Istituto per la storia del Risorgimento italiano, Rome	MRM	Museo del Risorgimento, Milan
		MRMO	Biblioteca del Museo del Risorgimento, Modena
BLLI	Biblioteca Labronica, Livorno	MRTO	Biblioteca del Museo del Risorgimento, Turin
BMF	Biblioteca Maruceliana, Florence	*RSR*	*Rassegna storica del Risorgimento*
BNF	Biblioteca Nazionale, Florence	*RST*	*Rassegna storica toscana*
BNNA	Biblioteca Nazionale, Naples	*RSS*	*Rivista storica del socialismo*
BODM	*Bollettino della Domus mazziniana*	SNSP	Società napoletana di storia patria, Naples
BPTO	Biblioteca della Provincia, Turin	SRSP	Società romana di storia patria, Rome
BRPR	Biblioteca Ronciniana, Prato	SSSP	Società siciliana di storia patria, Palermo
BUGE	Biblioteca universitaria, Genoa		

Notes

1. The Italian Revolution as a Cultural Revolution

1. On the attitude of the Italian revolutionaries toward the temporal power see A. C. Jemolo, *Chiesa e stato negli ultimi cento anni*, 2nd ed. (Turin: Einaudi, 1963), chap. 2, and Giorgio Candeloro, *Storia dell'Italia moderna*, 8 vols. (Milan: Feltrinelli, 1956–1978), vol. 2, chap. 5.

2. Felice Orsini, *Memorie politiche* (Turin: De Giorgis, 1858), p. 77.

3. For background see Giuliana D'Amelio, *Stato e chiesa: La legislazione ecclesiastica fino al 1867* (Milan: Giuffrè, 1961), and Adolfo Omodeo, *L'opera politica del Conte di Cavour, 1848–1857* (Milan and Naples: Ricciardi, 1968), pp. 59-81, and 166-178.

4. Giuseppe Mazzini, *Scritti editi ed inediti*, 100 vols. (Imola: Edizione nazionale, 1906–1953), 3:8. Hereinafter cited as *SEI*. For background on Mazzini's religious thought see especially Gaetano Salvemini, "Il pensiero religioso-politico-sociale di Mazzini," in *Scritti sul Risorgimento* (Milan: Feltrinelii, 1961), pp. 145-249, and Francesco Landogna, *Le idee religiose di Mazzini* (Livorno: Giusti, 1924).

5. Mazzini, *SEI*, 5:45; emphasis added.

6. Giuseppe Mazzini, *Note autobiografiche* (Naples: Centro studi maz-

ziniani, 1972), pp. 283-284.

7. For Giuseppe Ferrari's philosophical formation see especially his *De l'erreur* (Paris: Moquet, 1840) and the *Essai sur le principe et les limites de la philosophie de l'histoire* (Paris: Joubert, 1843).

8. See Giuseppe Ferrari, *Scritti politici*, ed. Silvia Rota Ghibaudi (Turin: UTET, 1973), especially pp. 390-405, and 901-908.

9. For references to the Italian masses see especially Ausonio Franchi's *La filosofia delle scuole italiane: Lettere a G. M. Bertini* (Capolago: Tipografia elvetica, 1852), p. xliv. For Franchi's views of religious sentiments among the upper classes, see his *Introduzione alla filosofia delle scuole italiane* (Italy, 1852), p. 43.

10. See especially Davide Levi's *Democrazia e papismo* (Milan: Robecchi, 1863).

11. Andreini to Cernuschi, Algiers, February 9, 1851, in Franco Della Peruta, *I democratici, e la rivoluzione italiana* (Milan: Feltrinelli, 1958), pp. 473-481. But see also Andreini's vitriolic tract *Il Pontificato* (Lugano, 1851).

12. Giuseppe Galletti, *La mia prigionia* (Bologna: Vitali, 1870), p. 43.

13. Ferdinando Petruccelli della Gattina, *Popery Exposed: An Exposition of Popery as It Is*, trans. Robert E. Peterson (Philadelphia, 1875). But see also Petruccelli's devastating portrait of lechery, greed, and ambition among the Italian upper clergy in *Pie IX: Sa vie, son regne, l'homme, le prince, le pape* (Brussels: Lacroix, 1866).

14. For the Wallon-Ferrari connection see C. M. Lovett, "Il Secondo impero, il Papato ed il nazionalismo italiano: Lettere inedite di J.-G. Wallon a G. Ferrari," *RSR*, 63 (1976): 441-448. For Holyoake's connections with the Italian exiles see his autobiography, *Sixty Years of an Agitator's Life* (London: T. Fisher Unwin, 1906), passim, and Della Peruta, *I democratici*, pp. 267-269. For the influence of Italian anti-Catholic opinion upon German democrats see Bruno Malinverni, "Gli Italiani negli stati germanici," *Il Veltro*, 5-6 (1961): 51-58, and the De Boni-Herwegh correspondence in Franco Della Peruta's *Democrazia e socialismo nel Risorgimento*, 2nd ed. (Rome: Editori Riuniti, 1977), pp. 341-377. See also Arnold Ruge, *Staat oder Papst? Ein Beitrag zum Ausgleichen zwischen Staat und Kirche, von einem Weltgeistlichen im Munsterlande* (Elberfeld, 1876). Ludmilla Assing, niece of Varnhagen von Ense and the editor of his controversial correspondence with Humboldt, was an important link between Italian and German anti-Catholic circles. See Emil Bebler, *Gottfried Keller und Ludmilla Assing* (Zurich: Rascher, 1952), especially pp. 146-155, and Assing's introduction to her biography of the Tuscan democrat Piero Cironi (*Vita di P. C.* [Prato: Giachetti, 1865]).

15. Mazzini, *Note autobiografiche*, p. 287.

16. Ibid.

17. Petruccelli, for instance, complained that in 1848 Mazzini's attitude had been that of a "European Brigham Young in charge of a gang of second-rate Mormons." (*I fattori ed i malfattori della politica europea contemporanea*, 2 vols. [Milan: Brigola, 1881], 2:365).

18. See Andreini to Cernuschi, Algiers, February 9, 1851, cited in Della

Peruta, *I democratici*, p. 479.

19. Angelo De Gubernatis, ed., *Francesco Dall'Ongaro ed il suo epistolario scelto: Ricordi e spogli* (Florence: Tipografia editrice dell' Associazione, 1875), pp. 308-312. Hereinafter cited as *Epistolario Dall'Ongaro*.

20. For the political implications of Mazzini's religious thought see especially Egisto Roggero, *La giovinezza morale di Mazzini* (Bologna: Zanichelli, 1920); Arturo Codignola, *La giovinezza di Mazzini* (Florence: Vallecchi, 1926); and Giuseppe Berti, *I democratici e l'iniziativa meridionale nel Risorgimento* (Milan: Feltrinelli, 1962), pp. 15-61.

21. See, for instance, Mazzini's "Agli Italiani e specialmente agli operai italiani," *SEI*, 25:3-20.

22. See especially Mazzini's series of essays entitled "Dell' unità italiana," *SEI*, 3:261-335.

23. See especially Quirico Filopanti's *Dio liberale* (Bologna: Zanichelli, 1880) and *Dio esiste* (Milan: Treves, 1881).

24. See, Gustavo Modena, "Un novizio e suo fratello," in *Scritti e discorsi di Gustavo Modena*, ed. Terenzio Grandi (Rome: Istituto per la storia del Risorgimento, 1957), pp. 31-57.

25. For background on the development of labor unions and of working-class political organizations, and for the activities of democratic leaders among them, see especially Gastone Manacorda, *Il movimento operaio italiano attraverso i suoi congressi: Dalle origini alla formazione del Partito socialista*, 2nd ed. (Rome: Editori Riuniti, 1963), and Daniel Horowitz, *Storia del movimento sindacale in Italia* (Bologna: Il Mulino, 1966).

26. This speech was delivered in Rome on November 24, 1875. See *Epistolario di Maurizio Quadrio*, 2 vols. (Milan and Rome: Golio & De Angelis, 1876–1879), 1:92-93. Hereinafter referred to as *Epistolario Quadrio*.

27. Ferrari, *Scritti politici*, pp. 390-391; emphasis added.

28. Ausonio Franchi, *Il razionalismo del popolo* (Lausanne, 1861), p. 254.

29. Carlo Cassola, *I misteri del Papato esposti al popolo* (Pavia: Tipografia degli artisti, 1864), pp. 3-4.

30. Ibid., pp. 85-87.

31. For background on Freemasonry in Italy, see especially Franco Venturi, *Settecento riformatore* (Turin: Einaudi, 1969–), vol 2. and Delio Cantimori, *Utopisti e riformatori italiani* (Florence: Sansoni, 1949). For the role of Masonic lodges in the Risorgimento see Alessandro Luzio, *La Massoneria ed il Risorgimento italiano* (1925; reprint ed., Bologna: Forni, 1966), and Aldo Alessandro Mola, *Storia della Massoneria dall'unità alla repubblica* (Milan: Bompiani, 1965), pp. 13-64.

32. Ludovico Frapolli, *La Franc-maçonnerie reformée*, (Turin: Vercellino, 1864).

33. Lemmi to Crispi, Gabbiano, September 17, 1894, BISR/Archivio Adriano Lemmi, busta 397, plico 17, no. 3. Hereinafter cited as BISR/Lemmi/397/17/3. For Mazzoni, who was active in the First Socialist International, see "Lettere di Mazzoni a Bakunin," ed. Gino Cerrito and P. C. Masini, *Movimento operaio*, 3 (1951): 617-623.

34. Giovanni La Cecilia, *Memorie storico-politiche dal 1820 al 1876*, 5 vols. (Rome: Gargiulo, 1894), 1:13.

35. Giuseppe Montanelli, *Appunti storici sulla rivoluzione d'Italia* (1851; reprint ed., Turin: Chiantore, 1945), p. 109.

36. For Pantaleo and his association see *Fra' Giovanni Pantaleo: Ricordi e note* (Rome: Tipografia economica, 1883) and *Fra' Giovanni Pantaleo: Memorie* (Rome: Bocca, 1891), both edited by B. E. Maineri.

37. See, for instance, the viewpoint of the agnostic Agostino Bertani, "Per la libertà di coscienza," in *Scritti e discorsi scelti*, ed. Jessie White Mario (Florence: Barbèra, 1890), pp. 169-176.

2. The Italian Revolution as a Political Revolution

1. For a good up-to-date introduction to "the problem of independence" see S. J. Woolf et al., *Storia d'Italia dal primo settecento alla unità* (Turin: Einaudi, 1973), pp. 240-379.

2. See, for instance, Giuseppe Mazzini's essay "Ai ministri piemontesi: Siete con l'Austria o contro l'Austria?" *SEI*, 51:121-129.

3. Rosario Romeo, *Il giudizio storico sul Risorgimento* (Catania: Bonanno, 1979), pp. 110-112.

4. For an introduction to the political values of the Risorgimento liberals see especially Gaetano Salvemini, *Scritti sul Risorgimento* (Milan: Feltrinelli, 1961), pp. 395-471; Giuseppe Maranini, *Storia del potere in Italia* (Florence: Vallecchi, 1967), pp. 61-96; and Raymond Grew, *A Sterner Plan for Italian Unity* (Princeton: Princeton University Press, 1963), pp. 3-66.

5. For pre-1850 attempts to reach a synthesis of liberal ideology see Massimo Taparelli d'Azeglio, "Proposta d'un programma per l'opinione nazionale italiana," in *Scritti e discorsi politici*, 3 vols., ed. Marcus De Rubris (Florence: La Nuova Italia, 1931-1938), 1:213-269; Michelangelo Castelli, *Saggi sull'opinione politica moderata in Italia* (Italy [but actually published in Switzerland], 1847); Luigi Torelli, *Pensieri sull'Italia di un anonimo lombardo* (Paris [but actually published in Switzerland], 1846); and Luigi Settembrini, "Protesta del Popolo delle Due Sicilie," in *Opuscoli politici*, ed. Mario Themelly (Rome: Edizioni dell'Ateneo, 1969), pp. 3-91.

6. For the contribution of liberal exiles to the political and cultural life of Piedmont-Sardinia after 1848 see G. B. Furiozzi, *L'emigrazione politica in Piemonte nel decennio preunitario* (Florence: Olschki, 1979). But see also Vittorio Bersezio, *Il Regno di Vittorio Emanuele II*, 8 vols. (Turin: Roux and Favale, 1878-1895), 6:35-130, and Domenico Giuriati, *Memorie d'emigrazione a Torino, 1849-1866* (Milan: Treves, 1897).

7. See, for instance, Camillo Benso di Cavour, "Lo Statuto di Carlo Alberto," in *Scritti del Conte di Cavour*, 2 vols., ed. Domenico Zanichelli (Bologna: Zanichelli, 1892), 1:31-36; Carlo Boncompagni, *Della monarchia rappresentativa* (Turin: Cotta & Pavesio, 1848); and Domenico Carutti, *Dei principi del governo libero* (Turin: Ferrero & Franco, 1852). For the post-1860 debates on the issue of political participation, see Maranini, *Storia del potere*, chap. 3, and Carlo Ghisalberti, *Storia costituzionale d'Italia* (Bari: Laterza, 1974), chaps. 4-7.

8. On the issue of women's suffrage see Franca Pieroni Bortolotti, *Alle origini del movimento femminile in Italia, 1848-1892* (Turin: Einaudi Reprints, 1975), pp. 11-78, and Judith Jeffrey Howard, "The Woman Question in Italy, 1861-1893" (Ph.D. diss., University of Connecticut, 1977), chaps. 1-3.

9. Felice Orsini, *Memorie politiche* (Turin: DeGiorgis, 1858), p. 41.

10. Giuseppe Mazzini, *Note autobiografiche* (Naples: Centro studi mazziniani, 1972), pp. 200-201.

11. Quadrio to the editor of *L'Italia del popolo*, July 30, 1857 cited in Silvia Pelosi, *Della vita di Maurizio Quadrio* (Sondrio: Arti grafiche valtellinesi, 1921), p. 185.

12. For Mazzini's views see "Agli italiani," *SEI*, 38:213-220, which began with the warning: "The King's war is over! The Nation's war has begun." For Pisacane's views see especially his *La guerra combattuta in Italia nel 1848-1849* (1851; reprint ed., Milan: Leonardo, 1946), pp. 332-333.

13. See especially the observations of Ferrari, who was present at the democratic birth of the Second French Republic and was caught up in its conservative demise (*Scritti politici*, ed. Silvia Rota Ghibaudi [Turin: UTET, 1973], pp. 245-253), and those of Macchi, a supporter of universal suffrage before 1848 ("Il sistema rappresentativo ed il suffragio universale," in *Studi politici* [Genoa: Delle Piane, 1854], pp. 325-385).

14. Ferrari made this point quite forcefully in his *La federazione repubblicana* (1851) and in several parliamentary speeches of the 1860s. See especially a speech of March 14-16, 1868, "*Atti del Parlamento italiano. Camera dei deputati. Discussioni,*" hereinafter cited as APCD. See also Michele Tenerelli, *Sul disegno di legge degli onorevoli Crispi e Petruccelli intorno al sistema elettorale: Considerazioni* (Catania, 1864).

15. See, for instance, Saffi's article "Situazione-Dovere," in *Ricordi e scritti*, 14 vols. (Florence: Barbèra, 1892-1904), 6:204-214.

16. Giuseppe Ricciardi, *Storia d'Italia dal 1850 al 1900* (Paris: Lacombe, 1842).

17. See especially Giovanni Battista Tuveri's *Saggio delle opinioni politiche del Signor Deputato Giovanni Siotto-Pintor* (Turin: Cassone, 1848).

18. Ferrari, *Scritti politici*, p. 169.

19. For an example of democratic arguments against the exclusion of the masses from political participation see Gustavo Modena, "Il negoziante ed il carrettiere: Dialogo," in *Scritti e discorsi di Gustavo Modena*, ed. Terenzio Grandi (Rome: Istituto per la storia del Risorgimento, 1957), pp. 17-30.

20. Saffi, *Ricordi e scritti*, 6:233.

21. Pisacane to Nicola Fabrizi, Turin, March 13, 1856, *Epistolario di Carlo Pisacane*, ed. Aldo Romano (Rome: Albrighi and Segati, 1937), pp. 247-250. Hereinafter cited as *Epistolario Pisacane*.

22. Macchi, "Monarchia e repubblica," in *Studi politici*, pp. 121-152; emphasis added.

23. Ibid., pp. 150-151.

24. Ibid., p. 139.

25. On this issue see C. M. Lovett, "Nineteenth-Century Italian Radicals and the American Republic: A Study in Ambivalence," in *The U.S. and Italy: The First Two Hundred Years*, ed. H. S. Nelli (New York: American-Italian Historical Association, 1977), pp. 29-38.

26. Orsini, *Memorie politiche*, p. 65.

27. See Mazzini's "Agli italiani," *SEI*, 39: 123-124.

28. Carlo Cattaneo, "La forza della nazione italiana," in *Tutte le opere di Cattaneo*, ed. Luigi Ambrosoli (Milan: Mondadori, 1967–), 4:779-882.

29. Carlo Cattaneo, *Dell'insurrezione di Milano del 1848* (1848; reprint ed., Milan: Feltrinelli, 1973), pp. 160-198.

30. See C. M. Lovett, *Carlo Cattaneo and the Politics of the Risorgimento* (The Hague: Nijhoff, 1972), especially chap. 3.

31. Giuseppe Montanelli, *Appunti storici sulla rivoluzione d'Italia* (1851; reprint ed., Turin: Chiantore, 1945), p. 127; emphasis added.

32. Ibid., especially chap. 10. These arguments were widely used in republican and democratic propaganda of the postunification period. See, for instance, Ferdinando Petruccelli della Gattina, *Storia della idea italiana* (Naples: Pasquale, 1877), and Aurelio Saffi, *Delle rivoluzioni di Firenze nel Medio Evo e di Michele Lando in relazione alla storia delle classi artigiane* (Florence: Tipografia cooperativa, 1880). Significantly, in the 1830s one of Modena's pseudonyms was Michele Lando, in memory of a republican and democratic hero of old.

33. Giuseppe Ferrari, "La révolution et les révolutionnaires en Italie," *Revue des Deux Mondes*, January 1, 1845, p. 172.

34. See especially Ferrari to Mazzini, October 1850, cited in Antonio Monti, *Un dramma fra gli esuli* (Milan: Caddeo, 1921), pp. 88-90.

35. See Pisacane, *La rivoluzione in Italia*, ed. Franco Della Peruta (1851; reprint ed., Turin: Einaudi, 1970), especially pp. 80-113, and his "Testamento politico" (1857), ibid., pp. 227-230.

3. The Italian Revolution as a Social Revolution

1. Giuseppe Mazzini, *Note autobiografiche* (Naples: Centro studi mazziniani, 1972), p. 201.

2. De Boni to Mazzini, Rome, December 31, 1848, cited in *Studi e documenti su Goffredo Mameli e la Repubblica Romana* (Imola: Galeati, 1927), pp. 59-63.

3. Mattioli to Dall'Ongaro, Ancona, January 16, 1849, *Epistolario Dall'Ongaro*, pp. 282-283.

4. Guerrazzi to Puccini, Livorno, September 16, 1848, *Lettere familiari*, ed. G. F. Guerrazzi (Milan: Albrighi and Segati, 1924), p. 353.

5. Giorgio Asproni, *Diario politico, 1855-1876*, 3 vols., ed. Bruno Josto Anedda, Tito Orru, and Carlino Sole (Milan: Giuffrè, 1974-1980), 1:483.

6. For Cattaneo's economic thought see *Scritti economici*, 3 vols., ed. Alberto Bertolino (Florence: LeMonnier, 1956).

7. Asproni, *Diario*, 1:480.

8. Giuseppe Ricciardi, "Cenni storici intorno ai casi d'Italia del 1848 e

1849 e documenti da ricavarsene," *Opere scelte*, 8 vols. (Naples: Stamperia del Vaglio, 1867-1870), 5:1-336.

9. This and the previous quotations are from Mazzini's essay "Agli Italiani, e specialmente agli operai italiani," *SEI*, 25:3-20.

10. Mazzini, "Un'ultima parola sul Fourierismo e sul Comunismo," *SEI*, 26: 81-105. For Mazzini's critique of Bentham and of the Utilitarian school, see "Pensieri sulla Democrazia in Europa," *SEI*, 34: 91-246. These six articles were originally published in *The People's Journal*.

11. See Mazzini's "Doveri della Democrazia," *SEI*, 46: 207-214.

12. Many of Mazzini's contemporaries noted his apparent lack of interest in the peasantry and in the land question. Among them were Ferrari, Pisacane, Mattioli, and Orsini. Della Peruta has summarized these criticisms as follows: "The Mazzinian social program then presented itself . . . basically as an *urban* program, which took into account the aspirations of the working class in the cities but neglected the problems and the needs of the rural populations" (*Democrazia e socialismo nel Risorgimento*, 2nd ed. [Rome: Editori Riuniti, 1977], pp. 7-35).

13. For an introduction to the role of the Società operaie and their connection with the democratic movement, see Gastone Manacorda, *Il movimento operaio italiano attraverso i suoi congressi: Dalle origini alla formazione del Partito socialista*, 2nd ed. (Rome: Editori Riuniti, 1963), chaps. 1 and 2.

14. For an introduction to Italian "Proudhonianism," see Franco Della Peruta, *I democratici e la rivoluzione italiana* (Milan: Feltrinelli, 1958), chap. 4. But see also Carlo Rusconi, *La rendita ed il credito* (Turin: Libreria patria, 1851); Carlo De Cristoforis, *Il credito bancario e i contadini* (Milan: Vallardi, 1851); and Pietro Maestri, *Annuario economico-politico* (Turin: Libreria patria, 1852).

15. Giuseppe Ferrari, *Scritti politici*, ed. Silvia Rota Ghibandi (Turin: UTET, 1973), especially pp. 383-405.

16. Mauro Macchi, *La conciliazione dei partiti: Risposta a Giuseppe Mazzini* (Genoa: Moretti, 1856), pp. 41-46.

17. For Ferrari's arguments see C. M. Lovett, *Giuseppe Ferrari and the Italian Revolution* (Chapel Hill: University of North Carolina Press, 1979), chap. 7. For Bertani see especially "Per i derelitti," *Scritti e discorsi scelti*, ed. Jessie White Mario (Florence: Barbèra, 1890), pp. 153-165.

18. See Rusconi's "Programma del Direttore," *Rivista d'agricoltura, industria e commercio*, (October 15, 1869): pp. iii-xi.

19. Except for Pisacane, the ideas of these ultraradical thinkers must be reconstructed largely from unpublished essays and correspondence. For Pianciani, the fundamental work is a book-length manuscript (*Della Rivoluzione*) in the Archivio di Stato, Rome. For Pisacane see especially "Testamento politico," in *La rivoluzione in Italia*, ed. Franco Della Peruta (1851; reprint ed., Turin: Einaudi, 1970), pp. 227-230.

20. Landi's manuscript on the revolution of 1848 and its social implications is said to be preserved in the private library of the Puzzolo-Sigillo family in Messina. I have not been able to gain access to that collection and

therefore have relied on a summary of Landi's work kindly provided by the late Professor Giuseppe Berti.

21. Francesco Siliprandi, *La rivoluzione dei contadini* (Mantua: Bortoli, 1884), especially pp. 3 and 28-30.

4. Family and School: Patterns of Political Socialization, 1830-1848

1. For background on the role of the family in the process of political socialization see David Eaton and Jack Dennis, *Children in the Political System* (New York: McGraw-Hill, 1969); Richard Niemi, *The Politics of Future Citizens* (San Francisco: Jossey-Bass, 1974); and Annick Percheron, *L'univers politique des enfants* (Paris: Colin, 1974).

2. For interpretations of the Risorgimento that focus on the relationship between the rise of a politically conscious and assertive "bourgeoisie" and the development of capitalism see especially Antonio Gramsci, *Il Risorgimento* (Turin: Einaudi, 1949); Rosario Romeo, *Il giudizio storico sul Risorgimento* (Catania: Bonanno, 1969) and his "La storiografia politica marxista," *Nord e Sud*, 21 (1956): 5-37, and 22 (1956): 16-44 and Aldo Romano, "Il problema chiave della storiografia del Risorgimento," *Rivista storica del socialismo* (*RSS*), 1 (1958): 210-228.

3. For the problems of historical interpretation that such social groups and subgroups pose for historians see especially Arno J. Mayer, "The Lower Middle Class as Historical Problem," *JMH*, 47 (September 1975): 409-436.

4. Angelo Brofferio, *I miei tempi. Memorie*, 20 vols. (Milan: Guigoni, 1857-1861) vol. 1, chap. 2.

5. Giuseppe Ricciardi, *Memorie autografe d'un ribelle*, 2nd ed. (Milan: Battezzati, 1873), especially pp. 18-24. For the family tradition see also his "Vita di Francesco Ricciardi," in *Opere* (Naples: Rondinella, 1861), pp. 219-272.

6. See, for instance, G. Mazzoni to Jacopo Martellini, Florence, May 20, 1836, BNF/Carteggi vari/72/43. For Sineo's family background see Ferdinando Bosio, *Ricordi personali* (Milan: Battezzati, 1878), pp. 249-268.

7. G. Mazzoni to G. Caffarelli, Paris, June 9, 1852, BNF/Carteggi vari/72/65.

8. Aurelio Saffi, *Ricordi e scritti*, 14 vols. (Florence: Barbèra, 1892-1904), 1: 19-25, 36-39, 137-143.

9. Casimiro De Lieto to his son Antonio, Genoa, May 6, 1858, BISR/174/28/3. For the De Lieto family tradition see M. Polimeni Serra, "Schizzo biografico di Antonio De Lieto," BISR/175/58 and G. Morabito De Stefano, *La famiglia De Lieto nel Risorgimento nazionale* (Rome: Libreria dello Stato, 1938).

10. For Govean, see Vittorio Bersezio, *Commemorazione di Felice Govean* (Turin, 1899), pp. 20-37. For Quadrio see Silvia Pelosi, *Della vita di Maurizio Quadrio*, chaps 1-2.

11. Francesco Angherà to his sister, 1851. Cited in Giulio Mellini, *Francesco Angherà, patriota calabrese del Risorgimento, 1850-1879*

(Bologna: Spe, 1948), p. 12.

12. Augusto Elia, *Note autobiografiche e storiche d'un garibaldino* (Bologna: Zanichelli, 1898), pp. 6-8.

13. Giuseppe Petroni to his son Raffaele, San Michele prison, March 16, 1864, Pisa, Domus mazziniana, Fondo Spatafora/G IV sc. a 30/25.

14. See Marietta Campo, *Vita politica della famiglia Camp dal 1848 al 1860* (Palermo: Lorsnaider, 1884), pp. 7-10, 16, 20.

15. See, for instance, Salvatore Morelli's preface to his *Sulla riforma delle leggi penali con riferimento all'ordine della famiglia* (Rome, 1878). For Bixio see Giuseppe Guerzoni, *La vita di Nino Bixio* (Florence: Barbèra, 1875), especially pp. 18-29.

16. See Saffi, *Ricordi e scritti*, 1: 63-67; and Amilcare Carlotti, *Lorenzo Valerio* (Turin: Stamperia reale, 1872), pp. 11-12.

17. See Carlo Arrigoni, *Un carteggio inedito di Giuseppe Lamberti, 1837-1847* (Turin, 1957), which contains many excerpts from family correspondence and from Lamberti's unpublished diaries.

18. For these relationships see especially Bianca Montale, *Maria Drago Mazzini* (Genoa: Istituto mazziniano, 1955) and E. Ghiglione Giulietti, ed., *Adelaide Cairoli ed i suoi figli. Lettere inedite dal 1847 al 1871* (Milan: Gastaldi, 1952).

19. ASR/Pianciani/49 and 52/passim.

20. For Albini see Saverio Cilibrizzi, *I grandi lucani nella storia della nuova Italia* (Naples: Conte, 1958), pp. 122-128.

21. F. D. Guerrazzi to M. F. Guerrazzi, Florence, April 1, 1849, *Lettere familiari*, p. 61. For Guerrazzi's family background and social aspirations see also Giosuè Carducci, ed., *Lettere*, 2 vols. (Livorno: Vigo, 1880), vol. 1, passim.

22. F. D. Guerrazzi, *Pagine autobiografiche* (1848; reprint ed., Bologna: Cappelli, 1969), pp. 85-90.

23. Brofferio, *I miei tempi*, 1:63-65.

24. Carlotti, *Valerio*, p. 11.

25. Guerzoni, *Bixio*, p. 24.

26. *Romana di cospirazione contro gli arrestati Montecchi Mattia del fu Nicola* . . . (Rome, 1844), pp. 133-138.

27. For a comparison of family motivations in this area, see Margherita Trabaudi Foscarini, *Francesco Dall'Ongaro* (Florence: LeMonnier, 1926), pp. 9-11; Robert Sylvain, *Clerc, garibaldien, prédicant des deux mondes: Alessandro Gavazzi, 1809-1889*, 2 vols. (Quebec: Centre pédagogique, 1962), 1:14-28; and Luisa Fiorini, *L'abate Luigi Anelli, storico del Risorgimento* (Bergamo: Cattaneo, 1958), pp. 5-11.

28. See, for instance, Domenico Cassiano, *Democrazia e socialismo nella comunità albanese di Calabria: Attanasio Dramis* (Naples: Il Rinnovamento, 1977), pp. 3-9.

29. See Ettore Montecchi, *Mattia Montecchi nel Risorgimento italiano* (Rome: Proja, 1932), pp. xi-lxxxvi.

30. See Jessie White Mario, "Della vita di Alberto Mario," in *Scritti scelti di Alberto Mario*, ed. Giosuè Carducci (Bologna: Zanichelli, 1884), pp. v-clxxvii.

31. Giuseppe Mazzini, *Note autobiografiche*, pp. 15-33.

5. The Emergence of a National Democratic Network, 1846-1848

1. Franco Della Peruta has documented this point, refuting the older view of a sharp break between the original Young Italy groups and the "new" Mazzinianism of the 1840s. See his *Mazzini e i rivoluzionari italiani* (Milan: Feltrinelli, 1974), pp. 220-277.

2. For background on the Mantua democrats see, in addition to Francesco Siliprandi's *La rivoluzione dei contadini* (Mantua: Bortoli, 1884), Renato Giusti, "Dalla presa di Mantova alla fine della prima guerra d'indipendenza," in *Storia di Mantova*, 3 vols. (Mantua: Istituto Carlo d'Arco, 1963), 3:261-526.

3. See Enrico Tazzoli, *Memorie inedite al Generale Culoz sulle cause della congiura del 1850* (Mantua: Eredi Segna, 1886).

4. See Achille Sacchi, *La pellagra nella provincia di Mantova* (Florence: La Rassegna settimanale, 1878), pp. 45-48.

5. For instance, Orsini's friends Eusebio and Rubicondo Barbetti were accused of spreading such ideas in the Ravenna area. ASR, Miscellanea di carte politiche e riservate, 3209B [1843-44].

6. An interpretive study of the Greek Orthodox communities during the Risorgimento comparable to Giorgio Spini's *Risorgimento e protestanti* (Naples: ESI, 1956), or to Attilio Milano's *Storia degli ebrei in Italia* (Turin: Einaudi, 1963), has never been written. But see Emilio Tavolaro, "Il contributo degli italo-albanesi al Risorgimento," in *Atti del II Congresso di storia calabrese* (Naples: Fiorentino, 1961), pp. 551-579; Gaetano Cingari, *Romanticismo e democrazia nel Mezzogiorno: Domenico Mauro, 1812-1873* (Naples: ESI, 1965), chaps. 1-3; Domenico Cassiano, *Democrazia e socialismo nella comunità albanese di Calabria: Attanasio Dramis* (Naples: Il Rinnovamento, 1977); and Renato Composto, "Le origini albanesi in Francesco Crispi," *Nuovi quaderni meridionali*, 12, (1974): 302-317.

7. For pre-1848 democratic propaganda in the Greek Orthodox villages of Calabria see, for instance, the political trials of Giovanni Mosciaro and of the Mauro brothers, ASCS, Processi politici, 152/8 bis and 157/72. For post-1848 democratic networks in the same villages see the trial of Agesilao Milano, ibid., 158/1-14.

8. See Giovanni Natali, *Il patriota bolognese Giuseppe Camillo Mattioli, 1817–1893* (Bologna: Museo del Risorgimento, 1931) and Rinaldo Andreini, "Cronaca epistolare dal 1843 al 1845," in Mario Menghini, *Rinaldo Andreini e i moti di Romagna del 1845* (Città di Castello: Tiferno Grafica, 1916).

9. On the Bandiera expedition see Luigi Carci, *La spedizione e il processo dei fratelli Bandiera* (Modena: Stem, 1939); Stanislao De Chiara, *I martiri cosentini del 1844* (Rome: Albrighi and Segati, 1904); and Alessandro Conflenti, *I fratelli Bandiera e i massacri cosentini del 1844* (Cosenza, 1862).

10. Massimo d'Azeglio, *Degli ultimi casi di Romagna, Riflessioni*, in *Scritti e discorsi politici*, 3 vols., ed. Marcus De Rubris (Florence: La Nuova Italia, 1931–1938), 1:1-94.

11. For the political climate in the early months of Pius IX's pontificate see Raffaele De Cesare, *Roma e lo Stato del Papa* (Milan: Longanesi, 1970), chaps. 2-5.

12. Giuseppe Montanelli, *Memorie sull'Italia e specialmente sulla Toscana dal 1814 al 1850* (1851; reprint ed., Florence: Sansoni, 1963), p. 284. For similar views expressed by a non-Catholic democrat see Davide Levi, *A Pio IX. Ode* (Florence, 1847).

13. Mazzini to De Boni, October 14, 1846, cited in Giorgio Candeloro, *Storia della Italia moderna*, 8 vols. (Milan: Feltrinelli, 1956–1978), 3:34.

14. See Giuseppe Ferrari, "Questione italiana," in *Scritti politici*, ed. Silvia Rota Ghibaudi (Turin: UTET, 1973), pp. 113-125.

15. Upon his return from a trip to Sicily in November 1847, the Tuscan Ermolao Rubieri recorded this very impression in his "Memorie auto-biografiche," part I, unpublished ms., in MFR/Sezione Manoscritti. But see also Nicola Campolieti, *La mente e l'anima di un eroe [Carlo De Cristoforis]* (Milan: Mondaini, 1907), pp. 83-88.

16. For the contacts between Asproni and other Sardinian intellectuals and the Brofferio circle see Ferdinando Bosio, *Ricordi personali* (Milan: Battezzati, 1878), especially pp. 3-23 and 249-268. For Pigli see Augusto Mancini, "Un patriota aretino: Carlo Pigli," *Atti e memorie della Accademia Petrarca di Arezzo*, 35 (1949–1951): 2-19.

17. Maestri's theories may be reconstructed from the series *Annuario economico-politico*, published in Turin in the 1850s.

18. See Carlo Cattaneo, *Dell'insurrezione di Milano del 1848* (1848; reprint ed., Milan: Feltrinell, 1973), pp. 86-91.

19. See Carla Ronchi, *I democratici fiorentini nella rivoluzione del 1848–49* (Florence: Barbèra, 1962), chaps. 1-2.

20. See Leopoldo Cattani-Cavalcanti, *Colonia e istituto agrario di Castelletti presso Signa. Regolamento interno e programma* (Florence: Capponi, 1865).

21. For background on Neapolitan democracy before 1848 see Giuseppe Ricciardi, *Memorie autografe d'un ribelle*, 2nd ed. (Milan: Battezzati, 1873), pp. 233-249; and Giovanni La Cecilia, *Memorie storico-politiche dal 1820 al 1876*, 5 vols. (Rome: Gargiulo, 1894), vol. 1.

22. For evidence of the Bourbon government's attempts to curb the influx of university students and of young professional men generally into the capital see ASNA, Ministero di Polizia, I/4236 (1840s).

23. Petruccelli della Gattina described this kind of life in a fictionalized account, "Il Marchese di Tregle," in *Le notti degli emigrati* (Milan: Treves, 1872), pp. 303-360.

24. Giuseppe Mazzini, *Note autobiografiche*, p. 358.

25. See Umberto Marcelli, "Il dibattito al Parlamento subalpino sulla questione degli acattolici," *Bollettino di studi valdesi*, 102 (1957): 57-61.

26. Cited in Rosario Romeo, *Dal Piemonte sabaudo all'Italia liberale* (Bari: Laterza, 1974), p. 115.

27. For the development of democratic groups in Piedmont before 1848 see Vittorio Parmentola, "Preconizzazioni e impegni sociali di repubblicani

piemontesi," *BODM*, 5 (1958): 49-60 and his "Repubblicani mutualisti e co-operatori in Piemonte," ibid., 15 (1968): 100-184; and Costanzo Maraldi, "Il partito democratico subalpino e l'azione politico-parlamentare di A. Depretis," *RSR*, 17 (1930): 105-173.

28. For background on the Five Days of Milan see, in addition to Cattaneo's previously cited account, Antonio Monti, *Il 1848 e le Cinque Giornate di Milano* (Milan: Hoepli, 1949), and Carlo Pagani, *Uomini e cose in Milano dal marzo all'agosto 1848* (Milan: Bocca, 1906).

6. Experiments in Democratic Leadership, 1848–1849

1. For the papal allocution and its impact on public opinion see Giorgio Candeloro, *Storia dell'Italia moderna*, 8 vols. (Milan: Feltrinelli, 1956–1978), 3: 217-224.

2. See Ferrari's "La rivoluzione e le riforme in Italia," in *Scritti politici*, ed. Silvia Rota Ghibaudi (Turin: UTET, 1973), pp. 135-137.

3. Casimiro De Lieto to his wife, May 1, 1848, BISR/172/15/2.

4. On this issue Mazzini clashed violently with the democratic leaders of the Five Days of Milan, especially Cattaneo. See the account of their dispute in Antonio Monti, *Un dramma fra gli esuli* (Milan: Caddeo, 1921), part II.

5. For general background on the revolution in the Two Sicilies see Aurelio Lepre, *Storia del Mezzogiorno nel Risorgimento* (Rome: Editori Riuniti, 1969); Harold Acton, *Gli ultimi Borboni di Napoli* (Milan: Martello, 1962); Michele Viterbo, *Il Sud e l'unità* (Bari: Laterza, 1966); and Rosario Romeo, *Il Risorgimento in Sicilia*, 2nd ed. (Bari: Laterza, 1970).

6. Confident of his ability as a revolutionary leader, La Cecilia wrote to Guerrazzi: "Trust me with the overall supervision of your National Guard, and I will show you miracles." Letter of October 6, 1848, from Livorno, BISR/548/60/1.

7. For background on the Tuscan revolution see, Ernesto Ragionieri, "Mazzinianesimo, garibaldinismo e origini del socialismo in Toscana," *RST*, 9 (1963): 143-158, and Carla Ronchi, *I democratici fiorentini nella rivoluzione del 1848–49* (Florence: Barbèra, 1962).

8. Cironi to his brother, Florence, September 25, 1848, BNF/C.V./76/38.

9. On Montanelli see Giovanni Spadolini, *Un dissidente del Risorgimento: G. M.* (Florence: LeMonnier, 1962); Clementina Rotondi, "G. M. a cent'anni dalla sua morte," *RST*, 8 (1962): 1-75; and Giovanni Monaci, "G. M. ed i suoi scritti politici" (thesis, University of Bologna, 1951–52). For excellent, up-to-date essays on Guerrazzi see *F. D. Guerrazzi nella storia politica e culturale del Risorgimento* (Florence: Olschki, 1975). For Mazzoni see Pietro Paolini, "Fonti documentarie risorgimentali presso la Biblioteca forteguerriana," *Bollettino storico pistoiese*, 3 (1961): 145-160.

10. Cited in Giuseppe Sforza, *Giovanni La Cecilia e F. D. Guerrazzi* (Turin: Bocca, n.d.), p. 13.

11. Montazio, *Il ministero toscano ed i democratici di ogni colore a proposito della dimostrazione del 12 dicembre 1848 in Firenze* (Florence:

Tipografia del Vulcano, 1848), p. 13.

12. Montanelli, *Programma di G.M. Governatore di Livorno detto dalla terrazza del palazzo governativo il dì 8 ottobre 1848* (Florence: L'Alba, 1848).

13. Guerrazzi to Gaetana Cotenna del Rosso, Florence, November 13, 1851. Giosuè Carducci, ed., *Lettere*, 2 vols. (Livorno: Vigo, 1880), 1: 300-301.

14. *Regolamento per il Circolo popolare di Firenze* (Florence, 1848), pp. 3-4.

15. Guerrazzi, for instance, published his *Predica per il Venerdì Santo* (Livorno: Poligrafia italiana, 1848), written in March of that year while he was imprisoned in Portoferraio. This uncharacteristic exercise in Christian populism emphasized the duty of all social classes to sacrifice for the national cause.

16. For a discussion of the dissidents' position see Ronchi, *I democratici fiorentini*, especially pp. 149-157.

17. Andrea Giannelli, *Cenni autobiografici e ricordi politici* (Milan: Unione tipografica, 1925), p. 47.

18. Montazio, *O repubblicani o tedeschi. Decidetevi! Parole al popolo e al governo provvisorio toscano* (Florence: Tipografia del Vulcano, 1849).

19. Mazzoni to Martelli, April 1849, cited in F. Fiorelli, "Lettere di Giuseppe Mazzoni a Carlo e Diego Martelli," *Archivio storico pratese*, 25 (1949): 3-20.

20. For general background on the revolution in the Papal States see, in addition to works cited previously, Giuseppe Leti, *La rivoluzione e la repubblica romana*, 2nd ed. (Milan: Vallardi, 1948); Domenico Demarco, *Pio Nono e la rivoluzione romana del 1848* (Modena: Stem, 1947) and his *Una rivoluzione sociale. La repubblica romana del 1849* (Naples: Fiorentino, 1944).

21. Pianciani to Eugenio Brizi, Rome, May 1848, ASR/Archivio Pianciani/7.

22. For the circumstances surrounding Rossi's assassination see Candeloro, *Storia dell'Italia moderna*, 3:325-333.

23. Mazzini to Michele Accursi, December 5, 1848, *SEI*, 37:187.

24. Demarco, *Una rivoluzione sociale*, pp. 33-38.

25. *Le assemblee del Risorgimento*, 15 vols. (Rome: Camera dei Deputati, 1911), 7:221.

26. For the activities of the Tuscans in Rome see Cironi's numerous letters to his brother, December 1848-March 1849, BNF/C.V./76/39, 54, 100.

27. Aurelio Saffi, *Ricordi e scritti*, 14 vols. (Florence: Barbèra, 1892–1904), 1:256.

28. *Assemblee del Risorgimento*, 7:265-270.

29. See Marco Minghetti, *I miei ricordi*, 2 vols. (Turin: Roux, 1888–1890), 2:132.

30. *Assemblee del Risorgimento*, 9:21.

31. Cited in Demarco, *Una rivoluzione sociale*, p. 95.

32. Ibid., pp. 110-114.

33. See, for instance, Ferrari, *Scritti politici*, pp. 872–880.

34. On this point see the essays by Valdo Vinay and Giorgio Spini in *Protestantesimo*, 1(1956): 24–50; 75–79; 80–86.

35. See Dall'Ongaro's preface to the Milanese edition of the *Stornelli* (Milan: Daelli, 1862).

36. See, for instance, Giuseppe Fratellini to Luigi Pianciani, Spoleto, early 1849, ASR/Archivio Pianciani/21.

37. See Savino Savini et al., "Al Consiglio dei Deputati i Circoli Nazionale e Popolare bolognesi," (December 1848), BABO/Sezione MSS/Fondi Speciali/Savini/1/3.

38. For the plight of the Ligurians, see Campanella's correspondence with A. D'Oria (or Doria), Rome, May-June 1849, IMGE/3/427–429 and 4/744–746. For Miceli's views see Emilio Frangella, "Luigi Miceli eroico patriota del Risorgimento," in *Atti del II Congresso di storia calabrese* (Naples: Fiorentino, 1961), pp. 635–652.

39. De Lieto to Valerio, October 6, 1849, BPTO/Archivio Valerio/7/12/5.

40. Precisely because he had this experience behind him, in the 1860s Salvatore Piccioni insisted that the Roman "underground" must be led by native sons, not by outsiders. See his letter to M. Corini, Marseilles, January 9, 1867, BISR/41/41/2.

41. According to the statute of the Circolo popolare bolognese, outsiders could become members by invitation but could not serve as officers or instructors. See BABO/Sezione MSS, Fondi speciali/Savini/1/3.

42. For the problem of corruption see especially Demarco, *Una rivoluzione sociale*, chap. 12, passim. For an example of revolutionary asceticism see Saffi's letters to his mother in *Ricordi e scritti*, 3:262–263.

43. See, for instance, Saffi's articles of the early 1850s for *L'Italia del popolo*, now available in *Ricordi e scritti*, 4:134–203.

44. See especially Carlo Pigli, *Risposta all'apologia di F. D. Guerrazzi* (Arezzo, 1852); and Ferrari, *Scritti politici*, especially pp. 351–358.

45. Paul Ginsborg, *Daniele Manin e la rivoluzione veneziana del 1848–1849* (Milan: Feltrinelli, 1978), pp. 97–124.

46. Angelo Giacomelli, *Reminiscenze della mia vita politica negli anni 1848–1853* (Florence: Barbèra, 1893), pp. 64–65.

47. Modena to Dall'Ongaro, Palmanova, April 16, 1848, *Epistolario di Gustavo Modena*, ed. Terenzio Grandi (Rome: Istituto per la storia del Risorgimento, 1955).

48. For general background on the revolution in the Two Sicilies see, in addition to the works cited in note 5, *Assemblee del Risorgimento*, vols. 10–11 (Naples) and 12–15 (Sicily).

49. Ibid., 12:6.

50. Of the eleven Sicilian democrats included in the sample, only four served in the Assembly. For their role as intermediaries between moderate liberals and radical dissidents see Crispi's journalistic and parliamentary activities, discussed in Renato Composto, "Sull'itinerario politico di Crispi nel 1848," *BODM*, 21 (1975): 319–333. For Friscia's difficulties as editor of the radical newspapers *L'Armamento* and *La Costituente*, see Antonio Riggio, *Per*

Saverio Friscia (Girgenti: Carini, 1886), pp. 7–12.

51. For the constitutional crisis in Naples see *Assemblee del Risorgimento*, 10:27–52.

52. ASCS/Processi politici/157/162. *Decisione della Gran Corte Speciale della Calabria citeriore* . . . (Naples: Tipografia del Fibreno, 1853), pp. 17-19.

53. For the Libertini-Maffei network see especially the records of Maffei's trial in 1853, ASNA/Archivio di Casa Reale/845/535/69. But see also Tommaso Pedio, *Emissari leccesi a Potenza nel 1848* (Lecce: Tipografia salentina, 1940); Raffaele Riviello, *Cronaca potentina dal 1792 al 1882* (Potenza: Santanello, 1888), pp. 160–163; and Saverio La Sorsa, *Giuseppe Libertini nelle carceri di Potenza* (Lecce, 1909). For the Albini-Ciccotti network see the records of the Albini trial in 1850-51, ASPZ/Processi di valore storico/87/1. See also Enrico Ajello, *Lucania 1860* (Bari: Laterza, 1960), chaps. 4–6, and Michele Lacava, *Cronistoria documentata della rivoluzione in Basilicata del 1860 e delle cospirazioni che la precedettero* (Naples: Morano, 1895).

54. See V. Valinoti-La Torraca, *Ferdinando Petruccelli* (Naples: Ricciardi, 1915), pp. 7–18.

55. Giuseppe Ricciardi, preface to "Cenni storici intorno ai casi d'Italia," in *Opere scelte*, 8 vols. (Naples: Stamperia del Vaglio, 1867–1870), 5:1–336.

56. Francesco Crispi, "Ultimi casi della rivoluzione siciliana esposti con documenti da un testimone oculare," in *Scritti e discorsi politici* (Rome: Unione cooperativa editrice, 1890), pp. 12–13.

57. ASSA/Gran Corte criminale/Processi politici/265/23 and 76/2. In 1849 two minstrels were arrested in the Maratea area for having improvised songs about Carducci's deeds and his death. See ASPZ/Processi di valore storico/99/3–4.

58. See Salvatore Calvino, "Appunti della spedizione del 1848 in Calabria," in Francesco Guardione, *Il dominio dei Borboni in Sicilia dal 1830 al 1861*, 2 vols. (Turin: Società tipografico-editrice nazionale, 1907), 1:393–396.

59. Francesco Campo, *Cenno storico sulla spedizione dei Siciliani in Calabria* (Genoa: Dagnino, 1851), pp. 55–63.

60. Domenico Mauro, *Vittorio Emanuele e Mazzini* (Genoa: Ponthenier, 1851), chap. 6.

7. A Question of Survival: The Democratic Experience in the 1850s

1. Costantino Reta to Carlo Negroni, Turin, March 17, 1848, cited in Guido Bustico, *Giornali e giornalisti del Risorgimento* (Milan: Caddeo, 1924), p. 116.

2. Milo Guggino to Fabrizi, Marseilles, August 30, 1859, BISR/524/48/1.

3. Rinaldo Andreini, "La dedizione di Comacchio," in *Intorno al* . . . *fatto bolognese*, ed. B. Del Vecchio (Capolago: Tipografia Elvetica, 1851, pp. 145–162.

4. Enrico Gentilini, *Riscontro allo scritto "Relazione delle operazioni militari . . . in Lombardia nel 1848"* (Capolago: Tipografia Elvetica, 1849), p. 19. But see also Cassola's *L'insurrezione di Brescia ed atti ufficiali durante il marzo 1849* (Capolago: Tipografia Elvetica, 1849), and Dall'Ongaro's *Venezia l'11 agosto 1848. Memorie storiche* (Capolago: Tipografia Elvetica, 1850).

5. See, for instance, Mazzini, "Letter to an English Friend," *SEI*, 39:107–120, and Saffi, "Storia di Roma dal giugno 1846 al 9 febbraio 1849," in *Ricordi e scritti*, 14 vols. (Florence: Barbèra, 1892–1904), vol. 2, passim.

6. See Savino Savini, *La Repubblica romana del 1849*, 2 vols. (Turin: Cassone, 1859), 1: iv-vii, and his "Memorie della Repubblica romana," ed. Giovanni Natali, *Bollettino MRBO*, 2 (1957): 64–90.

7. For Montazio see *Cenni storici sulla condotta di E. Montazio* (San Miniato: Ristori, 1853), pp. 6–27. For Pigli see *Risposta all'apologia di Guerrazzi* (Arezzo, 1852), pp. 8–13. For Cironi's views see *Dei fatti di Livorno* (Bastia, 1848).

8. Ferdinando Petruccelli, *La rivoluzione di Napoli nel 1848. Ricordi* (Genoa: Moretti, 1850), p. 23.

9. See Benedetto Musolino's *La rivoluzione del 1848 nelle Calabrie* (Naples: Di Gennaro & Morano, 1903); and Giuseppe Ricciardi's "Pensieri d'un esule," in *Opere scelte*, 8 vols. (Naples: Stamperia del Vaglio, 1867–1870), 1:407–448, and his *Guerra alla povertà. Cenni sulla questione sociale* (Naples: D'Orsi, 1877), pp. 25, 52–53.

10. Carlo Pisacane, *La guerra combattuta in Italia nel 1848–1849* (Milan: Leonardo, 1946), pp. 332–350.

11. See Giuseppe Ferrari, *Scritti politici*, ed. Silvia Rota Ghibaudi (Turin: UTET, 1973), p. 356.

12. Cattaneo to Mazzini, Lugano, September 30, 1850, *Epistolario di Carlo Cattaneo*, ed. Rinaldo Caddeo, 4 vols. (Florence: Barbèra, 1949–1953), 2:44–48.

13. Epigram to chap. 1 of Giuseppe Ricciardi's *Glorie, sventure e speranze d'Italia. Canti repubblicani* (Venice, 1848).

14. See the recollections of Tazzoli's friend Cesare Cantù, *Del prete Enrico Tazzoli* (Turin: Rivista contemporanea, n.d.).

15. See Alessandro Luzio, ed., "Lettere di Giuseppe Finzi dal carcere, 1853–55," *Rivista storica del Risorgimento italiano*, 1 (1895–96): 422–436.

16. Francesco Siliprandi, *Memorie storiche* (Mantua: Bortoli, 1884), pp. 65–71.

17. Handwritten note by Antonio Zambelli on the inside cover of Giulio Faccioli, *La scuola della sventura, ossia ispirazioni e reminiscenze d'un carcere* (Verona: Merlo, 1862).

18. Orsini to Carlo Arrivabene, London, July 19, 1856, *Lettere*, ed. A. M. Ghisalberti (Rome: Istituto per la storia del Risorgimento), p. 204. See also Orsini's *Memorie* (Turin: De Giorgis, 1858), pp. 150–159, 177–194, and 225–245.

19. For Nicotera see Jessie White Mario, *In memoria di Giovanni Nicotera* (Florence: Barbèra, 1894), pp. 26–29. For Calvino's imprisonment

see Lucia Ortoleva, *Salvatore Calvino* (Palermo: Corselli, 1934), chap. 2.

20. For Morelli's experiences see Irma Scodnik, *Salvatore Morelli* (Milan and Rome: Albrighi and Segati, 1916), pp. 11–13. For Angherà see especially his *Alcuni documenti relativi al governo napoletano ed alla ex-Legione Anglo-Italiana* (Italy, 1858).

21. See Domenico Albini, *Montemurro per la rivoluzione lucana* (Rome: Mundus, 1912), pp. 40–42. For the polemics of the 1850s between the Neapolitan Comitato d'insurrezione and Albini see Giovanni Greco, *Le carte del Comitato segreto di Napoli, 1853–1857* (Naples: Storia di Napoli e della Sicilia Società editrice, 1979).

22. See Giovanni Ferretti, "F. De Boni e i suoi soggiorni nella Svizzera," *RSR*, 37 (1950): 136–139 and Ferdinando Bosio, *Ricordi personali* (Milan: Battezzati, 1878), pp. 59–107.

23. For Montazio's plea to remain in Tuscany see "Dichiarazione di E. Montazio dal carcere delle Murate," Florence, March 9, 1859, BNF/C.V./453 bis/57. Montazio's letters to his daughter and to Pianciani (1852–1855) are found in ASR/Pianciani/34.

24. ASCS/Processi politici/157/93 and 162.

25. See Rosolino Pilo, *Lettere*, ed. Gaetano Falzone (Rome: Istituto per la storia del Risorgimento, 1972), pp. 18–20 and 55–57.

26. Zuppetta to De Lieto, Turin, March 21, 1850, BISR/173/12/2.

27. Both letters are in BABO/Fondi speciali/Savini/XI/10.

28. On this issue see Saffi's letters to his mother, summer 1849, in *Ricordi e scritti*, 4:123–132. Other examples are found in Mazzoni to Cironi, Paris, July 22, 1852, BNF/C.V./72/66; Dall'Ongaro to Brofferio, Arona, July 18, 1849, BISR/343/4(5); and Mattioli to Gioacchino Pepoli, Corfù, December 20, 1849, cited in Ercole Gaddi-Pepoli, *G. C. Mattioli e G. N. Pepoli, 1847–1849. Documenti inediti* (Bologna: Tipografia già Compositori, 1932), pp. 15–18.

29. For background see Angelo Giacomelli, *Reminiscenze della mia vita politica* (Florence: Barbèra, 1893), pp. 201–203, and Domenico Giuriati, *Memorie d'emigrazione, 1849–1866* (Milan: Treves, 1897).

30. Cited in Giovanni Ferretti, *Esuli del Risorgimento in Svizzera* (Bologna: Zanichelli, 1948), p. 158.

31. Giovanni La Cecilia, *Memorie storico-politiche dal 1820 al 1876*, 5 vols. (Rome: Gargiulo, 1894), 3:183.

32. For Mazzini's appeal to democratic solidarity see, for instance, his "Il Partito d'azione. Cenni," *SEI*, 51:87–104.

33. See Andreini to F. Lazzeri, Nyon (Vaud), March 22, 1850, cited in Lea Padovani, "Rinaldo Andreini," (thesis, University of Bologna, 1946–47), p. 77.

34. De Boni to Mazzini, August 31, 1853, BISR/415/5/7.

35. Mazzoni to G. Caffarelli, Paris, February 16, 1852, BNF/C.V./72/63.

36. Quadrio to Giovanni Grilenzoni, *Epistolario Quadrio*, 2:48–49.

37. See Crispi to Cesare Correnti, September 22, 1853, and Crispi to Francesco Pinelli, November 2, 1853, in *Lettere dall'esilio*, ed. Tommaso

Palamenghi-Crispi (Rome: Tiber, 1918), pp. 55–57 and 63–69.

38. See Giuseppe to Vincenzo Libertini, London, 1856, cited in Nicola Bernardini, *Giuseppe Libertini. Memorie e documenti* (Lecce: Lazzaretti, 1894), pp. 107–108. But see also Mazzoni to G. Buonamici, Paris, March 27, 1851, in *Archivio storico pratese*, 10 (1932): 123–125.

39. Excerpt from Cironi's diary, cited in Giacomo Adami, *Piero Cironi. Dibattiti e contrasti per la libertà nazionale e la democrazia* (Florence: Arnaud, 1962), p. 80.

40. Reta to Emanuele Celesia, Malta, July 31, 1849, cited in Guido Bustico, "Costantino Reta," *Il Risorgimento italiano*, 13 (1920): 295–296.

41. Pisacane to Cattaneo, Genoa, January 17, 1853, *Epistolario Pisacane*, 155–157. In a similar mood Pigozzi announced to Pianciani the birth of his third child. Letter of December 15, 1854 in ASR/Pianciani/39.

42. Numerous items in BABO/F.S./Savini/X/70.

43. Mazzoni to Cironi, Paris, September 19, 1854, BNF/C.V./79/109. But see also De Lieto's numerous letters to his wife (1850–1856) in BISR/174 and 175; and Orsini's instructions to his uncle Orso and his brother Leonida for the education of his young daughters in the event of his death, *Lettere*, pp. 155–159.

44. Dall'Ongaro to Nina, n.d., *Epistolario Dall'Ongaro*, pp. 375–378.

45. Giovanni Ruffini, *Doctor Antonio* (Leipzig: Tauchnitz, 1861), p. 329.

46. Cited in Giorgio Candeloro, *Storia dell'Italia moderna*, 8 vols. (Milan: Feltrinelli, 1956–1978), 4:233.

47. Ibid., p. 225.

48. See Eugenio Brizi, *Memorie autobiografiche, 1838–1862* (Assisi: Metastasio, 1898), pp. 45–50; Carlo Cassola, *Tentativo d'insurrezione del 6 febbraio 1853 in Milano* (Pavia: Tipografia popolare, 1897), and Giovanni La Cecilia, *Gli ultimi fatti di Milano del 6 febbraio 1853* (Turin: Biancardi, 1853).

49. For background on the attitude of the democrats during the Crimean War see S. J. Woolf, *Storia d'Italia dal primo Settecento alla unità* (Turin: Einaudi, 1973), pp. 436–466, and C. M. Lovett, *Giuseppe Ferrari* (Chapel Hill: University of North Carolina Press, 1979), pp. 92–96. For Pisacane's attempt see Leopoldo Cassese, *La spedizione di Sapri* (Bari: Laterza, 1969).

8. Loyal Opposition: The Democratic Presence in the National Parliament, 1860–1876

1. Cited in C. M. Lovett, *Giuseppe Ferrari* (Chapel Hill: University of North Carolina Press, 1979), p. 120. For background on parliamentary democracy in the 1860s see especially Alfonso Scirocco, *I democratici italiani da Sapri a Porta Pia* (Naples: ESI, 1969).

2. Ferrari to Giovanni Carozzi, Paris, May 11, 1860, MRM/Archivio Generale/Carte Carozzi/36524.

3. La Porta to Crispi, Palermo, April 19, 1861, BISR/656/35/1.

4. Regnoli to Antonio Montanari, Turin, 1868-69, several items in BABO/Montanari MSS/5 and Bargoni to Cadolini, Turin, November 3, 1865, BISR/273/34/8.

5. See Guerrazzi to G. A. Sanna, Livorno, November 1, 1863, *Lettere familiari*, ed. G. F. Guerrazzi (Milan: Albrighi and Segati, 1924), p. 309.

6. See the recollections of Salvatore Barzilai, *Vita parlamentare* (Rome: Tipografia editrice nazionale, 1912), p. 160.

7. Mordini to Bargoni, Barga, October 22, 1867, BISR/234/30/5.

8. See, for instance, Asproni's strong appeal to Friscia and other Sicilian colleagues to pursue this goal in preference to armed insurrection and separatism. Letter of December 23, 1863, cited in Francesco Guardione, *Saverio Friscia* (Palermo: Telestar, 1970), pp. 120-123.

9. For the background of this crisis, see Scirocco, *I democratici*, chap. 6.

10. Bargoni to unknown recipient, June 13, 1862, BISR/254/33.

11. See Agostino Bertani, *Intorno la [sic] condotta del governo* (Turin: Tipografia del Diritto, 1863).

12. Miceli to Garibaldi, Turin, January 16, 1864, BISR/928/8/1.

13. Alberto Mario, *Scritti politici*, ed. Giosuè Carducci (Bologna: Zanichelli, 1901), p. 120.

14. On the political significance and uses of Nullo's sacrifice, see Giuliana Donati Petteni, *Francesco Nullo cavaliere della libertà* (Bergamo: Bolis, 1963), pp. 93-117.

15. Agostino Bertani, *Della opposizione parlamentare* (Milan: Robecchi-Levino, 1865), p. 11.

16. Mordini to Bargoni, Florence, January 21, 1864, BISR/234/27/9.

17. Several items on this issue are found in MRM/Archivio Ferrari/14/22 (1868-69).

18. Bargoni to Cadolini, Turin, October 24, 1865, BISR/273/34/5.

19. Asproni to Guglielmi, December 2, 1863, MRTO/Archivio Faldella/13/7; and Guglielmi to Sineo, Strambino, April 9, 1867, BPTO/Archivio Sineo-Arnò/3/11/2.

20. Ferrari to Circolo elettorale di Luino, Milan, March 20, 1860, MRM/Archivio Bertani/11/12-2/11.

21 .The Montecchi-Pianciani controversy can be reconstructed from documents in ASR/Pianciani/7.

22. Giuseppe Zanardelli to Bargoni, Brescia, May 20, 1864, BISR/234/20/1.

23. See, for instance, Giorgio Asproni, *Ai suoi elettori del Collegio di Nuoro* (Naples: De Marco, 1867), pp. 31-33.

24. See, for instance, several speeches by Nino Bixio in APCD, Legislature 9 (1865-66), 5:73-A, 98-A, and ibid)., Legislature 10(1867-1869), 3:40-A, 146-A and 9:317-A.

25. For Musolino's plan see his *Gerusalemme ed il popolo ebreo* (1851; reprint ed., Rome: Rassegna mensile d'Israel, 1951). On the relationship between Risorgimento democracy, irredentism, and imperialism, see Giovanni Spadolini, *I repubblicani dopo l'unità*, 2nd ed. (Florence: LeMonnier, 1963), appendix, pp. 105-150.

26. For background on the educational debates of the early 1860s, see Giuseppe Talamo, *La scuola dalla legge Casati alla inchiesta del 1864* (Milan: Giuffrè, 1960). See also Mauro Macchi, *Dell'insegnamento professionale della donna* (Turin: Rivista contemporanea, 1868); Salvatore Morelli, *Programma organico per la riforma della istruzione pubblica nel Comune di Napoli* (Naples, 1876); and Giuseppe Finzi's report of January 7, 1872, in APCD, Legislature 8(1861), 2:528.

27. See Judith Jeffrey Howard, "The Woman Question in Italy," (Ph. D. diss. University of Connecticut, 1977), especially chaps. 3–5.

28. On these issues see Agostino Bertani, *La prostituzione patentata ed il regolamento sanitario* (Milan: Quadrio, 1881); and Giuseppe Ricciardi, *Il divorzio* (Naples: Tipografia strada S. Pietro a Maiella, 1876).

29. In the preface to Anna Maria Mozzoni's *La donna nella famiglia, nella città e nello stato* (Bologna: Pongetti, 1891), Regnoli wrote: "The yardstick of a civilization is the status of women within it . . . different does not mean inferior." For earlier evidence of Regnoli's ideas on this subject see also his *Del matrimonio civile: Memoria* (Milan: Redaelli, 1861).

30. Thus, in his letter of resignation to the president of the Chamber of Deputies, Calvino wrote: "Despite my very limited means . . . for a decade I have carried the burden of the parliamentary mandate at the cost of enormous sacrifices." Letter of June 9, 1871, cited in Francesco De Stefano, *Salvatore Calvino e la sua azione unitaria nel Risorgimento italiano* (Palermo: Ciuni, 1942), pp. 217–218.

31. See Giuseppe Ricciardi's "Un'elezione, ovvero i due candidati: Commedia politica in tre atti," in *Opere scelte*, 8 vols. (Naples: Stamperia del Vaglio, 1867–1870), 5:327–388.

32. See Giuseppe Romano, *Proposta economico-finanziaria* (Naples: Tipografia del Fibreno, 1868).

9. Dropouts and Deviants: Extraparliamentary Democracy, 1860–1876

1. For Mignogna's career see G. Pupino Carbonelli, *Nicola Mignogna nella storia dell'unità d'Italia* (Naples: Morano, 1889), pp. 249–256. For Maffei see Rocco Brienza, *Martirologio della Lucania*, 2nd ed. (Potenza: Unione lucana, 1882), pp. 47–50.

2. See especially G. B. Tuveri, *Il governo e i comuni* (Cagliari: Tipografia nazionale, 1860) and his *La questione barracellare* (Cagliari: Timon, 1861).

3. Undated anonymous letter in BCPA/Raffaele MSS/2 Q-q-H-255/folder 1.

4. See Giovanni Raffaele, *Della abolizione della ruota* (Palermo, 1876), and Rinaldo Giuffrida, "Orientamenti politici di G. R. e Francesco Crispi sui problemi dell'unificazione," in *1862: La prima crisi dello stato unitario* (Trapani: Corrao, 1966), pp. 129–141.

5. *Risposta di Giovanni Raffaele ad una stampa clandestina* (Palermo: Barravecchia, 1868), p. 11.

6. See C. M. Lovett, *Giuseppe Ferrari*, (Chapel Hill: University of North Carolina Press, 1979), pp. 166–167.

7. See Ricciardi, *La Repubblica di San Marino e l'Italia* (Naples: Stabilimento tipografico strada S. Pietro a Maiella, 1871), pp. 115–121.

8. For background on the democratic press see Valerio Castronovo and Nicola Tranfaglia, eds., *La stampa italiana del Risorgimento*, (Bari: Laterza, 1979), especially pp. 467–542.

9 .For examples of this genre see Gaetano Tallinucci, *I moderati, ossia i meriti e le ricompense* (Lucca: Cheli, 1866); Enrico Montazio, *I reietti: Storia contemporanea* (Prato, 1867); and Antonio Ghiglione, *Simone Kenton* (Genoa: Moretti, 1856).

10. Despite Lemmi's prominent role in the democratic movement and in Italian Masonry, a good biographical study has yet to be written. His activities in the 1850s and 1860s must be reconstructed from documents in BISR/397–399.

11. For a brief biographical sketch of Bruzzesi see G. C. Abba, *Ritratti e profili* (Turin: Società tipografica editrice nazionale, 1912), pp. 101–107. But the activities of Bruzzesi and his wife must be reconstructed largely from unpublished personal and family papers in BISR/98–99.

12. Bertani, "Prospetto di federazione dei giornali democratici italiani," BISR/237/96. The Bertani-Bargoni correspondence on this issue (May-September 1861) is found in BISR/235/9–12.

13. Mileti to Dolfi, Naples, November 6, 1863, BDM/E I c/12/12.

14. Mazzini's position, discussed in chap. 3 of this work, was restated in Maurizio Quadrio, *Il dovere degli eredi* (Florence: Il Prato, 1914). See especially the appendix (pp. 45–52), with quotations from the Pact of Brotherhood drafted at the Twelfth Congress of the Società operaie italiane.

15. Various items in BISR/430/34–35 (1861–1864) illustrate Dolfi's role as liaison between democratic deputies and Fratellanza artigiana.

16. See Quadrio's *Catechismo popolare del Partito d'Azione* (London: Tipografia universale, 1858).

17. Various items on the Società operaia of Potenza are found in ASPZ/Carte Ciccotti/III/28–20 and ibid./IV/30.

18. On Piccoli see Paolo Alatri, "Il moto repubblicano del 1870," *Almanacco calabrese*, 2–21 (1971): 19–28, and Claudio pavone, "Le bande insurrezionali nella primavera del 1870," *Movimento operaio*, 8 (1956): 42–107. But see also the recollections of the Sicilian Tommaso Alati, who criticized Piccoli for having departed from the Mazzinian program and having acted on his own (*Note storiche d'un mazziniano dal 1860 al 1882* [Reggio Calabria: Morello, 1911], pp. 31–37, 46–48).

19. Cited in Gastone Manacorda, *Il movimento operaio italiano attraverso i suoi congressi*, 2 vols. (Rome: Editori Riuniti, 1971), 1:81.

20. Ibid., pp. 93–98.

21. Mazzini to Filippo Spatafora, London, December 8, 1866, cited in A. M. Isastia, "Il Comitato d'Azione di Roma: Lettere inedite di Mazzini a Petroni e Spatafora," *BODM*, 23 (1977): 225–231.

22. For Niccolò Lo Savio's theoretical contributions see his *Importanza e*

destinazione della scienza economica nel sistema dei rapporti sociali (Florence: Galletti, 1867) and his *Istituzioni di economia sociale applicata all'agricoltura, all'industria ed al commercio* (Bari: Cannone, 1871). For Fanelli's role in the First International and his mission to Spain see Antonio Lucarelli, *Giuseppe Fanelli nella storia del Risorgimento e del socialismo italiano* (Trani: Vecchi, 1952), pp. 107–112, and Manuel Espadas Burgos, "La Primera Internacional y la historiografia española," *Hispanica*, 1 (1970): 181–196.

Bibliographical Essay

ALL historians of the Risorgimento are indebted to the international team of scholars who produced the impressive four-volume *Bibliografia dell' età del Risorgimento* (Florence: Olschki, 1971–1977), under the general editorship of Emilia Morelli. Dedicated to Alberto Maria Ghisalberti, the longtime president of the Istituto per la storia del Risorgimento italiano, this work covers all aspects of Italian history from the last decades of the eighteenth century to World War I.

The *Bibliografia* is somewhat difficult to use because the contributors did not follow uniform criteria in the preparation of the various sections. Moreover, simple lists of secondary works and published sources appear more frequently than annotated entries. Even with these limitations, however, the *Bibliografia* is the essential starting point for any research on nineteenth-century Italian history. Specifically, Franco Della Peruta's essay "I democratici dalla restaurazione all' unità" (vol. 1, pp. 245–346) provided the bibliographical foundation for this book.

For books and articles that have appeared since 1974, the interested reader should consult the excellent bibliographical section of the quarterly *Rassegna storica del Risorgimento*, the official journal of the Istituto per la storia del Risorgimento italiano. The *Rassegna* reviews all books on the

Risorgimento, including those published outside of Italy. Moreover, its editors scan several dozen specialized periodicals, many of which are available only in Italy, and they list relevant articles by topic.

Among the many general histories of the period, two are especially noteworthy for excellent, up-to-date scholarship: Giorgio Candeloro's eight-volume *Storia dell' Italia moderna* (Milan: Feltrinelli, 1956–1978) and the multiauthored *Storia d'Italia dal Settecento all'unità*, published by Einaudi of Turin (6 vols., 1972–1976). Candeloro's work is primarily a chronology of political events, interspersed with topical discussions of social and economic developments. The Einaudi *Storia d'Italia* is organized topically, and it emphasizes economic, cultural, and intellectual trends more than political events. Thus, in a sense, these two general works complement each other.

One of the most striking differences between these and older general works on the Risorgimento, for instance, Ettore Rota's *Le origini del Risorgimento* (2 vols., Milan: Vallardi, 1948) lies in their treatment of the democratic opposition to Victor Emmanuel II and to the moderate liberals. In contrast to their predecessors, Candeloro and the authors of the Einaudi series had access not only to the published writings of Mazzini but also to those of other, less famous proponents of republican or socialist ideas. These historians, in fact, were the first beneficiaries – and the disseminators – of postwar scholarship on the democratic currents of the Risorgimento.

The first historical works on the Risorgimento, such as Vittorio Bersezio's massive history of the reign of Victor Emmanuel II, focused on Cavour and the moderate liberals. Influenced by the political climate of the post-Risorgimento, historians such as Bersezio, Luigi Chiala, and others included democrats like Mazzini and Garibaldi in their vast canvases of the national revolution. But they discussed them as individuals, rather than as members of a movement. Above all, they stressed not the radical political and social solutions favored by those men but their contributions to and acceptance of the creation of a liberal state.

In the early 1920s, however, the crisis of the liberal institutions shaped by the victors of the Risorgimento struggles changed significantly the direction of Italian historiography. As they sharpened their own critique of the liberal state, intellectuals such as Antonio Gramsci, Gaetano Salvemini, and Piero Gobetti traced and reinterpreted the arguments of Cavour's opponents. This work of rediscovery and reinterpretation was continued throughout the Fascist period by younger political exiles such as Nello Rosselli. But the best fruits of this new wave in Italian historiography came after Italy's defeat in World War II.

Republican and socialist dissidents were mentioned only briefly, and sometimes pejoratively, in the papers and memoirs of the great liberal statesmen of the Risorgimento and in the public documents of the period. Thus, in order to assess the dissidents' historical importance and to explore their ideas in depth, the postwar generation of Italian historians found it necessary to delve into documentary collections and sources heretofore unknown. The first results of this effort began to appear in fragmentary form in the 1950s, especially in such periodical publications as *Il ponte, Belfagor, Rinascita,* and *Mondo operaio.* Then, in 1958, Franco Della Peruta published his ground-breaking study on the political fortunes and debates of the democratic revolutionaries after 1848–49, *I democratici e la rivoluzione italiana: Dibattiti ideali e contrasti politici all' indomani del 1848* (Milan: Feltrinelli, 1958). This first critical study of the democratic currents of the Risorgimento and their contribution to Italy's unification was followed by Luigi Ambrosoli's first monograph on Cattaneo (*La formazione di Carlo Cattaneo* [Milan and Naples: Ricciardi, 1960]), and by the late Giuseppe Berti's pioneering study of southern democracy (*I democratici e l'iniziativa meridionale nel Risorgimento* [Milan: Feltrinelli, 1962]). At the end of a decade of inquiry and research, Alfonso Scirocco published the first important work on the democratic opposition in the years of moderate liberal ascendancy: *I democratici italiani da Sapri a Porta Pia* (Naples: ESI, 1969). Five years later, Della Peruta's *Mazzini e i rivoluzionari italiani* (Milan: Feltrinelli, 1974) provided exhaustive documentation for a hypothesis advanced earlier by Emilia Morelli and others, to wit, that in the early 1840s Mazzinian republicans had established networks well beyond the Po Valley.

In preparation for these interpretative works, the aforementioned historians and many others edited the long-forgotten or previously unpublished writings of many Risorgimento democrats. Thus, for instance, Ernesto Sestan completed the edition of Cattaneo's historical and geographical works that Salvemini had initiated for Le Monnier of Florence, while Della Peruta edited Pisacane's essays on revolution and Silvia Rota Ghibaudi turned her attention to Ferrari. Even with these invaluable contributions, however, the history of the Risorgimento, and especially the history of its democratic currents, cannot be written without going to the archival sources. As should be obvious from the notes, such sources were, in fact, used extensively in the preparation of this book.

The first of the three different types of archival materials that I examined were well-known collections such as the *Fondo emigrati politici* of the Archivio di Stato in Turin or the documents of the *Ministero di Polizia* at the Archivio di Stato in Naples. These were examined not from the traditional perspective of the conflict between despotic regimes and noble patriots but rather for biographical information about the men in the sample and for evidence of conflicts among them or between them and liberal revolutionaries. Second, I explored specialized but fairly well-known collections, such as the Ricciardi papers at the Biblioteca Nazionale in Naples and the archives of the Istituto mazziniano in Genoa. These sources were useful not so much for the profiles of the major figues after whom they are named as for information about democratic networks before and after 1848. The third and largest type of archival sources were collections in local and regional libraries such as the Carte Lamberti at the Biblioteca comunale of Reggio Emilia and the Carte Raffaele at the Biblioteca comunale of Palermo. Until quite recently these collections were used, if at all, only by local historians, many of them amateurs more interested in colorful anecdotes and patriotic hagiography than in scholarly analysis. Although scattered throughout Italy and not always easily accessible, these collections proved most valuable for the reconstruction of many individual profiles and for clues to local and regional democratic networks. The difficulty of working with poorly catalogued materials typically available only for a few hours each day was offset, in most cases, by the eagerness of local historians and curators to share their treasures with an adventurous outsider.

As the notes indicate, I used a broad range of published sources to complement the archival materials. Most important for biographical information and for insights into democratic ideology were the published works of the democrats themselves. Again, these included such well-known and easily accessible sources as the writings of Mazzini, as well as hundreds of lesser-known pamphlets, tracts, and memoirs. Many of these are found in the H. Nelson Gay Collection of the Widener Library at Harvard University — an underutilized gold mine of resources on the history of modern Italy. Those not available in the Gay Collection surfaced in local or regional libraries more often than in national ones. Equally useful, and usually great fun to read, were the published letters of democrats such as Guerrazzi, Cattaneo, Pisacane, Modena, and Dall'Ongaro, who corresponded with scores of others in the movement. Correspondence, both published and unpublished, was especially important for reconstructing the experiences of the 1850s and the activities of extraparliamentary democrats after the unification.

Finally, I made use of an unruly, inevitably uneven mass of biographical material which I checked for accuracy, whenever possible, against archival or other primary sources. Scholarly, reliable biographies were available only for a handful of the democrats in the sample, in part because of the recent and still underdeveloped character of historical scholarship on the Risorgimento democrats. But the lack of good recent biographies also reflects the strong prejudice of Italian historians, especially those of Marxist intellectual formation, against biography as a historical genre. Be that as it may, except for a few major figures, I had to rely on scores of popular biographical sketches and articles. Predictably, most of these appeared not in major scholarly periodicals but in regional and local historical bulletins, *Festschriften* (a very popular genre in Italy), and even daily newspapers.

The writings of Ambrosoli, Berti, Della Peruta, and Scirocco, and my own contributions on Cattaneo and Ferrari have advanced the historiography of Risorgimento democracy to the point that a great deal is known about the major figures and the major themes of democratic ideology. However, local or regional studies of the development of democratic networks before 1848 and especially of their evolution after the unification still need to be done. Much more must be learned, for instance, about the role that followers of Mazzini, Pisacane, and other major figures played in the emergence of the predominantly middle-class Radical party and of the Partito operaio.

A few scholars are indeed moving in this direction. Scirocco, for instance, has turned his attention to the evolution of democratic networks in and around Naples after the unification (*Democrazia e socialismo a Napoli dopo l'unità* [Naples: Libreria scientifica editrice, 1973]). Angelo Varni makes particularly intelligent use of local archives in his *Associazionismo mazziniano e questione operaia: Il caso della Società democratica operaia di Chiavenna, 1862–1876* (Pisa: Nistri-Lischi, 1978). And finally, the English scholar Paul Ginsborg has made an important contribution to the pre-1848 history of the democratic movement with his *Daniele Manin e la rivoluzione veneziana del 1848* (Milan: Feltrinelli, 1978). It is obvious that more such studies are needed before the continuities and discontinuities in the history of democratic ideology and politics in Italy can be fully understood.

Index